Changing Times in Teacher Education

We would like to dedicate this book to the organizers, participants and supporters of the UNITE (Urban network for improving teacher education) project, designed to improve the preparation of teachers for the urban school.

mfw and ppg

Changing Times in Teacher Education:
Restructuring or Reconceptualization?

Edited by

Marvin F. Wideen
Peter P. Grimmett

RoutledgeFalmer
Taylor & Francis Group.

LONDON AND NEW YORK

First published in 1995
By RoutledgeFalmer, 11 New
Fetter Lane, London EC4P 4EE

Transferred to Digital Printing 2004

A catalogue record for this book is available from the British Library

ISBN 0 7507 0182 X cased
ISBN 0 7507 0183 8 paper

Library of Congress Cataloging-in-Publication Data are available on request

Jacket design by Caroline Archer

Typeset in 10/12 pt Garamond
Graphicraft Typesetters Ltd., Hong Kong.

Contents

Contents

Preface

What can be more important than the preparation of those who teach our young? Yet, the preparation of teachers has never been afforded the care, attention, and support given to other professions such as law, medicine and dentistry. Nonetheless, attempts at all levels have been made to improve the preparation of teachers since the Second World War. The move from the teacher's college setting to the university campus provides one example. We have also seen restructuring at national levels and several institutional attempts at improvement in various countries around the world. Research at all levels in teacher education has increased considerably over the past decade. But, as we reach the end of the twentieth century, teacher education appears to be more in a state of turmoil than in a state of continuous improvement. If fact, it is not stretching things to say that, in many countries, teacher education is under attack.

In preparing this book, we seek to understand why this state of affairs currently exists. We see the need to examine the issues confronting teacher education in selected Western countries in which restructuring efforts are taking place. We ask ourselves whether there are patterns among these restructuring activities that go across national boundaries, cultures and contexts. We wonder what meaning we can take away from the efforts of policymakers to reshape the preparation of teachers in these different countries. Further, we see the need to identify some policy directions for changing how we prepare teachers, and to provide examples of what that might mean at the level of action.

Some fundamental assumptions guide this inquiry. First, we firmly believe that restructuring without reconceptualization does not lead to genuine change in teacher education. Put differently, we see restructuring as opening up different opportunities for reconceptualization. Second, we are convinced that the future of public education rests ultimately on the shoulders of strong teachers who have been nurtured in viable and challenging programs of teacher preparation. Third, we find uncompelling the arguments made against connecting teacher preparation in some vital way to the university community.

We asked a variety of persons to contribute chapters to this book. All share a passion for the activity of teacher preparation; all work to support and enhance it in their day-to-day efforts as teacher educators or policymakers; all are leaders, or are destined to become leaders, in their respective fields.

We wish to acknowledge the technical assistance given by Ivy Pye in the editing of several drafts. We also wish to thank Ida Clayton and Eileen Mallory for word processing. Finally, we thank the staff at Falmer Press for their patience and support in bringing this manuscript to completion.

Chapter 1

Teacher Education at the Crossroads

Marvin F. Wideen

Introduction

This book examines teacher education in changing times in six countries in the Western world. It points up many of the problems facing faculties of education in several countries as they try to respond to the changes thrust upon them by an increasingly assertive and sometimes hostile external environment. It provides several examples of innovative practices that teacher educators can make to respond to these challenges and outlines a framework to view these innovations. Finally, it sets out a series of issues to which those in faculties of education must respond if indeed their institutions are to survive the twenty-first century.

Teacher education has been soundly criticized in every decade since the Second World War. In 1963, Koerner was among several American authors who focused their analysis on the inferior intellectual quality of education courses, faculty and students. He described what was being taught in education courses as 'vague, insipid, time wasting adumbrations of the obvious, and probably irrelevant to academic teaching' (pp. 55–6). Peterson and Fleming (1979) writing from a Canadian perspective criticized almost every aspect of teacher preparation including its organization, staffing and the curriculum. Joyce and Clift (1984) used the symbolism of the ancient story of the Phoenix rebirth to argue that the very dismal picture of teacher education provided an opportunity for dramatic reform. They criticized the institutions that prepare teachers, the practices that socialize teachers into adhering to a practicality ethic where concerns about survival dominate their thinking, and the channeling of teaching styles toward the persistence of student recitation. Teacher education, they argued, could rise from the ashes if the knowledge base developed through research were to become the basis for reform within a changed culture of teacher preparation. Goodlad's (1990) systematic study of teacher education left little doubt that major problems confronted faculties of education and highlighted the need for radical reform in teacher preparation. And recently, Tyson (1994), after a review of the problems in teacher education identified by different authors, points out that these problems have changed little over the last forty years.

As we approach the end of this century, it appears that little has changed in teacher education since the critiques of these authors. Meanwhile, as we reach the mid-point of the 1990s, we see substantive and far-reaching changes occurring in society. While these changes have been building for some time, they have coalesced in a way that sets a very different context for schools and for the faculties of education that prepare teachers for those schools. It is difficult to imagine how the 'old ways of doing business in faculties of education – critiqued so thoroughly and found so wanting – can possibly survive in this new context. Teacher education may have reached a turning point in its history.

Drucker (1994) argues that the twentieth century has experienced more social transformations than any other period in history. Although that transformation has been accomplished with relative ease to this point, it has only begun. In his words, 'the age of social transformation will not come to an end with the year 2000 – it will not even have peaked by then' (p. 54). We can expect the future changes to occur with much less ease, raising questions about the role of many institutions in our society, faculties of education among them. Hargreaves (1994) makes a similar proposition about the transformations facing society. But he speaks more directly to their impact upon schools. He describes it in terms of 'a major sociohistoric transition from a period of *modernity* to one of *postmodernity*' (p. 23). Although Drucker and Hargreaves use different terms to describe the periods that we are experiencing as a society, their descriptions point to a time of relative calm and gradual transition. Hargreaves describes the period in terms of a disintegrating modernity. Modernity came into its own after the Second World War; the application of science and technology was to provide a better life for people by lifting them out of paternalism and superstition – the accumulation of knowledge would be brought to bear on improving people's economic and intellectual lot. Modernity has meant the smokestack, the belief in the welfare state, and the belief that our problems can be solved through rational means and the application of scientific knowledge. Drucker sees this period in similar terms except that he examines it in terms of changing working patterns from the farming and domestic communities to the rise of the blue-collar worker. Such patterns occurred with relative ease as the skills required in one could be applied in the other. But future transitions will not be as easy. The point on which both authors and many others, such as Giddens (1991) and Grimmett and Neufeld (1994), agree is that the period we have enjoyed as a society is now ending, and we are turning to a future that is much less predictable.

Although predictions about the future remain unclear, four aspects of change appear to be particularly crucial in the decades ahead – the work people do, the knowledge and education they require to do it, the pace at which changes will occur, and the people who will be involved in determining change. Drucker identifies the emergence of what he calls the *knowledge worker* as being a most fundamental change. Knowledge workers will be the largest single working group by the turn of the century. Unlike previous transitions from the farm to the factory which occurred with relative ease, the transition to knowledge work will require a different preparation and a differ-ent attitude. Those who are not prepared may be left out, thus creating an underclass in society. In the class society created by the period of modernity, all classes had work. This may not be the case as we move into a period of postmodernity. Schools will increasingly be required to deal with these differ-ences in society, as well as in the preparation of the knowledge worker.

The emergence of the knowledge worker will see the very nature of knowledge and education become subject to dramatic change. In earlier soci-eties, and today, an educated person was somebody who possessed a pre-scribed stock of formal knowledge which was developed and disseminated in universities. Gaining an education was essentially a process of acquiring a given amount of that knowledge. Learning to teach was a process of beginning teachers becoming acquainted with the best available knowledge about teach-ing (Carter, 1990). In fact, many, such as Joyce and Clift (1984), saw this knowledge base as the basis for reform in teacher education. Drucker's asser-tions appear to be challenging that foundation. While he and others maintain that knowledge will be very instrumental in future changes in our society, it will not be the type of knowledge that we have traditionally courted in aca-deme. Knowledge will take on significance as it relates to the context in which it is understood, applied and remembered. Brown, Collins and Duguid (1989) use the term *situated cognition* to describe knowledge which is developed and understood within specific situations. Drucker uses the term *knowledges* to argue that what will matter in the decades ahead will not be the knowledge possessed by the nineteenth-century liberal arts graduate, but knowledge which has a purpose beyond itself. The value of that knowledge will not depend upon where it resides, but in its value in solving problems within an increas-ingly competitive marketplace. Programs of teacher education may have to recognize the value of practitioners' knowledge on a par with that of university courses.

The work done and the education that supports it will also be affected by the pace of change and by the emergence of additional players who will seek to determine the nature of education. Hargreaves (1994) argues that schools and teachers are already being affected by the demands of 'an increasingly complex and fast-paced postmodern world' (p. 23). The pace of change in society has increased as communication improves, to the extent that know-ledge can be everywhere. Knowledge itself can be used to monitor and shape change. The uncertainty of such rapid change, coupled with the sense of competitiveness that comes from the global marketplace invites more players into the decision-making arena. Education has apparently become too import-ant to be left to educators.

Although we may question many of the assertions made by writers such as Hargreaves and Drucker, we can hardly question their general assumption that we will experience a period of profound social transition over the next few decades. While the nature of that transition remains unclear and will continue to remain so, schools and faculties of education will most definitely

3

be at the center of such changes, and will be required to rethink how they do business if they are to survive. If they are to remain a force in the preparation of teachers, faculties of education will have to face up to these transitions.

Restructuring has become the popular new buzzword of the 1990s. In the corporate sector the term has become synonymous with downsizing and the management of retrenchment. In elementary and secondary education, we find it used to describe any number of reforms ranging from school-based management to student empowerment. In teacher education we have seen the term used in a vague and general way to suit the aims of the persons using it. Generally, it connotes a major educational reform designed to achieve some laudable objectives, laudable at least to the persons proposing the change. And typically, we see these restructuring efforts being proposed by those outside schools and universities.

As editors of this volume we envisage a major restructuring of teacher education over the next decade. The changes occurring in society will almost surely dictate that. We feel, however, that if restructuring is not coupled with a reconceptualization of teacher education, little will change. Moreover, such reconceptualization must occur at the level at which those preparing teachers come in contact with those learning to be teachers. Restructuring efforts, laudable as they may be, typically take aim several levels above where there will be any effect, or deal with issues that do not really matter.

In this opening chapter, we first set out the picture of teacher education as we understand it in the Western world by examining its problems and its promise.

The Problems and Promise of Teacher Education

Faculty of Education standards are low enough that, after a while, one wonders if this is not the last hope for most people who cannot make it in other faculties (Student's comment in Clifton, Mandzuk and Roberts, 1994).

I find it very annoying that all the courses and assignments in education are so useless. They are entirely theoretical and in many ways I find them unrealistic. The courses and assignments in this Faculty do not pertain to the teaching profession. What you learn here from your courses is hardly applicable to the teaching field. (Student's comment in Clifton, Mandzuk and Roberts, 1994)

I think that this faculty very adequately integrates theory and practice. There is the involvement program where students go to schools for half a day a week for a semester. Then in the entire second year (usually) students go to a school for a whole day a week, and finally the internship. There is sufficient theory taught prior to experience in the schools so the theories can be tested in practice (Student's comment in Fullan, Wideen and Estabrook, 1983).

Our methodology courses are excellent. We have ample opportunity to give demonstration lessons in class. They are discussed as to techniques and probable success in a real classroom situation (Student's comment in Fullan, Wideen and Estabrook, 1983).

These comments, made by graduates of teacher education programs and university students preparing to be teachers, illustrate the Janus-like, or twofaced, nature of teacher education. On the one hand, we find students viewing it as a wasted experience. These perceptions are supported by some chapters in this book, as well as in the literature in teacher education (see, for example, Gideonse, 1992). These sources have become increasingly critical of how many faculties of education prepare teachers, and the negative comments that I just cited merely reflect the tip of that iceberg. The problems run much deeper than one might suspect. One gains the sense that time is running out for faculties of education; they must either 'get their act together', or see the preparation of teachers taken over by others. One thing appears obvious: the status quo will not be good enough in the years ahead. Teacher education must be reconceptualized from the ground up.

On the other hand, we find students who react positively toward their experience in teacher education. Typically, such comments come from students attending or graduating from those institutions that represent a wedge of progressive practice in teacher education that has become increasingly evident in many of the Western countries. Such institutions sustain our hope for the future. Potentially, they can lead the way in showing how teacher education can provide exemplary preparation for beginning teachers, as well as providing a positive, constructive force for school reform.

Both the problems we currently see and the promising innovations that have developed rest within an evolution in teacher education over the past several decades. As we examine this evolution, it becomes obvious that the concept of teacher education within a university setting rests on a set of expectations arising from the move to the university. The wedge of progressive practice just mentioned came about in university settings we describe later where faculties of education to a large extent have lived up to those expectations. But, if the perception emerges among policymakers that such expectations are not being met, then faculties of education are indeed vulnerable. So the question is not whether faculties of education should change their programs, but rather whether they have the time to do so before preservice teacher preparation is taken over by other players. Should universities lose teacher preparation, the concept of faculties of education as we currently know it could come under serious threat since it becomes an easy target when universities seek solutions to funding cuts.

It will also become apparent in this chapter, and others in this book, that faculties of education can not merely be content with the prospect of administrative restructuring. Efforts to restructure must be tied to a thorough reconceptualization of what it means to prepare teachers. Old wine in new bottles does not fare well.

Background

Teacher preparation, as we know it today, at least in North America, began in the high schools in 1848 in the United States (Larabee, 1992). These high schools assumed the role of preparing teachers for the elementary schools of the day. Eventually they assumed more responsibility for teacher preparation and came to be known as *normal schools.*

At the normal schools, which later became *teachers' colleges*, the high school concept prevailed. Those of us who received our initial teacher preparation from a normal school recall attending classes for a full day which began with morning exercises, being disciplined for coming late to class, having homeroom teachers, and going about business much as we had done in the high school we had just left. The sole focus of the instructors, many of whom were former school superintendents, rested with teacher preparation. If they had research interests they carried them out on their own time.

The move of teacher education from the normal schools to the university to join either existing faculties of education or to become fullfledged faculties within the universities themselves, occurred between the years 1860 and 1950 in North America (Meyers and Saul, 1974; Cushman, 1977) and later in Europe. Thus, as Larabee (1992) describes, over the period of some one hundred years, the task of preparing teachers moved from the high school to the university. Over that one hundred year transition the problems in teacher education that I referred to in the opening paragraphs of this chapter had their origins. Some argue that faculties of education have never really developed a role within the university; that they have remained marginalized in that setting. Others suggest that the move to the university has served to isolate faculties of education from the field – a somewhat ironic turn of events. Nonetheless, in preparing this volume, we take the position that the transition of teacher education from the teachers' college to the university has provided us with the opportunity to improve the preparation of those who will teach our children. In the chapters that follow we provide examples of that improvement and also set out the conceptual and political framework in which they occur.

The Past Promise

First we turn to the promise. When teacher education moved into the university it did so with more than a hint of promise. During those times when economic growth was strong, the vision of a better future for teacher education seemed a natural expectation in what appeared to be the dawn of a new era. Schools and better-prepared teachers would be central to a vision of young people being prepared for the new society. It was in the university as opposed to the normal school setting that such improvement would be realized. From the literature, one finds three types of arguments being made regarding that promise.

One argument holds that the problems confronting the schools could only be resolved through systematic research and inquiry which would normally go on within a university setting. By creating faculties of education, then, such problems could be examined on a systematic basis. The second promise had to do with the problem of attracting quality students. Teachers' colleges did not necessarily attract students from the upper rung of the academic ladder. By moving teacher education into the university structure, it was believed that a better calibre of student would be attracted to teaching.

The third expectation held that a different kind of education would result in a university education. Myers and Saul (1974) put it this way, 'the university provides a setting and an atmosphere in which fundamental issues can be examined critically, fresh alternatives can be explored, and promising, imaginative programs can be developed' (p. 38). Thus, the people who would teach the young would then be better selected and nurtured within a research-oriented environment by people who were examining issues in education. Therein lay the promise for teacher education in the university setting.

Now, years later, how far has teacher education come towards fulfilling that promise? In attempting to answer that question, we can examine the problems in teacher preparation and also gain a sense of the improvements that have been made.

The Problems

The problems in teacher education surface when graduates are asked to comment on the value of their preservice experience in helping them learn to teach. The two quotations that opened this section, taken from a study of a Canadian university (Clifton, Mandzuk and Roberts, 1994), typify the comments made by graduates, especially with respect to on-campus components (e.g., Koerner, 1963; Flanders, 1980; Isher, 1992). For example, in summing up the comments made by teachers who appeared before the Select Committee on Public Education created in Texas, Isher (1992) had this to say, 'the only thing worse than their preservice courses was the in-service training they were having to put up with in their current districts' (p. 8). Such comments suggest that the fresh new initiatives that were to develop within the setting of the university have been slow in coming.

While dissatisfaction with university teaching is nothing new, the negative data presented by these follow-up studies pose real and fundamental concerns about the survival of teacher education. In the Clifton, Mandzuk and Roberts study, for example, 90 per cent of the graduates provided negative comments about their teacher education. Such data support the argument that faculties of education such as these are seriously in trouble if substantive changes do not occur soon. Can one imagine a business, or for that matter any organization where accountability exists, surviving for long when 90 per cent of their clients are unhappy? I must hasten to add, that this negative brush does not necessarily paint the entire spectrum of teacher education. Graduates from some programs extol the virtues of their teacher preparation (see Bowman, 1991).

Client dissatisfaction, however, represents only a symptom of a problem that has much deeper roots, roots which extend all the way back to the move from the teacher's college to the university campus, described earlier. That move provided a classic example of administrative restructuring without a reconceptualization of what it meant to prepare teachers. Patterson (1984) who conducted a case study of a large university where a normal school was moved to a university setting, found that little had changed. The same coursework instruction that had occurred at the teachers' college simply moved to the university campus. The anticipation of new and innovative programs did not materialize. Instead, teacher educators no longer found themselves the centerpiece of the institution, rather they were obliged to compete with other faculties. They also found themselves forced to adopt the norms of the university where publication became more important than teaching (Larabee, 1992).

Many teacher educators, particularly in North America, responded to this situation by moving away from teacher preparation into fields such as counseling, educational administration, philosophy, and sociology, areas which would gain them recognition within the university. In a Canada-wide study (Fullan, Wideen and Estabrook, 1983) in which faculty members were interviewed, issues of salary, program, and organization took a back seat to the concept of respect within the university community in the majority of cases. Faculty members expressed a feeling of alienation in the university setting. Hargreaves (in press) describes this anomie in terms of marginalization within the university where faculties of education find themselves in a weak position *vis-à-vis* other faculties. But as teacher educators struggle to gain status with their counterparts in other faculties, they distance themselves from the schools for whom they prepare teachers. Because the two cultures are very different ones, the balancing act often becomes an unmanageable feat. For these reasons, faculties of education have indeed become marginalized, both within the university in which they are housed and in the schools for which they prepare teachers.

But the problem of marginalization does not stop there. Robinson and Ryan (1989) have recently described how teacher education has also become a marginalized activity within their faculty of education. While they described the program of teacher education in their faculty in very positive terms, ironically the point that ended the paper was that the program occupied the time of few faculty members. Now that graduate students and sessional instructors ran the program, faculty busied themselves with other agendas. They had been marginalized within their own program.

What has been the effect of such marginalization? In a recent examination

of teacher education policy in the United States, Gideonse (1992) and a group
of case workers present a sobering picture of teacher education in that country. Their analysis finds faculties of education holding very weak positions in
the policy arena. Because they are marginalized by the field and the university,
teacher educators have few friends to come to their rescue in times of attack.
The negative feedback about teacher preparation that came from the teachers
themselves had opened the door for policymakers to move in with simple
solutions to very complex problems. Among these we find external control
over teacher education, testing programs to ensure minimum competency for
beginning teachers, and caps on the number of hours of education courses
that could be required for accreditation. Consequently, teacher education was
seen as overgrown, lacking in quality, and not providing an adequate response to the needs of the school and the larger society. In the closing chapter
of the volume, Clark holds out this problem and the challenge:

> No professional can take comfort from the action by policy makers
> that challenge the basic utility of their professional activity. To suggest
> [for example] that less pedagogical instruction will improve teaching
> is a challenge that cannot be left uncontested (1992:294).

A further problem facing teacher education is the strong and compelling
argument that the perceived failure of the schools rests upon the shoulders of
those who prepared teachers for those schools – the teacher educators within
faculties of education. Although schools have always been the scapegoat for
all the assorted ills of society, today's criticism seems to have adopted a stronger
tone and one that is much less forgiving. Politicians, business interests, the
press, and contributors to talk shows generally decry the state of education
and, by implication, those who prepare the teachers who deliver it. Today we
find governments issuing mandates with much stronger teeth in them. Ironically, in the present situation, we now see faculties of education having to face
the same type of reform that they have been so fondly recommending to
others, particularly those in schools.

Subsequent chapters in this book will take up these and other problems
raised in this short treatment. In Chapter 2, Howey describes teacher education
in the United States pointing out that those heading the reform agenda for the
schools have virtually by-passed teacher education as a player in that reform.
He also points out that no legal, political or economic incentive exists for those
in schools of education to collaborate with the schools. Yet, that collaboration
has become one of the perceived means of reforming both teacher education
and the schools for whom they prepare teachers. An even more sobering
picture is described in Chapter 4 by Pimm and Selinger who provide an account of events occurring in England. There we see teacher education now
being moved from the university to the school setting, a concept that would
have been hard to imagine a decade ago. Teacher preparation for the most
part has been relegated to the schools or conducted through distance education

in that country. In Chapter 3 by Tisher we see economic forces at work in Australia, the parallel to a lesser degree of those occurring in Great Britain. Tisher describes the criticisms being leveled at faculties of education which pay little or no attention to the ground level reforms that are occurring in that country. In Australia, as in other countries, we find teacher educators 'amazingly docile, silent, and ignored' (p. 34). Tisher ends the chapter with the sobering observation that there have been no visionary or revolutionary writers in that country in recent years.

The three other chapters that involve national issues include those from Norway, Portugal, and Canada, countries that are at different stages in their educational development from the three just described. In Norway (Chapter 5), we find teacher education engaged in the most profound changes in forty years. Besides lengthening the preparation time for teachers, a major reorganization is occurring linked to the changes in both the content and the curriculum in the schools. These changes create pressure for a major restructuring of teacher education. One of the major restructuring moves, similar to what occurred in Australia, finds some 129 separate institutions being compressed into twenty-six larger regional units. Chapter 6, by Isabel Alarcaõ, describes the situation in Portugal where teacher education has developed within a context of building a national educational community since the 1974 Revolution. Politicians realized the relevance of education to the country's development and educators recognized the role that teacher education would play within that development. Both high-ranking educators and politicians have demanded educational reform which is now in progress in that country. Alarcão presents Portugal as an interesting case of ecological interaction in a changing sociopolitical setting where she sees educational discourse influencing the action of policymakers. This chapter illustrates the limitations of attempting to draw upon the knowledge base of other nations as a basis for reform. In the Canadian chapter (7), we see developments in two provinces. One gains less of a sense of crisis here. In fact, the proactive developments occurring in those two provinces appear to be setting the stage for a major breakthrough in teacher education. However, the authors, Sheehan and Fullan, point out that much in the way of readiness has occurred with a limited amount of follow-through. As in other countries, the activity occurring on the ground seems poorly connected to the statements being made by policymakers. We see a world of practice and a world of proposals, though never the twain shall meet.

These six chapters provide vivid accounts of both restructuring and reconceptualization of teacher education in the different countries. Although the authors of these six chapters were not asked to address common problems or given a template within which to write their chapters, a number of common themes and issues emerged to which Peter Grimmett returns in the final chapter. Although the picture of teacher education is one of turmoil in some countries and despondency in others, throughout the chapters we see developments which do provide hope and promise for teacher education, a theme to which I now turn.

The Future Promise

At one level a very dismal picture emerges from at least three of these chapters representing six countries. And, as Tom suggests in chapter 9, teacher education has not changed much over the years – a point raised at the beginning of this chapter. The dismal mediocrity that pertains in teacher education was captured by Goodlad's words 'teacher education programs are disturbingly alike and uniformly inadequate' (1984:315). This dismal picture presents a problematic face to teacher preparation within the university. But, as I argued earlier, another face exists which has literally risen from the ashes as Joyce and Clift (1984) suggested it would. That face provides a promise both of better understanding of how teacher education occurs and also presents a picture of improved practice.

Five chapters in this volume offer new ways of reconceptualizing how teacher education can be carried out. These are set within a context of general principles which offer an improved vision of teacher education. Together they represent examples of a wedge of progressive practice which holds a promise of what teacher education can become through a reconceptualization of the process.

Chapters 8 by Tuinman and 9 by Tom posit a set of parameters for reforming teacher education. Tuinman speaks as a former faculty member and Dean of a faculty of education. He draws our attention to the need for teacher educators to dedicate themselves more centrally to teacher education and argues for closer links with other faculties and to the field. He raises the possibility that central to the problems we face in faculties of education is what he terms *intemperate individualism*. Tom's chapter critiques four commonly-held assumptions about teacher education: its intensity, its sequencing, its staffing and its grouping of students. His proposal for alternatives would compress teacher education, place practice in front of the presentation of knowledge, would staff vertically with the same people providing input as well as supervising students, and have students move through programs in cohorts. He contends that we must not wait for our status to be given to us. These two chapters set a general context for the five specific exemplars that follow.

The first of these, Chapter 10 by Selma Wassermann, outlines the advantages of the case teaching approach. Drawing upon the work of the Harvard business school, her case method provides both a different approach to teaching and also a philosophy which essentially challenges traditional ways of teaching in faculties of education. In Chapter 11, Terry Carson describes another approach to teaching, based on reflection. He describes how a group of faculty and students worked with beginning teachers who all used journal writing as an ongoing reflective activity. Although he describes reflection in terms of the program structure in which he worked, the way he and his team use the term, *reflection* becomes a metaphor for not only changing our teaching but also, in Tuinman's words, 'to transform structures and institutionalism, to influence the terms of social reproduction' (p. 105). The third example of an approach designed to radically change the teaching of teachers comes in Chapter 12 by Dittmer and Fischetti. They draw from their experience over a seven-year period in which they changed from a commonly-used traditional approach in teacher preparation to a program based upon principles derived from the work in the Foxfire program and the writings of John Dewey. These authors describe both the program they developed and the process they went through to implement it. These three chapters stand in relief to Tuinman's critical comments made in Chapter 8 where he doubted that the quality of teaching in educational faculties is any better than elsewhere in the university. While we cannot speak for the quality of these programs, we can recognize them as an attempt to address the question of teaching practice at this level. These programs form part of the promising practice we now see in teacher education.

The reconceptualization that would be required if one were to stir the embers, as Tom would have us do, is illustrated in Chapter 13 by Dawson and Chapter 14 by Scott and Burke. Dawson's concept of a faculty associate bears similarity to Tom's notion of vertical staffing. Here we see faculty associates, or clinical professors as they are called in some universities, carrying out the tasks of teaching and supervision of beginning teachers shoulder-to-shoulder with faculty. But, as Dawson shows, the transition to that model does not occur without its problems and stresses. From this chapter one gains the impression that faculty would prefer the horizontal staffing model. The chapter by Scott and Burke describes the experience of a teaching team similar to Dawson's description in working within a modular structure. The authors describe how a campus-based program worked in conjunction with a large urban school district to offer both strong preservice teacher education for their students but also inservice education for the cooperating teachers involved. This chapter illustrates Tuinman's clarion call for universities to connect more closely with schools.

Issues and Pointers

As we examine this face of promise against the backdrop of problems that have been so forcefully brought to the fore by countless writers, several issues emerge that render this work, and indeed the entire field of teacher education, problematic. These issues and many others will be explored further in the chapters that follow. I raise three issues at this point and Peter Grimmett returns to them in the closing chapter.

The Role of Universities in Teacher Education

The first issue concerns the role of teacher education within the community for which it prepares teachers and the university in which it is housed. The advent of school-based teacher education in many countries, particularly in Great Britain, as well as alternative routes to certification in the United States, have seen teacher education move from the campus to the school. This change requires a different kind of involvement on the part of faculty members and raises the question of the role of universities in teacher education. What do faculties of education do that no one else can do as well or better? That question might not have been asked a decade ago. Today it must be faced.

Two examples, discussed later in more detail, illustrate the point. In Chapter 13, where Dawson describes the role of the faculty associate, it becomes apparent that outstanding teachers can provide much grounding for beginning teachers by relating the theory they learn to practice in schools. What then becomes the role of the university professor in this situation? That question also comes up in the context of the British situation where teacher preparation has been moved entirely to the schools who will now contract with faculties of education for services. But what will those services look like? What does the university have to *sell* in this situation? Given that many faculties of education in the past have delegated teacher preparation to graduate students and temporary appointments, they may now find some difficulty in addressing these questions.

We can see this issue being played out when we consider what constitutes knowledge for beginning teachers and how that knowledge informs learning about teaching. The move of faculties of education into university settings emphasized the *technical-rationalist* view of knowledge which posits that through research we can arrive at propositional statements about teaching which, if implemented by teachers, will improve the achievement of students. The process–product research which has become an important foundation for school and educational reform provides an illustration. The findings of this research paradigm have met with considerable acceptance; they have been converted into applications for teachers to follow and have been adopted in numerous programs of preservice and inservice education (Doyle, 1990). In Chapter 12 Fischetti and Dittmer point out that the earning of a Ph.D establishes the notion that professors have knowledge and that beginning teachers will learn to teach as they acquire such knowledge.

The social science community has increasingly questioned this technical-rationalist approach to educational research and its technical application to practice (Smith, 1983). Many writers doubt that context-free generalizations are suitable for research that focuses on social systems, or that such generalizations are even attainable. Social interactions constructed by individuals with multiple intentions become very complex. Research that focuses on central tendencies reduces complexity, masks contradictions, and downplays human agency (Zeichner and Gore, 1990). At issue here is not the value of such knowledge, but rather its application to practice. The school-based notion of teacher preparation is challenging the view that the presentation of positivistic forms of knowledge provides an adequate grounding for beginning teachers. The influence of constructivism has emphasized the need for beginning teachers to construct their own meaning of how to teach within a social context.

13

At issue here is whether those in faculties of education can reexamine their traditional status as knowledge-givers and take on the different roles that are required to adopt and apply strategies such as those required in case teaching described by Wassermann in Chapter 10. The case method of teaching is rich in terms of knowledge, but the way in which such knowledge is applied takes a very different turn. It illustrates one of several ways that the traditional role of the university is being challenged by more innovative forms of teacher education.

Change Within Faculties of Education

An issue raised in Chapter 7 by Sheehan and Fullan and one that runs through several others is the question of change within faculties of education and how it occurs. Generally, we see two types of change (or proposed change) being described in these chapters. On the one hand, we see mandates at the national or regional level, some of which have involved major restructuring, such as the Norwegian case, and others which remain at the level of benign proposals, which seems to be the case in Canada.

Parallel to these proposed changes at the regional and national levels we see a number of changes at, what Sheehan and Fullan call, the ground level. These are innovative efforts that I described earlier under the heading 'the wedge of progressive practice'. The Foxfire approach described by Dittmer and Fischetti represents an approach to change at the ground level, as are the changes described by Scott and Burke, Carson, and other chapters in this book. What we see from Howey's analysis of the situation in the United States, however, is that such examples are not being acknowledged by those who drive the reform agenda, as improvements in teacher education do not appear to be part of their plans.

At issue in these attempts is the connection between large-scale mandates, which frequently involve restructuring, and changes within faculties of education where reconceptualization must take place. What connections exist between the two? Does restructuring lead to ground-level changes, or do teacher educators ignore mandates and simply go on about their business as usual.

The issue of change becomes crucial given the premise on which this book was based – that radical reconceptualization of teacher education is a must if the activity as we know it is to survive. A knowledge of improved practice in teacher education is only the beginning. Coming to understand how to put that knowledge into practice on a larger scale is the next step, a step which will involve changes to the way we do business in faculties of education.

Can Teacher Education Meet the Challenge?

The normal school concept provided a known status for teacher preparation. As free-standing institutions, they enjoyed a clear mandate for the preparation of teachers for the schools. The move to universities, however, meant that this central mission became only one concern of those who educated teachers. Not only do faculties of education find themselves in competition for resources with other departments in the university setting, but many of their faculty have developed interests that have little bearing on the preparation of teachers. For that they have paid a price. Both Howey, in describing the situation in the United States, and Sheehan and Fullan in describing the Canadian case, point out the missed opportunities of faculties of education for participating in the school reform agenda. What else might one expect from an institution that has virtually squandered its central mission and lost its sense of purpose?

The issue that faces us as we examine the chapters that follow is how do we regain that central focus? How can teacher education become an important process in the years ahead given that their members have become, as Tisher points out, weak and docile players?

The grand design that we might paint for teacher education can only be achieved through a sensitive balance between efforts to restructure and efforts to reconceptualize. But in the final analysis, it will be the efforts of individuals and communities that will make the difference.

References

BOWMAN, J. (1991) *A Report of the External Review Team of the College of Teachers*, Vancouver: British Columbia College of Teachers.

BROWN, J., COLLINS, A. and DUGUID, P. (1989) 'Situation cognition and the culture of learning', *Educational Researcher*, **18**(1), 32–42.

CARTER, C. (1990) 'Teachers' knowledge and learning to teach', in HOUSTON, W.R. (Ed.) *Handbook of Research on Teacher Education*, New York: Macmillan.

CLARK, D.L. (1992) 'Leadership in policy development by policy educators: Search for a more effective future', in GIDEONSE, H.D. (Ed.) *Teacher Education Policy*, Albany, NY: State University of New York Press.

CLIFTON, R.A., MANDZUK, D. and ROBERTS, L.W. (1994) 'The alienation of undergraduate education students: A case study of a Canadian university', *Journal of Education for Teaching*, **20**(2), 179–92.

CUSHMAN, M.L. (1977) *The Governance of Teacher Education*, Berkeley, CA: McCutchan.

DOYLE, W. (1990) 'Themes in teacher education research', in HOUSTON, W.R. (Ed.) *Handbook of Research on Teacher Education*, New York: Macmillan, 3–24.

DRUCKER, P.F. (1994) 'The age of transformation', *Atlantic Monthly*, 53–7, 62–80.

FLANDERS, T. (1980) *The Professional Development of Teachers*, Vancouver: The British Columbia Teachers' Federation.

FULLAN, M., WIDEEN, M. and ESTABROOK, G. (1983) 'A study of teacher training institutions in anglophone Canada, Vol. I: Current perspectives on teacher training in Canada: An overview of faculty and student perceptions', A report to the Social Science and Humanities Council, 28–9.

GIDDENS, A. (1990) *The Consequences of Modernity*, Oxford: Polity Press.

GIDEONSE, H.D. (Ed.) (1992) *Teacher Education Policy*, Albany, NY: State University of New York Press.

GOODLAD, J. (1984) *A Place Called School: Prospects for the Future*, New York, McGraw Hill.

GOODLAD, J. (1990) *Teachers for our Nation's Schools*, San Francisco, CA: Jossey-Bass.

GRIMMETT, P. and NEUFELD, J. (1994) *Teacher Development Authenticity and the Struggle for Authenticity*, New York: Teachers College Press.

HARGREAVES, A. (1994) *Changing Teachers, Changing Times: Teachers' Work and Culture in the Postmodern Age*, London: Cassell.

HARGREAVES, A. (in press) 'Towards a social geography of teacher education', in SHIMAHARA, N.K. and HOLOWINSKY, I.Z. *Teacher Education in Industrialized Nations*, New York: Garland.

ISHER, R.E. (1992) 'Teacher education policy: The Texas experience', in GIDEONSE, H.D. (Ed.) *Teacher Education Policy*, Albany, NY: State University of New York Press.

JOYCE, B. and CLIFT, R. (1984) 'The Phoenix agenda: Essential reform in teacher education', *Educational Researcher*, 5–16.

KOERNER, J.D. (1963) *The Miseducation of American Teachers*, Baltimore, MD: Penguin books.

LARABEE, D. (1992) 'Power, knowledge and the rationalization of teaching: A genealogy of the move to professionalize teaching', *Harvard Educational Review*, **62**(6), 123–55.

MYERS, D. and SAUL, D. (1974) 'How not to reform a teacher education system', in MYERS, D. and REID, F. (Eds) *Educating Teachers: Critiques and Proposals*, Toronto: OISE Press.

PATTERSON, R. (1984) 'Teacher education in Alberta's normal schools', In GRIMMETT, P. (Ed.) *Research in Teacher Education: Current Problems and Future Prospects in Canada*, Vancouver: Center for the Study of Teacher Education, University of British Columbia.

PETERSON, K.B. and FLEMING, T.C. (1979) 'Irrationality and teacher education', *Teacher Education*, 40–9.

ROBINSON, S.D. and RYAN, A.J. (1989) *An Analysis of the Internship Experience*, College of Education, University of Saskatchewan. Paper presented at the annual meeting of the Canadian Society for the Study of Education, Laval University, Quebec.

SMITH, J.K. (1983) 'Quantitative versus qualitative research: An attempt to clarify the issue', *Educational Researcher*, **12**(3), 6–13.

TYSON, H. (1994) *Who will Teach the Children?* San Francisco, CA: Jossey-Bass.

ZEICHNER, K. and GORE, J. (1990) 'Teacher socialization', in HOUSTON, W.H. (Ed.) *Handbook of Research on Teacher Education*, New York: Macmillan, 329–48.

Part One

Opportunities and Troubling Times in Teacher Education

The statement that teacher education will face major changes over the next decade probably could have been uttered at any time since the Second World War. But today the statement takes on a much more serious tone and the stakes have become much higher. In several Western countries various forms of restructuring have already begun. This section of the book describes the efforts to restructure teacher preparation in six Western countries. The situations in the United States, Australia and Great Britain, as described by Ken Howey, Richard Tisher, and David Pimm and Michelle Selinger respectively, provide cause for concern. The events in Great Britain, in particular, provide a grim reminder of what happens when radical restructuring is not accompanied by careful reconceptualization. Were this to become the pattern for the rest of the world, then the very nature of teacher education as we have known it would be at stake.

As we see in the Portuguese, Norwegian, and Canadian chapters, however, restructuring can take on quite different forms. Isabel Alarcão describes an ecological situation in which policymakers are being influenced by the dialogue and discourse of those in the educational community. Trond Eiliv Hauge presents the Norwegian case as one in the throes of a major change in which the lengthening of the time frame of teacher education is accompanied by a nation-wide reorganization of its institutions. In the case of Canada and the two provinces described by Nancy Sheehan and Michael Fullan, there is an optimistic sense that the pressure for reform can be a positive force.

Change, then, becomes the common element in all these cases. What remains to be seen, however, is whether this change will become instances of restructuring without appropriate reconceptualization or instances of restructuring that leads to a careful and rigorous reconceptualization of teacher preparation.

Chapter 2

The United States: The Context for the Restructuring and Reconceptualization of Teacher Preparation

Kenneth R. Howey

Certain forces exert pressure for change on teacher education in the United States including reform initiatives in elementary and secondary schools, teacher licensing, accrediting, standards-setting activities, and teacher education networks or consortia. Other factors, however, which one would expect to exert influence on teacher preparation in fact do not to any substantial degree. What has *not* influenced teacher preparation is as informative and points the direction for future action as much as what currently *is* influencing the initial education of teachers.

What isn't Exerting Enough Influence

One would assume that the changing condition of elementary and secondary schools in this vast and diverse country would influence teacher preparation and visa versa. However, this condition should be underscored at the outset: what transpires in attempts to restructure and reform schools in the United States and what takes place in the name of teacher education reform occur largely independent of one another. Beyond this fact, an overriding characteristic of educational change initiatives in the United States is that no *national* design exists for either the reform of elementary and secondary schools or schools of education. Further, we find no dominant trend which can be said to characterize the nature of curricular or instructional reform either in schools or in the preservice education of teachers.

I should add that a growing number of voluntary networks of schools concerned with restructuring do have common characteristics including those maintained by Levin (1991); Sizer (1991); and Comer (1992). They however, represent but a small percentage of the elementary and secondary schools in the United States, and none of them has demonstrated any interest in the reform of initial teacher preparation so that new teachers entering the teaching force are prepared to teach effectively in them. The parallel initiatives in teacher education such as Goodlad's National Network for Educational Renewal (1988) The Renaissance Group (1989), and the Holmes Group (1990) who do have an interest in school reform as well as teacher education reform are still in the initial phases of education reform. Many of the innovations espoused in the literature, however, such as interdisciplinary curricula or forms of authentic assessment are not common practice in either elementary or secondary schools, or colleges of education.

I should also add that no potent legal, political or economic incentives exist for those in schools and those in schools of education to collaborate in ways which would influence parallel changes in teacher preparation and elementary and secondary schools. Rather, policies are evolving which will likely widen an already considerable gap between the higher education/teacher education community and the elementary and secondary school sector. For example, some states provide modest venture capital to restructure elementary and secondary schools with no incentive for them to cooperate with the teacher education community. Moreover, while states often provide nominal financial support to local districts for the continuing education of first-year teachers, they neglect their preservice preparation and make no effort to engage higher education in this critical transition phase of education for teachers.

Higher education/teacher education's ability to influence such policies has been marginal, at best. The political muscle of teachers, administrators, and school boards on the other hand is exerted, not on matters of teacher education, but on what are understandably viewed as more fundamental problems: teacher's salaries and school funding. Many school reformers apparently take the view that preservice preparation is a relatively weak intervention and that in developing new models of schools, a culture will be created wherein the experienced licensed teacher will continue to learn, typical of the national strategy in countries like Japan. Educational policy, especially at the state and local district level where the primary responsibility for education rests, reflects a similar position; put the monies into school renewal with as direct a connection as possible to pupil improvement and where the effects are most visible to the public and voting constituency. Again, this seems an unnecessarily dichotomous strategy. Thus, school reform initiatives and the work in faculties of education appear to go on separately with little mutual influence.

Similarly, issues of social equity have not influenced teacher preparation as one would have thought they would. As in other countries, an overriding characteristic of schooling in the United States sees elementary and secondary schools often differentiated by their private and public character. But they are also very differentiated *within* the public sector because of major disparities in funding. For example, Chicago City Schools provide $5000 per year per student enrolled, while Niles Township, but a few miles from Chicago, spends $15000 per year per student enrolled. The racial composition and per-capita income of families in these two settings vary greatly and, while in close geographic proximity, the social distance between the two districts is as vast as is the difference in the quality of educational opportunities. Thus, we see so-called 'reform' of teacher education and the reality of reform of teacher education. Existing conditions have not driven a reform of teacher education which more centrally addresses how we recruit, prepare, and retain teachers for the many youngsters living in poverty and the special challenges they bring with them to school.

There are a number of reasons why this alarming condition has not exerted a greater force, but suffice it to say the great majority of the teacher education community is white, middle class, and conservative. They do not live in these settings. Prospective teachers represent a similar profile; they tend to come from small towns and suburbs and this is where they wish typically to teach. Another factor which curiously has not had the influence upon teacher education, and one which ought to be central to its mission, is the very nature of teaching and learning.

The society at large, the education community, and the teacher education community in the United States have begged the central question concerning the mission of schools in a stratified society. Teaching, in far too many instances, and certainly in the halls of academe, remains largely a teacher-centered activity which stresses the transmission of information. Learning, in turn, remains basically a passive, and largely an individual, activity, massively reinforced by pupils out of school watching hour after hour of television. And teachers continue to teach as they are taught.

Teaching has not improved because teacher educators, frankly, are limited in their pedagogical abilities, and no major pressures exist to change the nature of their teaching. College classrooms are truly private sanctuaries. These fundamental problems of pedagogy, underestimated by most and ignored by many in the teacher education literature, are nonetheless manifest everywhere. They speak both to how we as educators have failed to authentically engage many bright and materially-rich youngsters in their formal schooling as well as the problem of educating our equally able but less supported youngsters who live in conditions of poverty. We simply have *not* manifested widely the best of what we know about how to enable learning that is active, conceptual, and monitored both by individual learners and the group or learning community, – learning which simultaneously contributes to social as well as cognitive development. Thus, new pedagogy is a third major factor, along with changes in schools and the stratification of society, which has *not* greatly influenced teacher preparation. My perception is that most of us in the teacher education community do not know how to proceed in terms of adapting our programs to meet the demands these developments place upon us.

In attempting to call attention to the magnitude of these problems and the need to focus squarely on pedagogy, I recently put forward a series of interrelated premises for a network of elementary and secondary schools and colleges of education dedicated to addressing education problems in urban contexts.

1   The very nature of our social fabric, our quality of living, and our collective sense of social justice are inextricably tied to the character and quality of education in our elementary and secondary schools, and especially the quality of education in public schools in our major urban areas.

2   The quality of these schools ultimately hinges on the quality and dedication of teachers within these schools and on the nature and quality of the culture and conditions in which teaching and learning occur.

3   The quality of teachers and teaching which occurs in these schools is directly related to the quality of their teacher preparation.

4   The nature of how teachers are, or at least should be, prepared also speaks directly to the culture that evolves in schools and to some extent to the conditions in which teaching and learning occur.

5   In order to fundamentally alter the nature of teaching, teacher preparation needs to be deeply anchored in the intellectual foundations of the university and in professional schools and colleges of education while at the same tied in a continuing manner to the realities and practical problems of elementary and secondary schools.

6   This integrated notion of teacher education calls for more authentic partnerships between those in schools and colleges of education and those in elementary and secondary schools (Howey, 1994:25–26).

In addition to these concerns we have been less than creative in defining the broader construct of a school, especially in our urban contexts where so many youngsters are educated, or more accurately, not educated. Astuto and Clark (1992) share such a vision:

> Imagine an educational experience for adolescents and young adults that recognizes and is responsive to the economic and social contexts in which schools exist. *Community centers for young adults* replace traditional high schools. Teaching and learning occur in these centers, but the educational enterprise is sensitive to the range of needs and problems confronting today's youth. These centers exist for young adults for whatever assistance they need, to respond when they are sick or homeless or depressed or frightened or lonely. The full range of *community health, protection, and social services* converges on these sites so that the services are where the needs are.
>
> Educational professionals and the general public can no longer tolerate beliefs about the inevitability of below-par school performance of poor children and other historically underserved populations. Schooling for all children must deliver on the promise of a productive life in a just and equitable society for all citizens (1992, 107–8).

Thus, I assume that the major forces which *should* influence the nature of teacher preparation have to do with 1) a fundamental reexamination of the nature of a school in this society, and especially in communities where the education needs are the greatest; 2) the changing roles and responsibilities of those we refer to as teachers; 3) and the character of learning desired for our youngsters, and what this implies for teaching. As I have indicated, these factors have neither been addressed centrally nor deeply and when they are, they are largely considered in the abstract. If the focus on the reform of teacher preparation in the US is not here, then where is it? What is influencing school and teacher education reform?

A Brief Historical Perspective

A brief examination of what was attributed to a signal passage for school reform – and to some degree teacher education reform – in the United States is instructive in terms of explaining what is influencing teacher education today. The publication of *A Nation at Risk* by the US federal government a decade ago was referred to by some as a paper Sputnik. It was apocalyptic in its message, warning of a rising tide of mediocrity that threatens our very future as a nation as a people. The report was undergirded by pupil test-scores documenting the relatively poor performance of US students *vis-a-vis* other technologically advanced (and not so advanced) countries. The report called for improvements in four major areas: tougher high school graduation requirements; stronger admissions requirements for colleges; better *preparation* (emphasis mine) and salaries for teachers; and longer school days and school years. What progress has been made in these regards in the ten years since it was published?

In terms of graduation requirements, the Education Commission of the States (ECS) reported that by 1990, 37 per cent of the fifty states had achieved four years of English in secondary schools, albeit begging the ultimate question of their quality. However, only ten of the fifty states had met requirements in mathematics and only four in science. Measures of pupil achievement in this intervening time-period have been uneven at best. A recent Education Testing Service (ETS) document revealed that US 13-year-olds ranked 13th when compared to fifteen other countries in science, however, US 9-year-olds finished second out of thirty-six countries in reading scores.

In terms of the second recommendation, the large number of institutions of higher education in the United States competing in a depressed economy for students, suggests that it is folly to assume uniformly higher standards across these institutions. Virtually all students who want to pursue a college education can find a college to admit them.

Relative to the fourth major recommendation, neither longer school years nor school days have been achieved. Given model instructional practice at present, this may be fortuitous. The continuation of a depressed economy on the one hand, and the power of the teacher unions in terms of working conditions for teachers on the other, explain much of the lack of change here.

The third major recommendation called for better preparation for teachers and higher salaries. Higher salaries have been achieved in many instances, however, little evidence exists to show similar progress in teacher preparation and, as I have argued, forces which should have influenced teacher education, have *not*.

The Current Impetus for Reform

Thus, a decade later, what can we learn from the at-risk report which fueled so much ferment in terms of educational reform? It is quite clear now that from a governmental policy perspective, the primary strategy for improving schooling is to influence the education communities to focus on test scores and *outcomes*, rather than on any specific means, policies, resources, or conditions which are assumed to represent quality education. This focus on outcomes and testing pertains increasingly to teacher education as well. Expenditures for education – a great percentage of which are for salaries – have gone up significantly, but pupil performance has made but marginal progress. Patience has run out; it is time for results. The current pervasive strategy to influence education and teacher education are the development of new and more rigorous standards and the means to assess progress against these.

From this perspective one cannot argue with the need to achieve greater consensus and better clarity about what it is, if anything, that all students should know and be able to do. The same applies to teachers, and I would argue as well that more rigorous benchmarks for assessing our progress as educators and teacher educators are needed. From this perspective it is not axiomatic that a system of national standards, heretofore not established in the US, will necessarily result in a narrower, more convergent and less creative instruction. The problem is *not* standards as such, but rather the efforts by many to further uncouple and distance assessment from instruction and to focus on discrete pupil performance.

Nonetheless, one finds some encouraging movement. While hardly in the majority, a number of scholars are contributing to major new initiatives which suggest breakthroughs relative to student assessment and, more fundamentally, the notion of effective instruction, which I have argued should be a major force for change in teacher education. Most notable in this regard is the New Standards Project which is a joint venture of the Learning Research and Development Center (LRDC) at the University of Pittsburgh and the National Center on Education and Economy (NCEE). The project is viewed not so much as an evaluation effort but rather as a broader reform movement in American education attempting to blur the lines between curriculum, instruction, and evaluation. In order to underscore the major departure in this important assessment endeavor from what is measured on more traditional and conventional standardized tests, the project emphasizes what are referred to as the three Ps: performance tasks; projects; and portfolios. Each of these may take students days or even months to complete. The intent is that such forms of assessment, closely coupled with instruction, will often require students to work with their peers, consonant with the notion of a learning community.

The three types of national standards on which the New Standards Project is focused include *content* standards which specify what they should know in various subjects and domains; *performance* standards which address benchmark exemplars of student work on various tasks and assignments – as close to real life endeavors and responsibilities as possible; and finally, what are referred to as *school delivery* standards. This third type of standard will identify criterion guidelines for assessing whether schools are providing their students with the opportunity to learn – a critical concern given the unevenness across schools in this society.

Understandably, the very considerable political muscle of many in the testing industry along with numerous legal and political agencies concerned with increased accountability have raised major concerns about such forms of measurement. They assert the need for more standardized, external measures of student assessment. However, while standards and assessment, are embraced more than ever by governmental and regulatory agencies in the United States as the engine for reform, there is a growing, enlightened faction of the education community concerned about what constitutes standards and how performance over time can be assessed against these.

Teacher Education Standards and Assessment Activities

No major parallel initiatives exist that are concerned with teacher standards setting or outcomes identification. One of these is the vanguard effort supported by the National Board for Professional Teaching Standards (NBPTS). This board is concerned with establishing standards which signify *accomplished* practice. Unlike physicians, architects, or accountants in the US, the knowledge, skills, and dispositional behaviors that represent accomplished practice for teachers have not been codified. Results of empirical studies providing evidence of effective teaching patterns and agreement about what constitutes good teaching have not, to date, been addressed on any national performance measures. The NBPTS' ambitious agenda, however, calls for developing standards for accomplished practice in twenty of the thirty certificate fields that will comprise the National Board Certification System when it is fully operational. As with the New Standards Project, major piloting of assessment procedures is underway which engages sizable numbers of teachers with multiple means of documenting and assessing their teaching. The portfolio assessment phase of the project, for example, is examining the use of videotape in determining what teachers will bring with them to an assessment centre. NBPTS asserts that the state-of-the-art assessments which they are in the process of developing 'must be deeply rooted in self-reflection and class-room practice' and, as with the assessment initiatives in the New Standards Project, there is a considerable emphasis on the professional development of teachers and the closer coupling or blending of instruction and assessment.

The concept of advanced teacher certification is new, and a guiding assumption in NBPTS efforts is that by establishing high and rigorous standards for experienced teachers who have demonstrated accomplished practice, the linch-pin for educational reform will have been turned. Recall that I earlier underscored the emphasis on experienced teachers in many reform initiatives. However, NBPTS' initiative should have major implications in terms of the identification of teacher-leaders who will be able to assume new and expanded roles in the *initial*, as well as the continuing, education of teachers. A parallel standards setting project has been initiated by the Council of Chief State School Officers in the United States. The Interstate New Teacher Assessment and Support Consortium (INTASC) is addressing *initial* teacher licensing in a manner consonant with the initiatives of the NBPTS relative to *advanced* certification.

The effects of these endeavors are difficult to predict. I have highlighted them because at this particular time standards settings and assessment are the most discernible and pervasive activities in a myriad array of reform endeavors in both the elementary and secondary schools and teacher education sectors. Further, the best of these endeavors signal, at the very least, a more enlight-ened view than is generally manifest, not only of learning, but learning to teach. These enlightened assessment efforts move from a preoccupation with periodic evaluation of discrete behaviors to multiple measures of development over time. The evolving emphasis on *students' reasoning* in their instructional activities is parallel with increasing attention to preservice *teachers'* reasoning, as well as their classroom performance.

An optimistic view is that these endeavors will foreshadow an important shift in how teachers are prepared in the future: moving from an emphasis on technical skills to be eventually demonstrated in "students" teaching, to a focus on clinical abilities fostered first in pedagogical laboratories and then refined and examined over time in classroom settings. The pessimistic view is that these standards will drive changes in paper curricula and will not greatly affect the nature of teaching and learning. We have a history of such efforts. The major point here is that standards-setting and assessment occupy center stage at the present time in the United States and a number of key players are focused, rightfully from this perspective, on a more informed conception of learning and teaching as well as on learning to teach.

Teacher Education Reform Initiatives

While the major reform in teacher education, as in the elementary and secondary sector, is embedded currently in standards-setting and assessment activities, other initiatives with a teacher-education reform agenda occur as well. Although the impact of the Holmes Group, a consortium of almost 100 research institutions which prepare teachers, has waned considerably, its influence over the last decade has been considerable. Holmes served as a major wake-up call to the leadership in most of our major schools and colleges of education. Several dormant programs were revitalized over the last decade. Further, we have seen a positioning of teacher education within a post-baccalaureate endeavor that has carried symbolic and political significance. However, the effects of these attempts to protract the preparation of teachers and enhance the professional image of teacher preparation will not be determined for some time. The guiding principles which the Holmes Group has promulgated for Professional Development Schools have indeed spurred new and improved partnerships with elementary and secondary schools.

A major question at this juncture is whether the guiding principles which The Holmes Group (1995) have recently established for rethinking schools of education, will once more stimulate needed discourse between teacher education faculty and their colleagues in the schools. I, for one, am not optimistic in this regard. I believe the challenge for the Holmes Group is whether policies and products can be put into place to reward and sustain faculty working in Professional Development Schools in a manner that integrates research with teacher development and which engages school personnel more fully and responsibly in the education of preservice teachers.

The Renaissance Group is a consortium of higher education institutions which historically were *teaching* schools or colleges of education as opposed to research institutions. While considerably smaller in membership and more recently formed than the Holmes Group, this network has actively engaged the presidents of these institutions in its deliberations about the reform of teacher education, and for this they are to be commended. Teacher education is typically a more central enterprise to these universities as a whole than it is to many of the institutions in the Holmes Group. It may be that this consortium can help make teacher education more of an all-university responsibility, at least in the more regional and somewhat less comprehensive universities. As with the Holmes Group, however, there are at present neither major investments of money nor faculty to suggest dramatic reform will emanate from this consortium.

Fourteen diverse institutions across the country are working with John Goodlad to engage in a fundamental transformation of their programs of teacher preparation. Much of the change that is underway is guided by the nineteen postulates that Goodlad enunciated as a result of his major study of teacher education in *Teachers For Our Nation's Schools* (1990). Goodlad has further enunciated four guiding beliefs for the school/university partnerships in this National Network for Educational Renewal (NNER). These include first, that teachers should realize that education is primarily a means to enculturate the young into a democratic society, and hence they must possess a thorough understanding of the nature of a democratic form of government. Second, teachers must possess the intellectual tools and skills to meaningfully engage in conversation and in multiple ways introduce their students to that conversation; this includes the canons of reasoning that are central to an intelligent and satisfying participation. A third expectation is that teachers possess the pedagogical knowledge and skills needed to arrange more optimal learning conditions than are present for educating the young. And, finally, a fourth expectation is that teachers have the skills to participate in the renewal of the schools in which they will teach, and in this regard, will engage in sustained inquiry about the nature, quality and relevance of the educational enterprise. Goodlad and his colleagues have rightfully placed an emphasis on the moral and ethical dimensions of teaching and schooling. A second major strength in this network is the coordinated agenda for reform in the elementary and secondary schools and in schools of education. It must also be commended for its attention to the integrated human services approach to schooling, enunciated earlier as one response to the problems in the core of our cities. While its mission is on target, this network is small and the investment of faculty resources to meet a very ambitious agenda limited.

Another recent teacher education reform initiative, the Urban Network to Improve Teacher Education, directed by the author of this chapter, again involves a relatively small number of institutions. Nine highly respected schools and colleges of education located in urban settings have joined together to more fully address the very significant problem of preparing teachers able and disposed to teach in multicultural settings and in neighborhoods characterized by conditions of poverty. The project is also distinctive in its use of leadership teams and in its focus on faculty development. While focused in its agenda, its chances for success, as with all experiments, is problematic. Whether leadership teams can be sustained and exert influence in the highly idiosyncratic higher education culture is one of several questions which will be tested. This consortium, as with the Goodlad consortium, affects only a few institutions. The technical assistance and professional development, provided to individual institutions on-site, are also limited in this initiative and are a major shortcoming, just as in many other reform endeavors. Perhaps its significance lies in pointing to where broader efforts should be focused – preparing teachers for the urban context and squarely addressing teaching and learning and learning to teach through faculty development.

While each of these teacher education reform initiatives underscores the necessity of restructuring teacher education in concert with changes in schools and school communities, it should be emphasized again that little has been accomplished in the way of social policy and public support for the clinical aspect of teacher preparation to be taken seriously by those in schools. This is hardly to denigrate these various reform initiatives, but to place them in perspective within the very large and diverse enterprise of teacher education and teacher licensing. In addition to these networking and confederation efforts, the National Council for the Accreditation of Teacher Education also exerts an influence. On the horizon, more attention in the National Council for the Accreditation of Teacher Education will also be given to the assessment of programs over time and of preservice teachers graduating from these programs. While institutions are being reviewed in more rigorous ways and more are being cited for not meeting standards, it should be underscored that the majority of institutions preparing teachers do *not* seek NCATE accreditation.

In addition, we find a few alternative teacher preparation endeavors outside of higher education. They are few in number, however, and typically maintain some relationship to higher education. They are not that different than many programs of a concentrated nature in the vast and diverse higher education/ teacher preparation enterprise. Excellent marketing and their abbreviated character have typically allowed them to recruit a higher percentage of individuals from historically under-represented populations. The most common of these is *alternative credentialling* where several thousand teachers annually are temporarily licensed without preparation or with only minimum preparation in order to place teachers in diverse and difficult-to-teach-in classroom settings, especially in our major urban areas. This move is not an alternative teacher education movement, let alone a reform movement. Rather, it represents a most unfortunate, but necessary, response to the vacuum created by the lack of licensed teachers who can and will teach in these contexts, and reflects a lack of enlightened policy to recruit and prepare teachers for these settings, as well as absence on the part of education professions to focus collectively on an untenable situation – a problem I underscored at the outset.

The Most Common Catalyst for Change: Individuals and Small Working Groups

The efforts I have just described are ultimately very modest given the extremely large number of institutions engaged in teacher education (over 1200). It should be underscored that at the government level (whether federal, state, or local) no substantial venture money or experimental capital has been directed towards the improvement of initial teacher education. Public funds are, in fact, diminishing for initial teacher preparation, although some indication exists that under the Clinton administration more money will be diverted toward the professional development of experienced teachers which will typically be tied to teaching subject matter, such as mathematics and science and the standards attached to them. Thus, notwithstanding the efforts of standards-setting bodies, regulatory agencies, voluntary accreditation, and a few consortium arrangements, the matter of teacher education reform ultimately rests with small groups of individuals or individual teacher educators within their own institutions.

This author has been part of a small research team which has tracked changes in preservice teacher education across the United States over the last decade. Each year a national probability sample of institutions stratified by institutional type and geographic location is surveyed in the Research About

Teacher Education (RATE) study sponsored by The American Association of Colleges for Teacher Education (AACTE, 1990) one of its several initiatives designed to improve the preservice preparation of teachers. This ongoing study provides a vantage point from which to make some observations about the nature of reform promoted by individuals and small groups at their home institutions. The decisions and actions undertaken, I believe, provide the most accurate picture of what change is occurring in teacher preparation in the United States. Make no mistake about it, if elementary and secondary teaching is largely a private affair, this is even more the situation in higher education. Whatever the variety of external influences, the curriculum in teacher education is ultimately a very personal, idiosyncratic one.

Some would argue (Gideonse, 1994) that the states exert undue and unnecessarily prescriptive influence on programs of teacher preparation. I basically disagree. The State of Ohio – in which I live and work as a teacher educator – has fifty institutions which prepare teachers. Many of these are not NCATE accredited. They vary considerably in quality. However, none of these has been put out of business by the state because they fail to meet state standards. This is not atypical. The process of program approval across all states leaves much to be desired. Herein lies much of the problem of teacher preparation. It is not over-regulated, rather, mediocre programs proliferate because, among other things, we lack truly professional accounting. The attempt to coordinate NCATE accreditation and state program approval in many states is an initiative to be applauded, especially if it results in a more concentrated and educative self-study followed by rigorous review.

When one examines reform from this vantage point of individual and small groups of faculty making their way in their own settings, the picture is one of considerable unevenness. Let's take a look at the positive side first. In spite of numerous challenges and common reductions in what were limited resources to begin with, more than eight in ten of the teacher education faculty and preservice students polled annually rate the overall quality of their teacher preparation programs as high. The teacher preparation endeavor is uneven, but the situation simply is *not* as bad any many reformists would lead us to believe. In this regard, I suggest that you ask any individual teacher educator to rate the quality of his or her teaching and commitment to students. In the RATE studies students are invariably more positive than their faculty counterparts in assessing the quality of faculty and their teacher preparation overall. These perceptions are proxies for quality and they are seriously constrained since preservice students lack the experience to know what they don't know. Nonetheless, it appears that progress is being made by small groups of dedicated teacher educators on a number of difficult program issues in most institutions.

The annual RATE studies reveal that the teacher education curriculum at most institutions is in a state of continuing revision, albeit in a fragmented manner. New and improved relationships with elementary and secondary schools are being sought across all types of institutions that prepare teachers.

Holmes has been an important catalyst in this regard. More positive educational and socialization experiences are reported at many institutions through a wide variety of student cohorts. Improved evaluation and assessment through preservice student portfolios is increasingly seen. Inroads appear to have been made in several institutions on the reconceptualizing of the core abilities and dispositions desired in teachers, and in turn, these have then been manifested thematically throughout their programs.

A fairly high percentage of education deans recently reported in a RATE study (AACTE, 1992) that they have held their own, or even benefited slightly, in the common reallocation and retrenchment activities conducted by university budget officers. For example, four in ten deans of education reported that they gained in these prioritizing activities while one in eight reported diminishment in resources as a result of reallocation.

The considerable majority of faculty members surveyed over time report that in spite of increasing encroachments on their time and energies, they nonetheless maintain a considerable sense of efficacy relative to their abilities to prepare teachers and to engage in continuing renewal. It should also be noted that a fairly high percentage of administrators and teacher educators polled in the RATE studies indicated that recent rules and regulations at the state level relative to teacher preparation were, in fact, positive. Surely, not all state mandates relative to teacher education are uninformed, pernicious in intent, or largely negative in their manifold effects. Beyond this, respondents in the RATE studies report that elementary and secondary schools have been *more* willing, not less willing, to work with them in these difficult economic times. Finally, a great majority of those preparing teachers report that they are, in fact, engaged in sustained working relationships with urban and rural districts characterized by conditions of poverty. Schools and colleges of education are increasingly committing resources to schools and school districts where the challenges are the greatest.

One cannot, by any stretch of the imagination, however, paint a wholly positive picture based on these annual RATE inquiries. While some modest increases in terms of resources are reported in some institutions, it should be noted that in most institutions faculty are considerably stretched in their responsibilities with inadequate institutional support for them and their students. Further, resources to rectify this situation are not forthcoming. Schools and colleges of education are fighting to hold their own. This writer has had the opportunity to visit many of the new Professional Development Schools. While they have contributed to improving working relationships between schools and colleges of education and elementary and secondary schools, in most instances far more time, effort, and resources have been devoted to elementary and secondary school reform than to the fundamental improvement of teacher preparation or to a strengthened contribution from the teaching profession to preservice preparation. New faculty positions in teacher education are often difficult to come by and the RATE studies report that frequently when positions become available, the quality of individuals applying for these positions is not what it should be. Higher education/teacher education is, and will be for some time, in a period of down-sizing or 'right'-sizing. While some positive changes in the arts, sciences, and humanities relative to teacher education are reported in the literature, in most instances, the RATE studies reveal that teacher education faculty have little influence on curriculum matters in these academic units and only negligible impact in altering the fundamental nature of pedagogy that occurs within and outside of colleges of education.

The criteria for promotion remain disproportionately weighted towards research at the expense of instruction and service at many teacher education institutions. Further, in many institutions, it is reported that criteria for promotion are not fully accepting of the practice-oriented inquiry advocated in several reform initiatives. While the teacher education faculties wisely believe that they make a difference, increasing dissatisfaction with workload is reported and a lack of time and support of scholarship and for the new demands inherent in program redesign, especially of a school-based nature, are frequently cited.

Program evaluation in any systematic and ongoing sense remains uncommon. While many innovations are promulgated, again largely by individuals or small groups, full scale, well-planned experimentation with programs of teacher education, or planned variations in teacher education, are very rare. While a compelling case can be made for pedagogical cases grounded in domain-specific knowledge which state theoretical claims relative to the complexity of classroom life, instances of high-quality case development in teacher preparation with the full involvement of teachers are also extremely rare. Finally, and to the real heart of the matter, the fundamental nature of pedagogy, as it is provided for and in which prospective teachers engage on campus and in schools, is simply not what it should be.

Bold, coordinated action is largely lacking in teacher preparation and there is little in the way of policy, funding patterns, or changes in institutional culture to suggest that we will soon move beyond the creative, and not-so-creative, initiatives of individuals and small groups as the primary means of improving teacher preparation. While rhetoric and literature relative to teacher education reform continues to grow, from my perspective these are some distance from the reality of the lives of individual teacher educators and the prospective teachers with whom they interact. Ultimately, we need more accurate descriptions (like the RATE studies) of teacher education in the United States from the perspective of individual teacher educators and their students.

References

American Association of Colleges for Teacher Education (1990) *RATE IV: Teaching Teachers: Facts and Figures*, Washington, DC: AACTE.
American Association of Colleges for Teacher Education (1992) *RATE IV: Teaching Teachers: Facts and Figures*. Washington, DC: AACTE.

ASTUTO, T.A. and CLARK, D.L. (1992) 'The changing contexts of teaching', in LIEBERMAN, A. (Ed.) *Challenging the Limits of School Restructuring and Reform*, Chicago, IL: The University of Chicago Press, p. 90.

COMER, J.P. (1992) *A Brief History and Summary of the School Development Program*, New Haven, CT: Yale Child Study Center, Yale University.

GIDEONSE, H.D. (Ed.) (1992) *Teacher Education Policy: Narratives, Stories, and Cases*, Albany, NY: SUNY Press.

GOODLAD, J.I. (1988) *The National Network for Educational Renewal: Past, Present, Future*, Occasional paper no. 7, Seattle, WA: University of Washington, Center for Educational Renewal.

GOODLAD, J.I. (1990) *Teachers for our Nation's Schools*, San Francisco, CA: Jossey-Bass Inc.

HOLMES GROUP (1990) *Tomorrow's Schools: Principles for the Design of Professional Development Schools*, East Lansing, MI: The Holmes Group.

HOLMES GROUP (1995) *Tomorrow's Schools of Education*, East Lansing, MI: The Holmes Group.

HOWEY, K.R. (1994) *Leadership Teams and Networking: A Strategy for Faculty Development in Informing Faculty Development for Teacher Educators*. Norwood NJ: Abler Publishing Co.

INTASC (1992) *Model Standards for Beginning Teacher Licensing and Development: A Resource for State Dialogue*, Washington, DC: Interstate New Teacher Assessment and Support Consortium.

LEVIN, H.M. (1991) *Accelerating the Progress of all Students*, Albany, NY: Rockefeller Institute Special Report, No. 31, State University of New York.

NATIONAL BOARD FOR PROFESSIONAL TEACHING STANDARDS (1994) *What Teachers Should Know and be Able to Do*, Washington, DC: NBPTS.

NATIONAL COMMISSION ON EXCELLENCE IN EDUCATION (1983) *A Nation at Risk: The Imperative for Educational Reform*, Washington, DC: National Commission on Excellence in Education.

SIZER, T.R. (1991) 'No pain, no gain', *Educational Leadership*, **48**(8), 32–34.

THE RENAISSANCE GROUP (1989) *Teachers for the New World: A Statement of Principles*, Cedar Falls, IA: University of Northern Iowa.

Chapter 3

Readjustments, Reorganization or Revolution? The Changing Face of Teacher Education in Australia

Richard P. Tisher

Background

Australians praise the teachers of their own children and value what they do in their school, but criticize the profession and the preservice preparation teachers receive. They believe, as do many teacher educators, that little has changed from three decades ago (McWilliam and O'Brien, 1993).

The public criticism of preservice teacher education has intensified in recent years with calls at both state and national levels, from business, academic and political groups, for a review and a recasting of pre-service preparation programs. The academic critics have included University Vice-Chancellors who have instigated reviews of Schools of Education and staff from Schools of Law, Engineering and Medicine who value the content contained in the traditional disciplines and wish to see more of that in Education degree programs. In this debate teacher educators have been amazingly docile, silent, and ignored. They have been largely bypassed by the education employing authorities, politicians and business groups who maintain that Australian teacher education, like its American counterpart (Lanier and Little, 1986) has a weak and questionable knowledge base, a fragmented and shallow curriculum which provides little intellectual challenge, does not attract the intellectual high-fliers leaving school at year 12 (Hansford, 1992). The situation is exacerbated within the universities where teaching and Education are dealt a further blow. Schools of Education are accorded a lower status and receive a lower level of fiscal support than Schools of Science, Medicine, Business and Technology.

By and large, Australians' view of teacher education is not congruent with the image that teacher educators would like. Clearly there are difficulties to be resolved (Hansford, 1992) and certainly the public criticisms of teacher education cannot be ignored. Despite all the scrutiny and debate many contend that little change has actually occurred (McWilliam and O'Brien, 1993). Some teacher educators, however, suggest that criticism can be assuaged by making the public more aware of the changes made to teacher education programs to respond to educational, social and political demands, including educational

34

policy changes at national and state levels. For example, courses have been altered to enhance trainees' teaching repertoires and competencies to deal with new demands occasioned by alterations to school curricula, assessment practices, diversity in student learning styles, and policies and practices with respect to integration of students with disabilities. However, many contend that these changes are minimal and normal in any dynamic, interactive social setting. They do not constitute major changes to pre-service education.

Changes in program delivery have also occurred. For example, the increased acceptance amongst teacher educators of the diversity of talents and knowledge of the persons entering the programs of teacher education has led to some changes in the conduct of programs in several institutions. These involve the establishment of smaller interactive group settings in order to take better account of pre-service teachers' emerging concerns and needs, and collaborative, integrated teaching by educational psychologists, sociologists and curriculum specialists. But to many, these changes are also seen as normal expectations to changing circumstances. In Australia a three-year program is generally offered for primary teachers whilst a four-year program is offered for those aspiring to teach in secondary schools. These times are regarded as the minimum for relevant study. Some slight variations occur between the states as to the time trainees must spend in practice teaching.

Thus, we have seen a number of normal, evolutionary changes to the content and conduct of pre-service education arising from teacher educators' perceptions of how to improve teacher preparation and also to their responses to outside demands. But in general terms, the question is, have these internal and external pressures produced beneficial changes? Are they sufficiently significant or revolutionary to satisfy the demands of the 1990s?

Political and Structural Factors Affecting Teacher Education

Concerted national pressures for changes to teaching and teacher education have come from the federal government, professional associations, and nation-wide business and industry groups. As a consequence, national school curricula, national standards and procedures for school assessment, national 'agreed-to' basic competencies as the expected outcomes of educational programs (Finn, 1991; Lee, 1992; Mayer, 1992), and basic national qualifications for teachers (Schools Council, NBEET, 1990; 1991) are being formulated. The extent to which these national trends will continue, take hold and be successful remains to be seen. Warning cries now point to a downgrading rather than upgrading in teacher quality (Kennedy, 1993). But the return of the Labor Party in recent elections means work on many of these initiatives will continue. However, their implementation and adoption also depends upon the willingness of the states to forego some of their legislative rights with respect to education.

In Australia it is a historical and legislative fact that each of the eight Australian states and territories have the responsibility to provide education, including teacher education, for their residents. During the last three decades, however, the federal government has demonstrated an increased interest in all phases of education and has influenced state education, for example, through special education grants for specified educational initiatives. It also provides the major amount of the recurrent funds for universities which were initially established under state parliamentary acts. At present the federal government provides over $2 billion annually for the nation's schools and in the order of $420 million per annum to teacher education through its operating grants to universities. Consequently, pronouncements on education, including teacher education, by the federal government cannot, and will not, be ignored by state organizations. Of course tensions may arise between state and federal governments when their educational policies differ. For example, tensions arise when an Australian state government insists that all new teachers for its primary schools must have four years preservice education but the federal government maintains three years preservice as appropriate for primary teachers and funds universities accordingly.

The federal government's desire to influence state education, and teacher education, in particular, is found in a discussion paper on teacher education from the Commonwealth Department of Employment, Education and Training (1992) and a subsequent public statement by the Minister for Employment, Education and Training (Beazley, 1992). This discussion document encouraged teacher educators, other academics, teacher employers and the state governments to reassess the relevance of preservice and professional development programs to ensure a more rapid response to the changes occurring in the contexts in which teachers work, whether they be in primary or secondary schools, or the Technical and Further Education (TAFE) colleges. As might be expected the document was criticized for the quality of its arguments, contentious and unsubstantiated propositions, unsophisticated straw-man arguments and failure to recognize the foundational role of general education studies within pre-service programs (Barrie, 1993). The subsequent public ministerial statement, *Teaching Counts*, reaffirmed the government's stand on national competency-based standards and principles which underpin teacher education. For example, the key competencies (Mayer, 1992) which schools and teachers are to incorporate into the school curriculum are asserted to be:

- collecting, analyzing and organizing information;
- communicating ideas and information;
- planning and organizing activities;
- working with others in teams;
- using mathematical ideas and techniques;
- solving problems;
- using technology.

The key principles which underpin teacher education, and which must be maintained and enhanced, are asserted to be:

- a wide diversity of high quality teacher education courses between universities;
- partnerships between schools and universities which strengthen teacher education programs;
- the integration of pedagogy, research and discipline knowledge with teaching practice;
- a knowledge base which ensures that Australian teachers are given a strong grounding in their subjects and are exposed to recent developments in the relevant disciplines;
- flexibility within teacher education programs to facilitate appropriate shifts in the mix of theoretical and practical education;
- closer links between universities and teachers and trainers in their catchment areas, thereby encouraging the development of teacher education courses which are relevant and responsive to their professional needs and career development; and
- recognition by universities of employer needs and the most appropriate ways to respond to them.

The Minister for Employment, Education and Training also stated that the federal government would continue dialogue with teachers, teacher educators, and the Australian Vice-Chancellors' Committee on improving both preservice education and ongoing teacher professional development, according to the above principles. The release of the ministerial statement was followed by articles in state and national press focusing on an additional federal proposal to foster 'renewal of teacher education faculties' in order to address the issue of obsolescent teaching experience among staff, as documented by Turney and Wright (1992). The federal government promised a financial advance to assist schools of education with the early retirement of teacher education staff who had not taught in schools for two decades, and, consequently were out-of-touch, tenured, and 'inhibiting a flexible approach to the renewal of teacher education faculties' (Beazley, 1992:12).

These other federal funding proposals for teacher education were also made:

- the allocation of $60 million over three years for a National Professional Development Program which has as one of its objectives to renew teachers' knowledge of their subject disciplines;
- the establishment of a permanent Teacher Professional Development Fund, linked with the National Program, using $15 million per annum from the funds now provided to support trainee supervision during school field experience.

What will now happen to these proposals, post national election, remains to be seen. One gains the impression that the majority of teacher educators fear but are resigned to the political pressures.

One federal government action which has definitely affected the nature of teacher education is the abolition of the binary system of higher education. In this system Colleges of Advanced Education and Universities provided post-secondary degree and higher degree education programs. Now, these two kinds of institutions have amalgamated to form *mega-universities.* This restructuring has had an effect on schools of education with a consequent unique set of challenges for pre-service teacher education in particular.

It is appropriate to mention here, and a point to which I return later, that about three decades ago the majority of Australian teachers were trained in teachers' colleges controlled and funded by state governments and staffed by state government employees, the majority of whom had been teachers. The majority of trainees attending the colleges received state scholarships which bonded them for service as state teachers for three to five years. A proportion of persons aspiring to be secondary teachers completed their preservice education in the state universities and a smaller proportion of aspiring teachers attended institutions operated by the Catholic Church. A number of persons attending the state universities also received state government scholarships which provided a living allowance and covered university fees. They were also bonded to serve as teachers for a given period. As a consequence of these arrangements the state governments – the major employers of teachers – were able to exercise control over teacher qualifications and teacher supply. Both were governed by the state system's current educational needs.

During the seventies the umbilical link between state governments and the teachers' colleges was broken. The colleges became independent units, within a Colleges of Advanced Education sector, with the right to grant undergraduate degrees. The Colleges of Advanced Education were funded from the federal government to provide a high quality vocational education but were not expected to undertake research. Universities on the other hand were funded for undergraduate and postgraduate teaching and research. The Colleges of Advanced Education strove gradually, and with academic determination, to attain an educational status and recognition within the community equivalent to that held by the older universities. As part of this striving they increased their investment in postgraduate programs and research.

The Colleges of Advanced Education which had originated from teachers' colleges gradually added other than education programs. An aim was to give trainees an understanding of the substantive and syntactical nature of the subjects; an understanding which teachers could then foster in their own pupils. A number of teacher educators now believe that the shared responsibility and common purpose of teacher education as well as the nature of the understandings that were being developed, i.e., an interweaving of academic and pedagogical coursework, are under threat due to structural changes fostered in higher education by the Federal Government.

Now, three decades later, restructuring has occurred such that Australian Colleges of Advanced Education have been moved into Universities either through a marriage between a college and an existing university, or another one or two colleges of advanced education, to form a unit of an appropriate 'critical academic mass'. Some colleges have a new status as university colleges.

The amalgamations have, in a number of instances, led to some re-organizations in staffing. Individuals regarded as academically acceptable in a university discipline have been moved from the relevant discipline group in the college into the discipline department of the new amalgamated university where the emphasis is on research in the discipline, and rewards accrue to people who publish research papers. As a consequence, the commitment of persons to preservice teacher education alters, and there is a question as to whether the schools in the amalgamated universities will regard pre-service teacher education programs to be an institution-wide responsibility as they were in the colleges of advanced education.

The staff reorganizations and the expectation that the discipline departments will provide the general service courses within a preservice education program have created timetabling difficulties. Often the discipline departments refuse to cooperate with the education schools in the scheduling of the school experience components. As a consequence, doubts exist about the viability of concurrent programs. The alternative is a basic degree from one of the university's schools followed by a preservice pedagogical award, a Bachelor of Teaching, taken over two years. This move is being monitored by institutions in the Australian states, although there is an underlying concern about extending the overall length of preservice education for prospective teachers to five years.

Many, such as Bourke (1994) regard the federal interference as a short-sighted, short-term political expediency. Koop and Bezzina (1993) further argue that these associated national and state government initiatives are an attack on innovation, on the development of exemplary programs, and on quality and excellence.

Economic and Workforce Factors Affecting Teacher Education

Economic and workforce factors affect student enrollments in courses and the nature and quality of those courses. Altered levels of federal funding for universities, for example, affect the numbers of students who can be accommodated in university facilities and, consequently, the number of graduates who exit. Levels of funding affect the nature and quality of courses through the facilities and provisions that are available. Labor intensive programs, involving a great deal of one-to-one interaction in counseling and clinical situations, are the most likely ones to suffer when budget cuts occur. The quality of the practicum is one feature that has been greatly affected by reduced levels of funding to schools of education and the consequent reductions in staff. University mentors from some Australian institutions now only observe and counsel trainees in the practicum who are deemed to be at risk.

Economic factors in each state have also altered employment opportunities in the community. Unemployment generally is at an all-time high, and many mature persons, qualified as school teachers, are seeking to enter, or re-enter the teaching workforce. The level of teacher recruitment, however, has dropped in the government and non-government sectors due to such factors as a reduction in the growth rate in school enrollments and a lowering in the proportion of teachers who move into other occupations. School enrollments, and consequently the required number of teachers, in the non-government sector have also been affected by increases in school fees.

Universities on the other hand have continued to produce a large number of new teacher education graduates thereby adding people to the pool of qualified persons seeking school appointments. We now have, in Australia, a situation of over-supply where the younger teacher education graduates cannot be assured of a school teaching job. In some states, at present, fewer than 1 or 2 per cent are being appointed to permanent school teaching posts. Of course, recruitment policies will affect the proportion of mature and younger aged people who will be hired. These policies require further public analysis and revision bearing in mind that the Australian teacher workforce is an aging group with a mean age of about 40 and a likelihood that a high proportion of these people will retire in their fifties. If this occurs, the country may experience another teacher shortage in less than a decade. There are predictions, promulgated by the Australian Deans of Education from a survey they commissioned, that this shortage will occur well before the turn of the century.

The glaring fact that very few young teacher education graduates are obtaining employment as schoolteachers at present has prompted several rearguard actions. Teacher educators now are marketing their students as being skilled for a variety of occupations other than schoolteaching. Teacher education programs have been revised to include courses which are attractive to a variety of employers. The traditional academic disciplines offered in the extant teacher education concurrent programs have been strengthened.

The Victoria Experience

As the preceding discussion suggests, the response of Australian educators to societal and educational developments appears to be evolutionary rather than revolutionary reorganizations. Some teacher educators have grieved over the changes to their programs. A number maintain the changes are essentially structural with, in fact, no major substantive change in content or in process.

The State of Victoria provides an example of how preservice teacher education has evolved to develop links with industry, to provide credit for a variety of formal educational experience and improve supervisory practices. Victoria contains 19 per cent of the nation's 16 million people; 24 per cent of its 245,000 teachers; 20 per cent of the nation's 10,000 schools; 18 per cent of its 3 million students. Schoolteachers in Australia are employed by both state government and non-government (predominantly church) agencies.

Seventy-three are employed by the state government, 17 per cent in the non-government, Catholic sector, and 10 per cent in the non-government, non-Catholic sector. As in the rest of Australia, roughly 30 per cent of the students attend non-public schools.

Australian state and federal governments have used specially established advisory and consultative groups, as well as statutory boards, to advise on teacher education policies and practices. In Victoria this included a Ministerial Teacher Education Reference Group which has been recently superseded by a Standards Council. This group fostered debate and formulated advice on a number of key issues during its existence. The Group was to stimulate and change thinking about new ways of undertaking teacher education, provide exemplars of innovative practices, and thereby equip teacher educators to deal with the educational challenges of the next century.

The state-wide discussions on preservice education culminated in a statement including assertions that:

- universities should play a significant role in all phases of teacher education (preservice, induction and in-service);
- candidates with high university entry qualifications should be encouraged to undertake preservice programs;
- there should be an increase in the quality of the disciplines offered in preservice programs;
- a significant proportion of pedagogical studies should be undertaken in the workplace, i.e. in school and business and industry settings;
- preservice teacher education programs should provide some preparation for educational occupations other than school teaching; and
- whereas a basic degree followed by one year of education studies in a diploma in education (Dip.Ed.) can be appropriate, consideration should also be given to two years' of education studies with extensive workplace experience and the award of a second degree in education.

Teacher education can also be affected at the institutional level by consultative groups appointed especially for the purpose. In 1992 Melbourne University Council appointed two external consultants to consider the structure of its Institute of Education, the education programs being offered and the contribution being made to educational research and practice. The final Melbourne report (Maling and Taylor, 1992), which was endorsed by the University Council, has resulted in a number of actions including designating the Institute as a Faculty of the University, reducing the number of entrants to all preservice programs, a gradual phasing out of concurrent programs for secondary teachers and the consideration of whether that should also occur for preservice primary programs. The one-year Diploma in Education program for graduates will progressively be replaced with a two-year Bachelor of Teaching program to allow a high proportion of teaching experience in schools. The second year of the program is conceived as a period of internship for candidates.

A pilot program has been initiated in order to allow government and non-government employing authorities, the university faculty and the collaborating schools to evaluate and propose revisions to the program as well as resolve issues associated with supervision, legal liability and responsibility of the trainees, and payment for supervisory services.

Other Victorian universities are positioning themselves to follow the Melbourne University pattern should the new State Standards Council's recommendations regarding internships for beginning teachers be endorsed by the Minister for Education. Universities in other states are also monitoring the developments with varying degrees of caution as the addition of the extra period of internship has financial and other resourcing implications.

Business, Industry and Preservice Liaisons

Several, structural, evolutionary changes to preservice education programs have occurred in response to calls to change the mind set of teacher education graduates about being locked into one job for the whole of their working career, to make graduates more appealing to employers in business and industry, and to make teachers more aware of what happens in the world of work. One change, instituted at Deakin University, is the offering of a four-year double degree program where one degree is awarded by the School of Education and the other by another school, such as Humanities, Social Sciences or Economics. This development, which must cope with intra-university difficulties associated with differences such as entry requirements, is also being considered by other institutions as a viable offering. A matter of concern for the Deakin School of Education is that the degree in Education is locked into a degree from another school and that there is now no free-standing undergraduate degree in Education.

Another change, such as that which has occurred in the School of Education, Royal Melbourne Institute of Technology, involves the inclusion of business and industry placements during the times allocated for field experience in the preservice programs. As a consequence, stronger links are established between businesses, industries and teacher education; trainee teachers gain a rich understanding of business practices and the kinds of on-the-job training which occur in different work place settings. Employers learn that teacher education graduates have competencies which equip them for employment in a variety of settings other than school teaching.

Supervisory Practices

The quality of a preservice education program is affected by the nature of the supervision trainees receive from university mentors and supervising teachers during the field experience or practicum. There are contrasting supervisory styles. At one end of the spectrum is the *deficit-dependency* model where the trainee is assumed to be deficient in a number of pedagogical skills and must therefore depend upon and follow the advice of a more experienced person. At the other end is the partnership model (Rudduck and Sigsworth, 1985) where trainee and experienced teachers are both regarded as having different kinds of skills and knowledge to be pooled collaboratively during a practicum.

In several places in Victoria and elsewhere steps were being taken to foster partnership supervision. This was, however, by no means a prevalent movement throughout the country. More has been written about partnership supervision than has been practised. But now budget cuts and a national industrial change threaten what was being attempted. Reductions in the budgets of Schools of Education, for example, have led to a decrease in the number of university mentors who supervise and who favour partnership supervision. As has been mentioned already, in a number of institutions the university mentors now only visit those trainees who are not coping with teaching and consequently are at risk.

A recent industrial change within the teaching service can hinder partnership supervision. We now have an *advanced skills teacher*, a newly created promotions classification within the teaching service. Specific responsibilities are assigned to these experienced persons, including the supervision of trainees. This has been deplored as supervisors are now designated by position rather than by commitment to supervision (Koop and Bezzina, 1993). The industrial move has been labeled a ham-fisted approach to reform and one which does not address the broader issue of an industry-wide restructure (Kennedy, 1993; Koop and Bezzina, 1993). Now, when, as has occurred in Victoria and NSW, these advanced skills teachers are specifically designated for the supervision of trainees during a practicum, immediate limitations are placed upon the nature of the field experience. For example, Advanced Skills Teachers are not necessarily the most suitable people for partnership supervision or trained in supervisory practices. They are not uniformly distributed across school grades, subjects in the curriculum, metropolitan and country schools, males and females, and younger and older teachers. As a consequence appropriate and relevant supervision, suiting the needs of individual trainees, cannot be guaranteed. There are also questions about the personal care and attention which will be given to trainees' *stages of concern* during a school field experience. For example, what personal help will trainees receive as they try to learn how to become teachers and to grow as professionals? Matching trainee and supervisory teacher is now much more difficult than previously. In fact it has been stated that this industrial move 'by government bureaucrats makes the achievement of high quality teacher education a near impossibility' (Koop and Bezzina, 1993).

Credit for Work Done Elsewhere

Educational employers have produced disappointedly vague statements about their own responsibilities, preservice teacher education, professional qualifications and professional development (Tisher, 1987). But there are pressures, for example, from universities through the Australian Vice-Chancellors' Committee, to have them articulate their expectations more clearly. One incentive to do this is linked to the national discussions occurring on credit transfers. That is, discussions on the kinds of credit persons are entitled to receive towards a formal award for work done elsewhere, other than in the usual program leading to that award. A national Teacher Education Reference Group, which is a subset of the National Credit Transfer Project supported by the Australian Vice-Chancellors' Committee, is making recommendations for pilot projects where people will receive credit in preservice programs for work done in other compatible undergraduate programs; for example, credit in a preservice primary program for work done in a child-care program.[1]

Whereas the preceding discussions and recommendations regarding credit transfer between compatible undergraduate award programs are proceeding slowly and with due caution, they herald a new era and encourage education-employing authorities to state employment criteria clearly. They also open the way for consideration of the issues associated with credit transfer between compatible award and non-award programs where the latter may include offerings by professional associations. It will be interesting to see whether any related recommendations appear in the next decade!

Concluding Comments

An OECD publication, *The Training of Teachers* (OECD, 1990), states that world-wide educational developments such as, (i) shifts in decision making from central governmental authorities to local government schools, and (ii) changes to the school courses and teaching strategies to cater for a highly diverse student population, will produce changes to the face of teacher education worldwide. This is occurring in Australia as the preceding sections indicate. Other factors too have impacted on Australian Higher Education including teacher education, so much so that they are both in a steady state of flux. Evolutionary changes, to meet emerging societal requirements, are occurring continuously.

The previous sections indicate that educational policies and practices at state and national levels, economic factors, employment prospects, and university and college amalgamations are among the factors that have occasioned evolutionary alterations to the face of Australian teacher education. The visible alterations include increases in the amount of school experience for trainees, reduced participation in the supervisory process by university mentors, supervisory teachers appointed by position rather than commitment, a phasing out of concurrent programs, a 'strengthening' of the subject discipline base in the programs for prospective primary teachers, and the inclusion of business/industry experiences. Most changes to programs appear to be of a structural nature in response to the changing external circumstances rather than revolutionary reconceptualizations of teacher education: what it should be and how it should be practised. Bureaucrats and politicians regard the changes as appropriate, but uncertainties, disappointments and fears about the nature and quality of the changes and of teacher education are still around. Regrettably there have been no visionary or revolutionary writings by teacher educators, but there is no doubt that further 'face lifts' will occur. Whether there will ever be a satisfactory revolution remains to be seen!

Note

1   Copies of the reports produced by the Ministerial Teacher Education Reference Group, for example, The School Teacher Work-force in Victoria; The Future of Pre-service Education in Victoria. A Discussion Paper; Telematics: Implications for Teacher Education, are held at the Directorate of School Education, Melbourne, Victoria, Australia.

References

BARRIE, J. (1993) 'What future for teacher education? Reflections on a DEET discussion paper', *Australian Teacher Education Association (ATEA) Newsletter*, **16**(2), 30–7.

BEAZLEY, K. (1992) *Teaching Counts.* A Ministerial Statement by the Minister for Employment, Education and Training. Canberra: Australian Government Publishing Service.

BOURKE, S. (1994) 'Some responses to changes in Australian Education', *Australian Educational Researcher*, **21**(1), 1–18.

COMMONWEALTH DEPARTMENT OF EMPLOYMENT, EDUCATION AND TRAINING (1992) *Teacher Education.* A discussion paper. Canberra: Commonwealth of Australia.

FINN, B. (1991) *Young People's Participation in Post-compulsory Education and Training*, Report of the Australian Education Council Review Committee. Canberra: Australian Education Council.

HANSFORD, B. (1992) 'Teacher education: The image problem', *South Pacific Journal of Teacher Education*, **20**(2), 113–20.

KENNEDY, K. (1993) 'National standards in teacher education – why don't we have any?', *South Pacific Journal of Teacher Education*, **21**(2), 101–10.

KOOP, T. and BEZZINA, M. (1993) 'Quality assurance and accountability in teacher education: The Australian agenda?', *South Pacific Journal of Teacher Education*, **21**(2), 93–100.

LANIER, J. and LITTLE, J. (1986) 'Research on teacher education', in WITTROCK, M. (Ed.) *Handbook of Research on Teaching* (3rd Edition), New York: Macmillan, 527–69.

LEE, P. (1992) 'Whatever happened to those Mayer competencies?', *Independent Education*, **22**(4), 8–15.

MALING, J. and TAYLOR, W. (1992) *Consultancy on Future Directions for the Institute of Education Report*, University of Melbourne.

MAYER COMMITTEE (1992) *Employer-related Key Competencies: A Proposal for Consultation*, Melbourne: Mayer Committee.

McWilliam, E. and O'Brien, P. (1993) 'Towards teaching in partnership: Lessons still to be learned', *South Pacific Journal of Teacher Education*, **21**(1), 45–9.

OECD (1990) *The Training of Teachers*, Organization for Economic Cooperation and Development. Paris: Centre for Educational Research and Innovation.

Rudduck, J. and Sigsworth, A. (1985) 'Partnership supervision (or Goldhammer revisited)', in Hopkins, D. and Reid, K. (Eds) *Rethinking Teacher Education*, London: Croom Helm, 153–71.

Schools Council (1990) *Australia's Teachers: An Agenda for the Next Decade*, Prepared for the National Board of Employment, Education and Training. Canberra: Australian Government Publishing Service.

School Council (1991) 'A national professional body for teachers: A discussion paper'. Prepared for the National Board of Employment, Education and Training, Canberra, Australian Government Publishing Service.

Tisher, R.P. (1987) 'Research on teacher education in Australia', in Eltis, K. (Ed.) *Australian Teacher Education in Review*. Inaugural Yearbook of the South Pacific Association for Teacher Education. Marrickville: Southwood Press, 157–81.

Turney, C. and Wright, R. (1992) *Where the Buck Stops: The Teacher Educators*, Sydney: Sydmac Academic Press.

Chapter 4

The Commodification of Teaching: Teacher Education in England

David Pimm and Michelle Selinger

> Governing a large country is like frying a small fish. You spoil it with too much poking.
>
> (Lao-Tzu, verse 60).

In the last century, there was a theory linking the level of economic activity to sunspot activity, the average gap between major eruptions occurring every forty-two years. There appear to be comparable forces at work in education in England.[1] The dramatic and far-reaching wartime Education Act of R.A. Butler (1944), built on the Balfour Act (1902), established amongst other things universal secondary education (to age 15). In 1988, Parliament passed the third major education act of this century, the second longest piece of domestic legislation since the Second World War, the Education Reform Act (Maclure, 1990; Fludde and Hammer, 1990). This established for the first time ever statutory National Curricula[2] in Britain, and additionally (among many, many other things) abolished university tenure, the potential relevance of which for the concerns of this chapter we shall return to later.

Since then, however, the eruptions have failed to die away. It is the dramatic effects *on*, along with subsequent reforms *of* teacher education both initial and in-service, that we start to explore here. We shall endeavour to address these two areas of teacher education separately, focusing mainly on initial teacher education (ITE), though part of our account will indicate ways in which the former boundaries and distinctions have been altered or even erased.

These effects have come about in large measure due to the radical re-alignment of the *partnership* (a term which recurs in recent government proposals for reforming initial teacher education) among central government, local government agencies, tertiary institutions and teachers in schools themselves. In particular, the authority and power for teacher education is moving rapidly from higher education institutions to schools as a result of central government mandate. For an excellent, detailed analysis of the political history of the recent changes to initial teacher education in England (see Gilroy, 1993).

It would be wrong, however, to give an impression of a previously static system suddenly overrun by radical change. There had been many changes in the decade before this most recent Act, such as the abolition of the 'O'-level/ CSE distinction at 16-plus and the introduction of the GCSE examination system, as well as other major developments in curriculum and in the varied structurings of schools themselves. But they were all predominantly implemented within the existing framework, and generally came with the backing (and sometimes at the instigation) of the teaching profession. Nonetheless, it is hard to offer an overall sense of the dramatic scale of the transformation and shift in locus of control that has been wrought in structures and attitudes concerning schools, teaching and the preparation of teachers in England over the past five or so years.

Tomlinson (1992:48) has summarized the major transitions as follows:

> The 1988 Education Act, of course, contained both 'old' and 'new' Conservative thinking. The drive towards centralization continued. By 1990 the school curriculum, assessments at 7, 11, 14 and 16, all public examinations, the initial teacher training curriculum, in-service training, teacher appraisal, teachers' pay and conditions, capital building and the formulae for fixing individual school budgets, to mention only the obvious, were all directly under the control of central government. It is a breathtaking list not to be found in any other modern state.

As ever, one place to start to identify change is through the new rhetoric, particularly as the current discourse stems from other sections of the Thatcher Conservative, consumerist philosophy. Substitution of language in any institutional context is never innocent. Government education documents and reports are now full of the language of the market economy, of *choice* and *competition*; of *consumers* of education (parents or employers apparently, rather than the pupils themselves); of schools forming a *market place* with open enrollment rather than catchment areas, and public performance rankings of schools. The curriculum is now to be *delivered* by teachers (having been decided on and manufactured elsewhere it would seem). Schools are to *purchase* in-service from *providers, management of resources* is to the fore, and *quality assurance* is required for school-based initial education.

Notions of schools as having anything to do with *community* or *collaboration* – of devolved local education authorities providing a comprehensive, authoritative education *service* – seem discredited and are apparently no longer to be mentioned. Instead, schooling has been commodified to a remarkable degree and is seemingly to be thought of in the same way as all other goods in a market economy (Elliott, 1993).

The ideological nature of these radical changes is attested to by former Labour prime minister James Callaghan (1992:10):

> It has been obvious that many of the changes [in education] of the last decade have been inspired as much by the Government's ideology –

a dislike of local government, a disrespect for those working in the public services, a fixed idea that all problems can be solved by privatization – as by a serious attempt to get to the root of the nation's educational shortcomings.

Reorganizing the Business of Schools

Under the Orwellian-phrased guise of *less government*, and in thrall to a late twentieth-century Western preoccupation with increasing spurious *choice*, the last decade has seen a dismantling and in some cases destruction of many middle-level forms of social organization in England. This has happened directly with local politics and governance (for example, with the disenfranchisement of London's population and massively-decreased funding of local authorities).

More recently, it has also happened dramatically in medicine (with hospitals opting out of Regional Health Authorities to become self-governing Trusts and General Practitioners creating individual, fund-holding practices to buy services from different hospitals in an internal market). It has also happened in education, with the introduction of local management of schools imposing legal requirements on local education authorities to pass a substantial proportion of money for educational matters directly to schools, with an increasing number of schools initiating a comparable opting out from local education authorities control, spurred on by government sponsored financial intentions.

Before going on, we must make some comments about the background economic situation of the past decade. In 1985–6, a long, protracted and bitter national teachers' strike occurred over pay and working conditions, the eventual failure of which resulted among other things in the loss of collective bargaining rights for teachers' pay and conditions. In some ways, this was the first recent nationalization in the area of education. The playing out of the community charge (poll tax) fiasco meant that although the substantial grass roots non-payment protest was aimed at central government, it was local authority funding that was markedly depleted by withheld payments (which among other things resulted in massive under-maintenance of school buildings). Government rate-capping also meant that authorities were given ceilings on the amount they could try to raise via the community charge.

From 1988 to date the country has been gripped by a severe economic recession, which has substantially increased demands on central government for social security payments at a time of decreasing revenue from those in employment via direct and indirect taxation, resulting in a second squeeze on local authority funding via decreased government transfer payments. This background, together with the new ability of schools to influence their own economic situation via local management of schools, has set the scene for extensive financial bribery on the part of the government to influence schools' choice.[3] One school known to us was opposed to the notion of opting out of local authority control, but the financial incentives were such, that instead of losing up to ten teachers, they would gain two more. Armed with such 'information', how could parental 'choice' make any other decision than to vote for opting out?

In the wake of these continual 'reforms' came massive, form-filling bureaucracy, rapidly-changing statutory requirements, intrusive and extensive examination regimes and the rise of management apparently as the primary business of schools. We have also seen a massive public expenditure on the monitoring of schools. We used the word *Orwellian* above, because the upshot of this supposed lessened government has been far *more* powerful and centralized government presence in education, a massive process of nationalization (LESS is MORE). It has taken more and more powers for itself in many spheres and changed the role of local authority institutions to one of being at best merely an arm and agent of central government policy.

As with the health service, local management of schools has suddenly become a major issue, displacing teaching and learning as the primary focus. Budgeting and financial issues have become far more salient and preoccupying. Individual schools are now responsible for hiring and firing and the professional development of their teachers. Schools need to recruit pupils and retain them in an atmosphere of league tables and competition, accountability in particular forms, and both increased external demands and the power of school governors. There is a growing use of public examination results not only to provide information to parents and potential employers, but also to provide a basis for judgments about the worth of individual teachers and particular schools. Parents are seen not only as a school's customers (and therefore always right?), but also as if they had as much right to determine the direction of a school as those who taught there.

A division between administration and teaching in schools is increasingly opening up in England. The majority of headteachers, and deputy headteachers, were former teachers often working their way up inside the school where they taught. Many small primary schools had actively teaching heads. Since the local management of schools, economic and other purely external administrative concerns have increasingly prevented former teachers from occupying these positions. We predict there will emerge, precisely as with managers within the health service, a new breed of professional school administrators, at precisely the moment when those individuals who were formerly available from the local education authority for consultation and advice about such matters are losing their jobs in the run-down of local education authorities. It is as if the concept of 'economies of scale' had never been developed (Marks, 1992).

This much-strengthened, centralized government is confronting small, isolated and weak individual schools, hospitals and people. Individual schools are suddenly the sole unit of education. The fragmentation of former school *systems* has resulted in many changes, not least in the funding and organization of in-service education. As we shall mention later, the hemorrhaging of many advisory staff from local education authorities is having a dramatic effect on the organization and nature of in-service education in England.

Teachers were relatively autonomous in curriculum content before 1988. There was certainly plenty of advice, whether from school schemes, text series, local education authority guidelines or other colleagues. But the ultimate control of the curriculum was in the hands of individual teachers. Teaching has now become quite simply *delivering* the National Curriculum, the curriculum is no longer theirs.[4] It comes from outside and for many teachers has imposed serious demands, particularly in primary schools. The current removal of much of the initial teacher education curriculum from college control into schools and the additional burdens this imposes will be discussed in the next section.

Having briefly indicated some aspects of the changing nature of schools in England, we now turn to examine more recent changes in initial teacher education. The context and atmosphere just described is the one in which student teachers will be henceforth receiving much of their education.

The Preparation of New Teachers: Learning About Life in the Market Place

All those wishing to teach in a maintained (state) school are required to have *qualified teacher status* or to be on either the licensed teacher scheme or the overseas-trained teacher scheme. There are several routes into teaching, but traditionally there have been two main ones. The first is a four-year B.Ed degree (or BA/B.Sc leading to qualified teacher status) and the second is a one-year, full-time, specialist Post-Graduate Certificate of Education for holders of a three-year subject degree; both routes are available either at primary or secondary levels.

Initial teacher education stands on the threshold of being nationalized, starting now with secondary schools, with plans for primary schools about eighteen months to two years behind. These proposals are intending to:

- give schools a strong role in initial training and the funding to support increased responsibility. Schools can use their knowledge of the demands placed on new teachers to become active partners in designing and running courses;
- give students more time in schools. The best way to learn classroom skills needed for effective teaching is by observing and working with teachers, as well as by discussing classroom practice with teachers, tutors and other students;
- require courses to equip students with essential competencies, including the subject knowledge and professional and personal skills which new teachers need to manage, maintain order, and teach effectively in their classrooms. The development of complete

profiles of new teachers' competencies will help ease the transition from initial training to induction (DFE/WO, 1993:4).

In these proposals, the involvement of higher education institutions is substantially decreased and it seems their role is intended to become more one of accrediting and evaluating school-based schemes in which secondary student teachers spend far more of their time in school (originally proposed as 80 per cent, currently some two-thirds of a 36-week course). The then chair of CATE[5], William Taylor, declared:

> There is much that is new in these requirements. School-based training is not just extended teaching practice. It involves a fundamental change to the design, organization and management of initial training. It requires a much more substantial and continuous contribution from teachers (1992:2).

The government's belief in an apprenticeship model of learning is demonstrated in the second of these proposals (Gilroy, 1993). It takes little account of the developments in educational research that have demonstrated many failings of traditional teaching. In fact, the 'progressive movement' has been increasingly ridiculed by the government with attacks on the 'trendy progressive views of "expert" educationalists' (Ball, 1993:206), and a 'distrust of theory and research' (p. 208). Ball, with thinly-veiled anger, dubs the views of the government as those of *cultural restorationists*:

> And knowledge in the traditional classroom is realized via the traditional curriculum. The preservation and transmission of the 'best of all that has been said and written'; itself a pastiche, an edited, stereotypical, unreal, schoolbook past. A curriculum which eschews relevance and the present, concentrating on the 'heritage' and the 'canon', based on 'temporal disengagement' . . . *the curriculum of the dead* . . . The canon is unchallengeable. The selections are done elsewhere, at other times, they are 'handed down' by the unassailable 'judgment of generations' (Ball, 1993:210).

The advantages of a higher education-based teacher education course in which students spend more time reviewing a wide range of practice and discussing the relative merits of different ways of working will be lost. (See NAHT, 1993; SCETT, 1992.) Within this model, many teachers found that having a student in their classroom who has spent time working in other schools or sharing a range of practice can offer the supervising teacher a fresh perspective and can be viewed as a form of professional development.

Also, given the other responsibilities of teachers at this time, it is not hard to imagine their reactions to proposals for their substantially increased involvement in teacher education. Many do not wish to do all the training themselves; they are concerned that students' experience will be limited by the localized experience they receive from working closely with only one teacher. They see their school settings as necessarily limited and complain of no time – yet pressure to revise their roles.

However, the financial incentives that are now being offered to schools are hard to resist in a time of local school management and financial cuts (until these new regulations came into force schools demanded no payment for taking student teachers). It may not be a teacher's or even an individual subject department's decision to take on students, but perhaps that of the head teacher more concerned about dwindling resources.

The role of higher education has changed considerably under the new arrangements. Tutors are now required to coordinate student placements, and prepare teachers for their new role as *mentors* – experienced teachers prepared to supervise a student's subject work. However, most crucially, there has been a considerable direct transfer of resources from the colleges to the schools which has grave implications for those involved in teacher education in higher education institutions. Individual schools are rapidly making decisions to strengthen their partnerships with only one institution for reasons of time and practicalities. As a result, many university departments of education are considering moving out of initial teacher training altogether, as competition for school placements increases and financial inducements reduce, with schools actively searching for the highest bidder in the marketplace.

The third proposal listed above, to revise the accreditation of teachers by moving to a competence-based model, is but a particular instance of government principles for training in all occupations. Evidence of competence in six aspects of teaching is required and institutions have been allowed to set up their own competence criteria subject to fairly stringent guidelines within the Department of Education and Science circular 9/92. Some institutions are having to work with schools that they might not have chosen under the previous model and to develop new sets of competence criteria which might not meet with their approval. With typical bureaucratic understatement, the Department for Education document (DFE/WO, 1993:2) outlining the government's proposals observes: 'The role of higher education will need to be adapted in discussion with schools.'

The government had also hoped for a rapid move to *school-centred teacher training* in which schools take on the full role of training teachers with or without accreditation from higher education institutions. One hundred-and-fifty places in secondary schools were made available in September, 1993, with plans to increase this number quite dramatically over the foreseeable future. However, the uptake of such schemes has been slow, and of those schools that have taken it up, some have already pulled out. Reasons offered include too much work, and the money does not allow them to do the job properly: economies of scale afforded to higher education institutions are no longer present when working with perhaps only ten students in one school.

In primary education there have been moves to produce a three-tier system of teachers: subject specialists (Post Graduate Certificate of Education route), generalists (B.Ed route reduced from four years to three years, encouraged via funding incentives) and teaching assistants (qualified to teach up to the end of pupil age 7).[6] The move from main and subsidiary subject for primary teachers to six-subject courses has meant that less time need be devoted to academic studies in any particular subject area. However, there is real concern that a two-tier structure will emerge with academically more qualified graduates in National Curriculum subjects commanding more senior posts than will B.Ed generalists. There is confusion over government policy in this area which has placed more value on the role of teachers' subject knowledge than pedagogic knowledge.

Although the language is of *partnership* between schools and colleges, devolution might be more accurate. Very few teachers feel they want as large a role as is being required by Government, particularly in the area of subject methods which are legislated (in circular 9/92) to be taught in the school. One new higher education provider, in a location where there is no obvious existing institution, is able to offer schools more than double the average fee-per-student than others elsewhere because their Post Graduate Certificate of Education course was only established under the new regulations, and they lack the overhead and staffing costs of other institutions. But the schools then buy back the college staff to help in schools with professional tutorial support of students (thereby subverting circular 9/92 which lays down the differing responsibilities of schools and initial teacher education institutions).

Models of supervision for school placement under the new arrangements vary considerably. Many higher education institutions are unable to send tutors to visit students in school on a regular basis because of devolved funding. Some have revised their arrangements and only see students when they are requested by the school, and the assessment of teaching competence is made by the mentor and the training manager in the school. All students are required to have experience of teaching in a second school; this is often accomplished by pairing students within institutions, so that they can either do a direct exchange or team teach in each other's school.

This change obviously represents a coming loss of jobs in higher education. Considerable anecdotal evidence exists about teachers wondering why department lecturers are willing to hand over their jobs (the relevance of the loss of tenure here is obvious). The government document on the reform of initial teacher education disingenuously notes:

There will inevitably be some implications for the number and nature of staff in higher education involved in initial teacher training . . . Institutions can take their own steps to ease potential problems through redeployment, the use of short-term contracts and the management of staff turnover (DFE/WO, 1993:14).

The Open University: Action at a Distance

The Open University is a large, national, distance-teaching, degree-granting university for adults that has been in existence for about twenty-five years, offering a wide range of undergraduate and some graduate courses. It has a large School of Education with courses on a wide range of educational concerns, as well as satellite groups such as the Centres for Mathematics and for Science Education based in their respective academic faculties. During the 1970s and 1980s, many thousands of teachers studied individual courses as part of their in-service education as associate students, in addition to the substantial number of teachers who were studying for a bachelor's degree with the Open University.

We have chosen to separate out developments involving the Open University partly because of the differing nature of the courses it provides, but also because of its rapidly expanding roles in initial teacher education, in professional development at the masters level, and as a strong foretaste of things to come (Prescott and Robinson, 1992).

As a response to the teacher shortage that existed in the late 1980s and early 1990s in England and Wales, the Open University received extensive funding to develop a part-time, distance-learning Post Graduate Certificate of Education for primary and secondary teachers. A commissioned survey in 1990 of Open University students in the West Midlands found that a large proportion were interested in obtaining a teaching qualification. A significant factor arising from this survey was that many of those canvassed were interested in teaching shortage subjects like mathematics and science. Of those interested in primary school teaching, their mathematics and science qualifications were higher than students entering a conventional B.Ed course at the age of 18 or 19.

A second national survey commissioned by the Department of Education and Science in 1991 revealed many potential teachers living in urban areas where a shortage of teachers was equally matched by the problems of teacher retention. A part-time route into teaching could address this shortfall by providing access and opportunity to large numbers of students not only in these geographic areas, but in many areas around the country where, for financial or family reasons, potential students did not have easy access to conventional one year, full-time Post Graduate Certificate of Education courses. For the government which had already spent many thousands of pounds in recruitment campaigns, the Open University route appeared to be an excellent solution to the problems of teacher shortage. They therefore made the decision to fund the development of the Open University Post Graduate Certificate of Education course with an initial plan to train 1000 students per year across both the primary and secondary sectors.

The first cohort of students started in February 1994. The part-time, Post Graduate Certificate of Education course (leading to Qualified Teacher Status) lasts eighteen months and the first-year intake was some 1200 students, 500 of whom intend to be primary teachers. It is the students' (who must be over 21 and under 55) own responsibility to find a school near them where they wish to train and that is willing to take them (with whom the Open University then negotiates an agreement). The course is divided into three stages, each of which is linked to a school experience which accounts for a total of sixteen of the eighteen statutory weeks laid down by Council for the Accreditation of Teacher Education (part-time courses require less time spent in school than full-time courses). Students are attached to their chosen school for the whole of the course, but they also have to complete at least two weeks in a second school and make up the final week in any of a specified range of teaching-related activities.

Throughout the course, students are supported by the Open University through part-time tutors and staff tutors and by the partner schools through a subject or class mentor and a school coordinator who is normally a member of the senior management team. The school is responsible for the assessment of teaching competence and the tutor is responsible only for marking and assessing written assignments. Schools can draw on Open University support if they have any concerns about students they wish to share. There are regular tutorials and day schools for students throughout the duration of the course. Students are paired for their second school experience which ensures that all schools involved are aware of the nature and demands of the course. Regional briefing meetings are held with tutors, mentors and school coordinators at each stage of the course.

A big issue with all initial teacher education reforms is the accreditation (quality assurance) of teaching experience, as this remains the responsibility (and hence directly concerns the reputation) of the higher education institution, but is not under the control of their employees. With the Open University Post Graduate Certificate of Education, this devolution of responsibility to schools is complete – and these are not schools either suggested or vetted by the University. The covering letter to schools from the University states:

> This is an innovatory programme which is planned to run alongside existing provision. We hope, therefore, that you will feel able to provide support, whether or not your school is currently involved in Initial Teacher Education. The Open University will pay partner schools £1000 in respect of each student, for the professional support provided.

Schools working within the Open University model this year have initially reported that both the school experience guide and the mentor notes have been helpful in supporting them and indicating a desired direction ('letting us know what you want'). School mentors do not see themselves as experts in teacher education, as they do in teaching, and are actively seeking guidance and reassurance.

One of the strengths of the Open University position is that, despite the legislated separation of roles, it too does not leave subject method teaching solely to the individual schools. It can force schools, by means of its course assignments, to allow students to do things (such as investigative work or problem solving in mathematics) that might not be part of that school's rationale, and thereby perhaps in a small way challenges the ethos of certain schools.

Although the initial costs of setting up the Open University scheme meant that the costs per student were not substantially lower than in conventional institutions, due to, among other factors, a different structure of overheads and marginal staff costing, the Open University course may well cost less per student. In the event, a national pattern of school-based training supported by such distance education materials could easily become a reality, despite many obvious drawbacks to distance education training.

There is a small but present pressure on the Open University to sell its materials to consortia of schools and merely accredit school-centred schemes through its validation. It already sells its materials to institutions as support for their own schemes. It remains to be seen whether such pressures will diminish or increase, and whether the Open University has the institutional will to resist them, as this will provide the government with its perfect, deinstitutionalized model (a franchise which disenfranchises) of teacher education in schools alone. Despite the original intent of tapping different pools of applicants, the distance Post Graduate Certificate of Education programme has put the Open University into direct competition for the increasing number of mature students wanting to be teachers, and in some cases into contention with other initial teacher education providers.

The same is true at the masters level. In 1987, the School of Education offered the first modules (there are now ten, any three of which suffice for the degree) in an MA programme. In 1993, there were 2800 students studying with the Open University towards a part-time, taught, modular MA in Education – well over one-third of the national total of such students, which easily renders the Open University the major provider at this level. Some reasons for these increasing numbers are explored in the next section. A mentoring module is under preparation, in order to assist the massive amount of training that will be required, not just for Open University Post Graduate Certificate of Education mentors, but for any teacher involved in school-based initial teacher education.

The Demise of In-service Education of Teachers: Individual Development at Personal Cost

Although the main focus of this chapter has been on the changes in initial education of teachers, some important concomitant changes in the pattern of in-service education have also occurred as well as some blurring of boundaries that we address in the next section. In the heyday of the 1970s and 1980s, practising teachers who wished to go on courses would apply through their local education authority. Many one-day courses were held during the teaching day and supply teaching was covered through a pool of experienced teachers. Some courses were longer and involved secondment for a term or even a year. Others involved day or half-day release over a year or two years and led to the awards of Diplomas and Advanced Diplomas in various aspects of education. The one-year secondments often led to Advanced Diplomas and, more latterly, masters degrees.

The general demise of in-service education had started somewhat prior to the introduction of the Education Reform Act when teachers had taken issue with the government control of their pay negotiations. As part of their action, many teacher refused to give up time after school to attend courses, refused to supervise pupils at lunch time or run after-school events. In any event, the 1988 Education Reform Act specified the required number of hours a teacher must work – 1265 hours, which included five statutory training days per year. Many teachers were dissatisfied with this deprofessionalization and refused to work *over* the prescribed number of hours (as they had so consistently and willingly before the strike).

Government money had been made available in the early-to-mid-1980s in the form of extra support grants to help improve teaching in many areas of the curriculum, but particularly in the core subjects (see for example, Straker, 1988). This initiative had led to a vast increase in the number of advisory staff available to support teachers in professional development and a rise in the number of short and twilight (4:30–6:00 p.m.) courses. But as the 1980s progressed, local education authorities were increasingly forced to cancel large numbers of twilight and weekend courses as teachers voted with their feet. The heyday of professional development had ended.

By 1989–90, extra support grants and other sources of in-service funding dried up rapidly as local education authorities became strapped for funds for the reasons listed earlier. For example, the change in funding arrangements saw a massive drop in full-time, one-year MAs in education whose students were seconded teachers. Nationally, in 1986–87 there were 2112 such students; in 1988–89 there were some 439; in 1992 there were a mere handful. Ironically, about this time, the demand for very particular forms of in-service increased dramatically, driven first by changes in the examination system, and then by the introduction of the National Curriculum and Assessment at 7, 11, 14 and 16.

With the 1990s, new national funding arrangements came into force aimed at providing support for a range of educational priorities including training for teachers. This money was available only for specific purposes determined by the Department for Education. In addition, local education authorities' funding arrangements were altered to a system whereby the bulk of funds available for in-service have been devolved to the schools for them to buy back expertise from local education authorities. The reality has been very different.

At first, schools used the extra funds in other ways as they found loopholes in the regulations which allowed them to divert unspent monies into improving the fabric of the school. Many schools had been starved of cash needed for essential repairs, or their salaries bill had been too high due to an aging staff, so resources had to be diverted from other areas in order to pay teachers. Here was an ideal opportunity to make use of extra cash. Schools started to use their own expertise within their school or clustered with other schools to pool and share their skills.

Many of the training days were, and still are, used for working on whole-school issues; rewriting the school aims, considering corporate action on discipline, and so on. Very few of these days actually focus on teaching. In addition there is loss in the cross-fertilization of meeting colleagues from other schools. Also, who negotiates the course? In-school preoccupations are hard to move away from, as are the complexities of the existing matrix of relations between staff.

The actual cost of in-service also became apparent as the local management of schools took hold. Previously, the only cost to the school for a teacher's absence was perhaps the phone calls for supply cover. Now, not only did the school have to pay course fees, they also had to pay for this teaching cover. No longer was it seen as acceptable for a teacher to go on a course to further a personal interest or their own personal professional development; the interests of the school also had to be furthered. Thus, management courses became important, as did courses on pastoral care, discipline, etc.

The latest trend in in-service is now *designated courses*. Each year the government announces those areas of the curriculum they are prepared to fund for the next one or two years (another instance of 'choice' and 'less government'). This funding is the only source from which schools only have to pay a small proportion of the cost of the training and therefore, unsurprisingly, represents areas in which there is the highest demand for in-service. This has led to second guessing on the part of in-service providers so that, within this new market economy, they can prepare themselves to be the first to offer suitable courses. Latterly, it has been suggested that sources of funds in this area will soon cease.

Blurring of Boundaries: An Uncertain Future

The proclaimed intent of the government in many of their proposals has focused on the rhetoric of increasing choice and diversity, whether of forms of education or routes into education for teachers. One effect has been massive shifting of boundaries and loss of definition, as well as *diversity* which serves as a guise for a radical re-emphasis, as with *opting out* moving from being one *option* to being revealed as the new desired general state. And we believe school-centred initial training for teachers to be the next one.

Other shifting patterns include moves from institution to individual, from free-will to coerced (despite the rhetoric of *choice*) action. In in-service, there are yet-unresolved tensions between individual needs and institutional needs at the school level and allocating resources between them. Rather than an outside entity making decisions at a general level, devolved funding means confrontation The locus of responsibility for a teacher's own development seems to be moving away from themselves. We seem to be heading for a time of *ad hoc* provision, as providers are unable to predict and, therefore, plan provision. With the pressure on higher education via initial teacher education, no structures will be left in place for offering in-service education.

Where is the energy to come from to create a new coordinated and coherent approach to in-service and initial teacher education? Blurring of boundaries has occurred in part as a result of the loss of infrastructure of education. Yet, it is nonetheless important to remember that there are always opportunities in periods of change and turbulence: in particular, inertia is consequently a less omnipresent force than is usually the case in more static educational systems.

We end by summarizing briefly three *boundaries* that we see as shifting.

School/College

Schools are now seen as *the* place of learning – for higher education staff, for teacher-mentors, for newly-qualified teachers and for teachers-in-training, as well as for pupils! There is pressure for everyone to look at their own teaching, but is there similar pressure for everyone (including pupils) to look at their learning? There is the chance to increase the permeability of institutional boundaries and revise the sharing of responsibilities, for instance with teachers coming into colleges to teach groups while higher education staff teach in schools.

Buying in student supervision by seconding practising teachers to the higher education institution is common. But with this model, the students and teachers involved are *both* seen as part of the higher education institution rather than being affiliated primarily with the individual school. The demarcation of responsibilities is quite different with this model, as are all the relationships involved. Co-ordination is obviously needed, but who is in a position to take this overview? Could it come from within the institution or would a member of a local education authority be best placed to look objectively at such a situation? Perhaps the local education authorities ought to be resurrected in order to perform this role with the emphasis moved from inspection back to advising and co-ordinating.

Another instance of this boundary blurring is the springing up of mentoring courses for teachers and accreditation of mentoring as components of some qualification. So, what was previously solely a job (often learned on the job) carried out by Department of Education staff, has been (unwillingly given and frequently so received) in large part devolved onto teachers.

There is a further tension among teacher–educators at the moment. Funding in higher education is being determined by research ratings more than in previous times, so there is a stronger experiencing of the tensions between teacher–educator and researcher, particularly when there is falling money due to the payments made to school partners. One consequence has been an increase in the amount of research *on* teacher education and mentoring (rather than this merely being my 'day-job') at the moment, as a brief look at current journals and recently published books will attest.

In-service/Initial Teacher Education

As in the above instance, the helpful call for initial teacher education as being merely the first part of continuous, expected professional development through the induction year and into service, argues for a continuity of experience rather than strong boundaries. In some other countries, many institutional courses are open both to pre-service and in-service students equally (and are timed for after school hours to allow this). An increased need for related in-service education is appearing with mentoring, as teachers and departments get a continuous flow of students and can no longer avoid issues that were avoidable before.

For example, the Open University's Post Graduate Certificate of Education program illustrates this blurring. For ten years, the Centre for Mathematics Education has been producing long courses (160 hours) in mathematics education, intended primarily (but not solely) for practising teachers with some considerable school experience. While there were many teachers in the Open University system, and a well-funded and local education authority-supported programme of in-service education, many practising teachers availed themselves of such courses (up to 1000 a year at the height across these two courses alone). Moreover, teachers could work towards a professional diploma to assist them in gaining advancement.

With the declining size of the teacher population in the Open University undergraduate program and with the virtual collapse of this sort of in-service, the only growing audience for these particular courses (whose numbers have much dwindled) is Open University students doing a degree and subsequently planning to become teachers via the Open University Post-Graduate Certificate of Education scheme. One upshot of this (not necessarily a deleterious one) is that courses intended for practising teachers are being studied by neophytes *before* they start their teacher education course which will necessarily be at a less sophisticated level. The decision then becomes whether these courses are remade or are replaced by courses more suitable to non-practitioners.

State versus Private

England has a relatively small (about 10 per cent) but very influential collection of private schools. In order to obtain a qualifying teacher certificate, any teacher has to have taught in state schools. Current newspaper cuttings include discussions of dissension over higher education institutions not being willing to make partnerships with private schools (transfer payments which would offer yet another back-handed government payment to support private education). A similar deliberate blurring of boundaries can be seen in the hospital service with fund-holders able to buy private hospital services and even generate a two-tier service within the ostensibly National Health Service. By demolishing the state educational system, resulting in individual schools funded in diverse ways, funding of private schools may be increased.

The Open University has found in its first year that many existing teachers in private schools are endeavoring to gain Qualified Teacher Status by training through the Open University Post Graduate Certificate of Education scheme, using the school in which they are working as a partner school. This would enable them to move into the public sector at a later date should they so wish. The only institutional stipulation is that their school must teach the National Curriculum and that they must have a second school experience in a state school in order to meet Council for the Accreditation of Teacher Education requirements.

Conclusion

The National Curriculum is an imposed curriculum with the force of law and was not introduced by consensus – a requirement that has been felt to have disappeared in the wake of the legislative dictatorship that the make-up of Parliament in the 1980s allowed. Tomlinson (1992:47), addressing the methods and rate of change in education of the late 1980s and onwards, writes of the deliberate ignoring of the traditional mechanisms of consultation and obtaining consensus:

> Consultative bodies were disbanded and procedures compressed –
> often into the summer holidays to the intended discomfort of teachers
> and local authority associations. Where new consultative or executive
> machinery was created, its members were not appointed to represent
> a range or balance of interests but were nominated by government.

The interim Dearing report (NCC/SEAC, 1993) entitled *The National Curriculum and its Assessment* places considerable emphasis on:

- the need for lessening dramatically the overwhelming burden (much of it administrative) on teachers, particularly primary teachers;
- the importance of trusting teachers and decreasing government prescription;
- most of all the priority that there be a period of stability over the next few years for consolidation.

It seemed that the governors of England had finally been told that they must stop poking the fish.

We need to recognize that a major element in teachers' present concern about workload arises from the attempt to respond to all the changes (not just those necessitated by the National Curriculum and its assessment) that have been taking place, and from the pace at which change has been sought.

The balance between what is defined nationally and what is left to the exercise of professional judgment needs to be reviewed.

I recommend that the curricular and administrative complexity must be reduced and the excessive prescription of the National Curriculum removed, particularly outside the core subjects. This is a recognition that the professionalism[7] of teachers must be trusted (NCC/SEAC, 1993:5–6, 10).

Nonetheless, other moves taking place are still in the direction of the deprofessionalization and dismissal or discrediting of teacher concerns and voices. Political forces have repeatedly acted to diminish the status and legitimate control of schooling by the teaching profession. From positioning teachers as mere *deliverers* of the curriculum while also castigating them as having *vested interests* (rather than being a legitimately, centrally-interested party) in its reorganization, and hence enabling the critical reaction to be ignored as mere special pleading, political forces have repeatedly acted to diminish the status and legitimate control of schooling by the teaching profession.

Recently (summer, 1993) the teachers' unions successfully mobilized massive public support for their complete boycott of National Curriculum testing at 14. This boycott, in protest against the trivialized form of testing proposed for English at this level, is really the first successful, large-scale resistance against an educational onslaught and is continuing to reshape the face of schools in England. In the seven years since the 1988 Act, we have seen substantial moves toward total state, legislated control of education. The political realities of the distress among parents as well as teachers is reflected in the Dearing Report's first small step back, and also signals moves to pull back from the domination of the business of schools by national level examinations.

But the changes in Initial Teacher Education and the (we believe) unintended effects on in-service education currently being seen continue the pressure and demands on teachers in schools. We fear that the firing of professionals with particular responsibilities in local education authorities' financial, managerial or advisory roles will continue, and the debacle in higher education institutions (pre-service and in-service) aided by the loss of tenure, has yet to come. All this work has been devolved onto schools and teachers, in addition to the pressures and public demands of national curriculum and assessment. Despite such enormous market pressures, schools must not focus solely inwards and become isolated – we feel it important that they invest in something larger than themselves.

We still believe that schools should be predominantly about pupils learning and teachers teaching, and not about management or assessment, and not primarily training teachers. Yet, it is as if the government is taking seriously the ironic ideal set out by Catherine Clément:

> The logical end of teaching, then, its secular ideal, really is – out there on the horizon – to train other teachers, to transmit the process of transmission itself (1987:67).

Teaching is an art as well as a craft. According to Hyde (1983), the essence of any artistic activity is the giving of a gift. It is certainly true that to teach successfully, a teacher must be generously disposed towards the pupils. The essence of a gift, for instance teaching, results in the generation of a feeling bond established between teacher and pupil and establishes an obligation that is usually unequal but reciprocal. It involves the creation of a shared bond and shared purpose.

If teaching becomes so dramatically commodified, it is rendered simply an exchange, without the accompanying social, communal, gluing function which generates social cohesion. Current government interference – the continual, neurotic poking of the fish – makes this far less likely to occur. Instead of generosity, teachers are filled with emotions of frustration, distraction, resentment, and exhaustion from overwork at the wrong things.

We end, as we began, with a quotation about the role of the state:

> A well ordered society would be one where the State only had a negative action, comparable to that of a rudder: a light pressure at the right moment to counteract the first suggestion of any loss of equilibrium (Weil, 1952:151).

The role of the State with regard to education in England in the last seven years has been so far removed from this view as to suggest that Orwell's, 'LESS is MORE' has become inscribed on the gubernatorial rudder, which seems intent on moving schooling ever towards greater disequilibrium.

Acknowledgments

We are very grateful to members of the Open University Centre for Mathematics Education for helpful discussion of many of these issues. Most of the teacher statistics come from Department for Education/WO, 1993.

Notes

1 In this chapter, we shall refer to the education system of England. Education in Wales is most similar to that in England (apart from substantial issues concerning

use of the Welsh language). Education in Northern Ireland is quite similar, while Scotland's educational system and traditions retain substantial differences.

2 As has been commented elsewhere (see, for instance, Dowling and Noss, 1990), however, what was established was neither *national* (in that private schools do not have to follow its dictates), nor a *curriculum* (in that the legal Orders which enshrine the curriculum consisted primarily of a sequence of *attainment targets* for ten different academic subjects – the basis for formal state school assessment at ages 7, 11, 14 and 16).

3 For instance, there has been a recent problem of surplus school places, some 1.5m places in English schools. The problem of overseeing education in a co-ordinated way has been hampered by opting-out proposals, even in schools threatened with closure.

4 However, continual pressure from teachers about these constraints has promoted a review of the National Curriculum under the auspices of Sir Ron Dearing, chairman of the new Schools Curriculum and Assessment Authority (SCAA), formed by a merger in 1993 of the National Curriculum Council (NCC) and the Schools Examination and Assessment Council (SEAC). In his final report (SCAA, 1994), Dearing made recommendations to reduce the National Curriculum that were acceptable to the government. These included slimming down the statutory content of what must be taught, leaving schools with approximately 20 per cent of time to use 'at their own discretion.' In this report, however, Dearing nevertheless suggested the first priority for this discretionary time must be 'to support work in the basics of literacy, oracy and numeracy,' while the remainder 'should be used for work in those National Curriculum subjects which the school chooses to explore in more depth.' The notion of teacher autonomy is still barely acknowledged.

5 The acronym CATE stands for the Council for the Accreditation of Teacher Education, a DFE advisory body formed in 1984.

6 The original proposals for teaching assistants was to give them qualified teaching status (QTS) after completing a one-year course. The criteria for entry, mature non-graduates with *considerable* experience of working with children, caused a wave of anger and the proposals were subsequently modified so that they will not be given QTS, but allowed to work alongside a teacher with either B.Ed or PGCE qualifications. See also Gilroy (1993).

7 This overt and deliberate refusal to acknowledge the professionalism of those who have spent their lives teaching in schools, as well as their effective exclusion from what was laughingly called *consultation,* is at the heart of the distress felt by many teachers. See, for instance, Francis (1992) or Gilroy (1993).

References

BALL, S.J. (1993) 'Education, Majorism and "the Curriculum of the Dead"', *Curriculum Studies,* **1**(2), 195–214.

CALLAGHAN, J. (1992) 'The education debate I', in WILLIAMS, M., DAUGHERTY, R. and BANKS, F. (Eds) *Continuing the Education Debate,* London: Cassell, 9–16.

CATE (1992) *The Accreditation of Initial Teacher Training Under Circulars 9/92 (DFE) and 35/92 (WO): A Note of Guidance from the Council for the Accreditation of Teacher Education,* London: CATE.

CLÉMENT, C. (1987) *The Weary Sons of Freud*, London: Verso.

DFE/WO (1993) *The Government's Proposals for the Reform of Initial Teacher Training*, London: Department for Education/Welsh Office.

DOWLING, P. and NOSS, R. (Eds) (1990) *Mathematics Versus the National Curriculum*, London: Falmer Press.

ELLIOTT, J. (1993) 'Three perspectives on coherence and continuity in teacher education', in ELLIOTT, J. (Ed.) *Reconstructing Teacher Education: Teacher Development*, London: Falmer Press, 15–19.

FLUDDE, M. and HAMMER, M. (Eds) (1990) *The Education Reform Act, 1988: Its Origins and Implications*, London: Falmer Press.

FRANCIS, P. (1992) *What's Wrong with the National Curriculum?* Shropshire: Liberty Books.

GILROY, P. (1993) 'Back to the future: The de-professionalization of initial teacher education in England and Wales', *The Australian Journal of Teacher Education*, **18**(2), 5–14.

HYDE, L. (1983) *The Gift: Imagination and the Erotic Life of Property*, New York: Vintage Books.

MACLURE, S. (1990) *Education Re-formed*, London: Hodder and Stoughton.

MARKS, J. (1992) *Value for Money in Education*, London: Centre for Policy Studies.

NAHT (1993) 'School-based initial teacher training', a briefing paper, National Association of Head Teachers, Haywards Heath, Sussex.

NCC/SEAC (1993) *The National Curriculum and its Assessment: An Interim Report*, London: National Curriculum Council/School Examinations and Assessment Council.

PRESCOTT, W. and ROBINSON, B. (1992) 'Teacher education at the Open University', in PERRATON, H. (Ed.) *Distance Education for Teacher Training*, London: Routledge, 287–315.

SCAA (1994) *The National Curriculum and its Assessment: Final Report*, London: Schools Curriculum and Assessment Authority.

SCETT (1992) 'Responses to the DES consultation document on the reform of initial teacher training', *SCETT News*, **21**, Autumn, 2–6.

STRAKER, N. (1988) 'Advisory teachers of mathematics: The ESG initiative', *Journal of Education Policy*, **3**(4), 371–84.

TOMLINSON, J. (1992) 'Retrospect on Ruskin: Prospect on the 1990s', in WILLIAMS, M., DAUGHERTY, R. and BANKS, R. (Eds) *Continuing the Education Debate*, London: Cassell, 43–53.

WEIL, S. (1952) *Gravity and Grace*. London: Routledge and Kegan Paul.

Chapter 5

Teacher Education in Norway: Images of a New Situation

Trond Eiliv Hauge

As the year 2000 approaches, Norwegian preservice teacher education finds itself in a changing position. Three particular changes are noteworthy. The first and most visible change involves a lengthening of the teacher education year[1] and a reorganization of the preparation programs. The second concerns the grounding philosophy in teacher education which covers the teacher's role, the supervision and mentoring of new teachers, and the relation between educational theory, subject matter knowledge and pedagogical content knowledge[2]. The third change is part of a nationwide institutional reorganization of all higher education outside the university system.

What are the reasons for these changes? Whose needs are the changes fulfilling? Who has spoken for them? What do these changes mean for the professionalization of teachers? These questions and other questions are now being asked as we witness one of the most profound changes in the Norwegian teacher education system in the last thirty to forty years. The central question is whether these changes will become real change or just surface movement. And, in relating these questions to the underlying theme of this book, we may also ask: Do we have any real chances of developing a new conceptualization of teacher education through these ongoing changes, or are we just entering another reorganization phase and nothing else?

The Main Structure of Teacher Education

Preservice teacher education in Norway can be characterized along two main lines: Elementary teacher preparation given by twenty teacher education colleges, and secondary teacher preparation given by four universities and eight to ten national higher education institutions. In addition, there are roughly twenty various regional colleges that give subject education relevant for teaching in secondary schools. Students from these colleges wanting to enter teaching have to take their final teacher education program at the universities.

To become an elementary teacher in Norway requires four years of study, a recent change (1992) from a three-year program. Secondary teacher education, which builds on previous academic studies, occurs in the universities and was lengthened to a full year in 1993. This represented a change from the half-year program that had been in place since 1907. Teachers in lower secondary schools (upper level in the nine grade comprehensive school) are recruited both from the universities and colleges. By contrast, teachers in upper secondary schools are mostly educated at the universities.

Reasons for Expanding Teacher Education

University-Based Teacher Education

The primary reason for the lengthening of university-based teacher education from a half- to a one-year program is based on the view that half a year of study is too short to build those understandings of pedagogy and learning processes that student teachers need to know to fulfill professional requirements in schools. The recent reforms in secondary education (1994) have also made the need for better prepared student teachers quite clear. Nevertheless, despite such a strong need for a reform, the universities themselves have, for a long time, been rather unsupportive of any attempt at strengthening their teacher education programs. We may explain this attitude by the fact that the university teacher education departments have, for a long time, been locked into a rather subordinated position by the universities themselves. The problem seems to be that teacher education is perceived to be embedded in a conservative-minded craft[3] tradition that does not really belong to *real* university studies.

Given this situation, it is not surprising that arguments behind the expansion rest on strengthening teachers' school subject education and teaching methods in those school subjects. The need to strengthen student practice in school or teaching in pedagogy at the university have played a minor part in the argument put forth both by the universities and the central government.

Nevertheless, the new situation has brought some optimism regarding the future of teacher education at the universities. The reform has given the teacher education departments a strong impetus to reconceptualize their educational program, to rethink essential content components, and to develop a more reflective learning situation for students. The reform has opened a door for experimentation with new models of student practice in school and theory components in the actual program. The greatest challenge for university-based teacher education in the long run, however, will be to raise their reputation as a professional program both among teachers in schools and at the universities themselves.

College-based Teacher Education

Among many reasons for prolonging elementary teacher education by one year is the need to strengthen in depth and breadth the subject education for new teachers. The fourth year is reserved for optional specialized subject education including education theory. As a consequence, the students' free course options are narrowed in the first three-year period compared to the previous model. The additional fourth year is reserved for optional specialized subject education, including educational theory.

The specialization in the fourth year is strongly related to education needs in lower secondary school where the reform tries to compensate for a lack of subject matter exposure in teachers coming from the colleges who must also compete for jobs with those educated at the universities.

The narrowing of the free course options in the first three years in college may be looked upon as an attempt to produce better-educated teachers in the main subjects taught in elementary school. Since elementary teachers follow their pupils for three to six years, a solid knowledge base in the main subjects taught is essential. This reform cuts off the possibility of producing elementary teachers who lack, for example, a math education.

The reason behind these changes rests on a need for upgrading content knowledge in teacher education. The motive here is similar to the one behind the reform in secondary teacher education. Neither education in general nor student practice in school are the focus of the reform. The difference, however, will be that in elementary teacher education an integration of subject-matter knowledge and teaching methods in the subject will occur in the same course.

Political Perspectives

The political context surrounding elementary teacher education reform has been rather turbulent. The reform was introduced by a Labour government. The minister responsible originally proposed a different solution, one which required in-service education for all teachers given by local education authorities and schools. The proposal was voted down by a majority in his own party.

Initially the whole reform idea was initiated by a right-wing government, but neither they nor the Labour government seemed to agree upon the desired length of teacher education. Despite a rather strong political rhetoric, led by the conservatives, about strengthening the qualifications of teachers in Norway, the political will to prolong teacher education has been rather fragile.

The final decision to extend teacher education occurred in 1992. It followed recommendations by the teacher unions, the professional teacher educators themselves, as well as from the many proposals made to Parliament. Varying motivations lay behind those recommendations and, due to political decisions made by the government at the last moment, the structure of teacher college reform took a somewhat different form from the one preferred by the professionals.

Pedagogy or School Subject Knowledge

The conflict between education theory in general and subject-matter knowledge has been exacerbated through the reform process, particularly in elementary teacher education. This aspect of the reform has met with severe criticism from professionals in pedagogy[4] who work in the colleges. They argue that the reform will destroy a well-considered balance between educational theory, school subject-knowledge, and student teaching in schools that has been developed since the middle of the 1970s. They foresee and fear a more atomized educational structure, an academization of education, and unclear expectations about who is ultimately responsible for the student teacher. However, some see this debate simply as part of an internal fight between various groups of teacher educators in the colleges. For it has become apparent that, *vis-à-vis* the responsibility for practice teaching in schools, teacher educators in school subjects have, to a greater degree than before, taken over the task of mentoring student teachers when they are in schools. From an organizational point of view, then, this means that teachers of pedagogy have moved into a less powerful position regarding supervision of student teachers in schools.

On the one hand, the debate over the role of educational theory in elementary teacher education may be interpreted as an internal cultural problem in the colleges rather than as resistance to the reform itself. On the other hand, however, the debate indicates that these institutions are facing great internal challenges in attempting to implement the reform.

By contrast, secondary teacher education, located in the universities, does not find itself in the same conflictual position regarding educational theory and subject matter. This is because universities have a tradition of ascribing low prestige to general education knowledge, as distinct from academic subject matter. Moreover, subject-matter teachers in the teacher education departments have had a much stronger position in relation to the field than do their colleagues in the colleges. Nevertheless, the outstanding characteristic of the reform for elementary and secondary teacher education is precisely that *the focus of the reform is on the education of teachers in subject matter.* This conclusion is well supported by the political rhetoric about prospective schooling in Norwegian society and by the policy passed by the union of secondary teachers.

A National Curriculum

An outstanding feature of the reform is a new common national curriculum plan for all teacher education colleges. This national curriculum plan states aims and goals for teacher education, characterizes its main structure, and proposes its frames of content (MER, 1994). The first general part of this plan is the same for all teacher education programs in the country, including secondary teacher education at the universities (MER, 1992).

The Norwegian school system has a tradition of making common national curriculum plans at different levels of the education system. The tradition is quite strong for elementary and secondary schools. The Ministry of Education is responsible for the development of the documents and is the final arbiter in decisions about using them. However, a common set of intentions and guidelines for *all* teacher education institutions has never been in place before. The colleges are used to having such national guidelines, but this move breaks the traditional mould of professional autonomy at the universities.

The background for this practice is found in the common legislative framework (1976) for all teacher education institutions in the country, but it has never been enacted in this way before. Despite a broad consultation process involving the university-based departments of teacher education for developing these common guidelines, it is still not clear how seriously the universities will take these obligations. Nevertheless, the curriculum signals a distinctive perspective on schooling in society, on teaching and learning, on supervision and mentoring, and on the role of the teacher that is worthy of note. It also provides a useful basis for reflecting on the professionalization of teachers in preservice teacher education.

The Role of the Teacher

To understand the redefined perspective on the teacher role in the new teacher education curriculum we have to look at how elementary and secondary schools have developed since the early 1980s and at the ongoing reform (1994) in upper secondary schools. Without elaborating the situation too much, two important trends may be mentioned:

1 In 1985–87, the nine-year comprehensive school was given a completely revised national curriculum, which stated that all schools should develop their own local curriculum based on national intentions and guidelines.[5] Every school was also required to make its own school development plan. These plans were to take care of at least two key dimensions in schooling: a) every child should have the opportunity to have instruction and learning adapted to his or her needs and abilities and b) collaboration between teachers was recommended as a principle for teaching and school development.
2 From 1994 onwards, all higher secondary schools are going to be restructured. By this reform the government has established the principle of twelve-year comprehensive schooling. To support this principle, the Ministry of Education has worked out a common national curriculum for elementary and secondary schools (1993). The question of teacher qualifications is highlighted throughout this document.

Within this changing school situation, teacher education institutions must now restructure their own programs. At the same time they have to keep pace with the curriculum reforms implemented in elementary and secondary schools in the middle of the 1980s.

The role played by teachers is of utmost importance in implementing these national reforms. In the new common curriculum plan 1992/94 for all teacher education programs we find the main role perspectives clearly stated and outlined in the text. New concepts, such as *transformational leadership* (Leithwood, 1994), teacher collaboration, teamwork, collective school planning and evaluation, take their place alongside the more familiar ones of assuming responsibility for role modelling and instructional tasks.

For elementary teacher education, these perspectives are not entirely new. Contact with schools in which student teachers are placed has essentially exposed elementary teacher educators to concepts of the teacher's role and practice as being inherently collaborative. By contrast, secondary teacher education, situated as it is in the universities, seems to lag behind this development, primarily because of the later reform act 1994 in upper secondary education.

Looking ahead to the next decade, we may say that the principles about the teacher's role expressed in the curriculum plan (1992/94) for all teacher education programs provide a common base upon which both elementary and secondary teacher educators can work further on implementing the new important aspects of the teacher's role.

Supervision and Mentoring of Student Teachers

Supervision and mentoring of student teachers is a collective responsibility for all teacher educators. This is a task that includes the subject teacher, the teacher in pedagogic theory, and the actual supervisor in practice. Moreover, every teacher education college has to develop a plan for supervision, which has to be revised each year. These statements are found in the national curriculum plan for elementary teacher education (MER, 1994). They set out a rather new philosophy about collective responsibility for student mentoring. For some teacher education colleges these guidelines merely confirm existing practice, but for the majority they imply a new situation.

Puzzling, but interesting enough, we do not find such recommendations for the departments of teacher education at the universities. There are no such guidelines for these institutions (see MER, 1992). It is difficult to find any reasonable explanation for this, other than it represents a reflection of the dominant conservative and individualistic tradition of mentoring at the universities.

Mentoring has been a focus for development in teacher education colleges during the last 5 to 10 years. This is due in part to initiatives taken by the National Council for Teacher Education during the period 1989–92, when four national conferences were held aimed at stimulating development in the mentoring of student teachers (NCTE, 1991a; 1991b). As a result of this activity the colleges have worked out a national network on mentoring in teacher education, based on collegial interest (R and D Network, 1993).

The underlying philosophy for mentoring in teacher education expressed in the national curriculum plan 1994 is heavily influenced by constructivistic learning theory and theories on the reflective teacher (Grimmett and Erickson, 1988; Handal and Lauvaas, 1987; Schön, 1983; 1987). This would suggest that the old apprenticeship traditions in teacher education are facing serious competition. This is, of course, an interpretation based only on stated intentions. However, looking at reports on mentoring in the teacher education colleges, we do find evidence to believe that these intentions are not that far ahead of practice. Nevertheless, supervision and mentoring in teacher education are embedded in a fragile organization, caught between faculties of education on the one hand and schools on the other. Since it belongs to an 80-year-old tradition, university-based teacher education seems to be in the worst position and attempts are being made to restructure and reorganize it.

Institutional Reorganization and Teacher Education

Two sets of reforms confront Norwegian teacher education in the nineties. One important set focuses on the structure of education. Another set addresses the content and curriculum in education. In both cases the reforms give impetus to a reconceptualization of teacher education.

In 1993 these intra-institutional changes in teacher education were challenged by a nationwide inter-institutional reform movement for all higher regional education outside the university system. Teacher education colleges are part of this regional system, together with technical education, health and nursery education, marine education, economic education, music education and other professional schools. This differentiated regional education structure expanded strongly in the 1970s during a good economic climate and under a strong national policy of decentralization. The growth was especially concentrated in regional colleges designed to give education options to people not able to travel to the big cities or universities. At first these institutions did not compete with the old professional education institutions, such as the teacher colleges. However, in the 1980s this situation became much more complex.

The regional reform is an exclusive restructuring movement forging 129 separate institutions into twenty-six big administrative regional units with a differentiated department system. The aim is clear: to rationalize administration, to cut down competing course options given by different institutions in the same region, to stimulate cooperation across professional borders, and to strengthen research and development work in a more efficient institutional network (MER, 1991). Economic motives also drive the implementation process.

Looking at the regional education structure (up to 1993) from a non-Norwegian perspective, an obvious question arises – how is it possible for a small country with only four million people to afford such a differentiated education structure? This question was highlighted by an OECD expert group which evaluated the Norwegian education system in 1987–88 (MER, 1989). This evaluation may be seen as a forerunner to, and a legitimation for, acting politically to change the situation. Since then, we have seen several national reports and white papers to Parliament about the case for reorganization. The articulation of restructuring is now placed under the rubric: *The Norwegian education network.*

Many of the teacher education colleges – 30- to 70-years-old – find themselves in a conflicting position, pulled in different directions. First of all, they have an obligation to be loyal to their own educational tradition and to assist student teachers in their professional development. Second, they have to revise and develop their preparation program in accordance with the revised teacher education structure and curriculum. Third, they have to adjust their prevalent organization to other institutional structures. Several questions arise: How do they work it out all at the same time? Do the colleges really have the capacity to change, adjust and improve themselves with regard to these great challenges?

The fact is that the fusion process has started and new structures have already been implemented. In several cases teacher education institutions are going to become departments or faculties in a centralized regional college structure. In the restructuring process we may ask about the outcomes. One serious threat to the identity of teacher education seems to be the internal competition between the various professional and academic programs in the regions. Considering the traditional high status of academic studies, it will not be surprising if teacher education and other practice-oriented professional education become the losers in the system.

Some twenty Norwegian teacher education colleges now find themselves in a position of having to restructure and reconceptualize at the same time, both internally and externally. We do know the likely results of this rather complicated process. Assuming that teacher education survives, the question that arises is whether or not it will be able to fulfill its original mandate: namely, to be the model for school teaching and the front agent for school development recommended in the revised national curriculum.

Student Explosion

In the last four to five years there have been an increasing number of students applying for the positions in teacher education. Both teacher education colleges and university departments have been asked by the central government to increase their student intake. Extra resources have been allocated for this purpose. In many instances, the colleges have made provisional physical and organizational changes and are obliged to reorganize their staff and teaching conditions. This increase in student intake coincided with the time when teacher education reform was being enacted.

The message from the teacher education institutions seems clear: the new education structure will be implemented and adjusted to the increased student number, but the critical question is whether or not they have any energy left to rethink their education content and improve their practice according to the new curriculum. Once again, an imposed structural regulation seems to compete with conceptual changes outlined in the curriculum reform.

Conclusion

Three significant reform movements have swept through the Norwegian teacher education system in the late 1980s and early 1990s. Two of these are strong restructuring movements, which alter basic elements of education. The first one may be called a *pure* teacher education reform, which provides for an expansion of preservice education for elementary and secondary teachers. This reform has been heartily welcomed by the education institutions themselves, because it is seen as a consequence of structural and curriculum changes in elementary and secondary schools through the 1980s.

The second reform, designed to establish twenty-six big regional institutions out of 129 separate units, involves an inter-institutional reorganization of all higher education at the regional level outside the university system. This reform, which sets a foundation for collaboration between various institutions, has been imposed on the institutions by the national government. The main reasons seem to be purely economic and rationalistic; however, they also seem embedded in a vision of inter-professional collaboration. It is hard to assert that it is welcomed by the teacher education colleges. They fear that the reorganization will undermine teacher professionalism and the very identity of teacher education.

The third change, a curriculum reform, gives content to the regulated expansion in elementary and secondary teacher education. The reform has two faces, which may be seen as competing partners in the implementation process. The strengthening of subject education has a heavy emphasis in the reform. On the other hand, a significant part of the reform is a common national curriculum plan for all of the various teacher education institutions, which is in addition to the emphasis on the specific subject curriculum. This common part of the curriculum reflects prevalent educational views on teacher education with a focus on the reflective teacher and a collaborative mentor culture. This philosophy was influenced by nationwide curriculum reforms in elementary and secondary schools in the 1980s. The motives seem to be political in nature; it is an attempt to establish improved cohesion between different parts of the education system and to adjust education content to prevalent trends or needs in Norwegian society.

The reform picture for Norwegian teacher education in 1994 is rather complex. Some initiatives are suggested by a genuine interest in improving teacher education. The expansion reform and part of the curriculum reform

	Intra-institutional change	Inter-institutional change (outside universities)
Restructuring	College teacher education: from 3–4 years University teacher training: from 1/2–1 year Revised education structure Increased number of students	Institutional reorganizing at the regional level: – from 129 to 26 units – resource effectiveness – course options across professional education borders – networking between institutions
Reconceptualization	A common national curriculum for all teacher education Subject education in focus Profiling of the reflective teacher Collaborative planning between teacher educators	Academization of teacher education (?) Research-based teacher education Disintegration of theory and practice (?)

Figure 5.1: Intra- and inter-institutional change viewed as restructuring and reconceptualization

are examples of that interest. Others, such as the regional restructuring reform of all higher education, are imposed political innovations without any deep concern for teacher education. The student explosion and the concomitant adjusted restructuring is another uncontrolled change force in the system. These two changes can be looked upon as serious threats to efforts which attempt to improve teacher education at the local level.

In sum, some of the important challenges described in Figure 5.1 may give an overview of the conflicting conceptions at issue between the various components of the reform. Restructuring and reconceptualization are the two main dimensions in the figure. Both of them have to be analyzed with respect to intra- and inter-institutional change processes.

Figure 5.1 indicates that teacher education for elementary teachers given by regional colleges is pulled in different directions. The restructuring initiative internal to the college system, based on a genuine interest in improving teacher education, is confronted by a rather heavy cross-institutional change, influenced by economic and political motives for structural change but which do not correspond to the *stated* political and somewhat controversial aims for teacher education. These two initiatives seem to be on a collision course in the college system.

The new structures are followed by explicit as well as implicit changes in the content of teacher education. Curriculum changes are put through as a consequence of the expansion reform. This explicit change in the college system is met on the other side by implicit cultural changes forced on the agenda by the regional inter-institutional change. The danger is that the external restructuring demands placed on the teacher education colleges are coming too fast and allow no room for consolidation of attempts to revitalize and reconceptualize teacher education. The worst-case scenario could be a degeneration of teacher education standards and professionalism in the colleges.

We may criticize the government for not being aware of the conflicting conceptions they impose on teacher education when implementing the reform of 1993. From an organizational point of view, it seems clear that the government has put too many change demands on the system at the same time (Fullan, 1993). The consequences may be a rather slow adaptation of the new grounding philosophy of teacher education, either because of a lack in structural readiness to work out the philosophy, or a mismatch between structural priorities and intentions in the reform. This conclusion may be particularly true for the teacher education colleges, since they find themselves in the most constrained position.

Notes

1   College-based teacher education was lengthened from three to four years in 1992. University-based teacher education was lengthened from six months to one year in 1993, being preceded by three to five years of academic studies.
2   The concept of pedagogical content knowledge borrowed from Shulman 1987 is not equivalent with the Norwegian term *fagdidaktikk* used to describe the specific course content. The course is subject specific, curriculum-oriented and based on questions like what, how or why in teaching subject matter. It covers a rather broad concept of the German word *didaktik*.
3   Grimmett and MacKinnon (1992) distinguish between conservative, progressive, and radical traditions of craft in teaching and suggest that an emphasis on the conservative tradition that has led to a lacuna in scholarly appreciation of teachers' craft knowledge in the progressive and radical traditions. They go on to document the kind of craft knowledge that teachers derive from these traditions and suggest ways in which such knowledge can be used in the education of teachers.
4   Teachers in pedagogy have for a long time been in charge of interrelated courses in educational theory and practice in school.
5   A new revised version of this national curriculum is going to be developed and will be implemented in 1997. Its consequences for teacher education are still somewhat unpredictable.

References

FULLAN, M. (1993) *Change Forces: Probing the Depths of Educational Reform*, London: Falmer Press.
GRIMMETT, P.P. and ERICKSON, G.L. (Eds) (1988) *Reflection in Teacher Education*, New York: Teachers College Press.

GRIMMETT, P.P. and MACKINNON, A.M. (1992) 'Craft knowledge and the education of teachers', in GRANT, G. (Ed.) *Review of Research in Education*, **18**. Washington, DC: American Educational Research Association, 385–456.

HANDAL, G. and LAUVAAS, P. (1987) *Promoting Reflecting Teaching*, Milton Keynes: The Open University Press.

LEITHWOOD, K. (1994) *Transformational Leadership*, Paper presented at the International Congress of School Effectiveness and Improvement, Melborne.

MER (Ministry of Education and Research) (1989) *OECD-vurdering av norsk utdanningspolitikk*. Aschchoug, Oslo: Ministry of Education and Research.

MER (Ministry of Education and Research) (1991) *St. meld nr. 40, Fra visjon til virke, Om høgrc utdanning*, Oslo: Ministry of Education and Research.

MER (Ministry of Education and Research) (1992) *Rammeplan for praktisk pedagogisk utdanning ved universitet og vitenskaplige høgskoler*, Oslo: Ministry of Education and Research.

MER (Ministry of Education and Research) (1994) *Studieplan for allmennlærerutdanningen*, Oslo: Ministry of Education and Research.

NCTE 1991a (National Council for Research Education). *Kunnskapsbehov i lærerutdanningen*, Oslo: National Council for Research Education.

NCTE (National Council for Teacher Education) (1991b) *Veiledning i lærerutdanningen*. Oslo: National Council for Teacher Education.

R AND D NETWORK (1993) *FoU-nettverk, Veiledning i lærerutdanninga*, Oslo: National Council for Teacher Education.

SCHULMAN, L. (1987) 'Knowledge and teaching: Foundations of the new reform', *Harvard Educational Review*, **57**, 1–22.

SCHÖN, D.A. (1983) *The Reflective Practioner*, New York: Basic Books.

SCHÖN, D.A. (1987) *Educating the Reflective Practioner*, San Francisco, CA: Jossey-Bass.

Chapter 6

Ways into Teacher Education: The Case of Portugal

Isabel Alarcão

Introduction

The case of Portugal is an interesting example of ecological interaction occurring in a changing socio-political setting in which it became possible for educational discourse to emerge and at the same time exert influence upon the action of policymakers. This fact has to be understood in the context of the building of a national educational community since the 1970s. In the post-1974 Revolution era politicians realized the relevance of education to the country's development. Educationists also grew aware of the substantial role of teacher education in this changing process. Both parties demanded an educational reform which is now in progress and puts some pressure on in-service teacher education programs. In this chapter I analyze recent legislation in its guidelines, and highlight recurrent themes as they emerge from writings in the educational field. I also comment on fears and as yet unsolved problems.

Background

In January 1993 the Education Department of one of the fourteen state universities in Portugal commemorated the twentieth anniversary of secondary school preservice teacher education at the Portuguese university. Before 1973, secondary school teachers received school-based training after graduation from the university; because of the shortage of teachers, however, a great proportion entered the profession with no training. Elementary school teachers graduated from professional teaching schools at upper secondary level after following a three-year integrated teacher education program. In the eighties these teaching schools were replaced by higher level colleges of education. At about the same period, some universities initiated preservice courses for elementary school teacher education as well.

We could say that the 1970s and 1980s were expansion years for teacher education in Portugal. Twelve higher colleges of education were established, and in ten universities, education departments came into existence. Seminal work was developed in these institutions between 1980 and the present time which greatly affected educational discourse both in newspapers and journals and also at national and international seminars and conferences. These changes in turn influenced political decisions on education.

After two decades of teacher education at the tertiary level, we now look critically at our programs of initial training. Confronted with a financial crisis in higher education, the institutions face the task of restructuring courses within parameters of cost efficiency. In the process of discarding what is felt to be less relevant, departmental staffs reflect upon the essence of professional teacher education and not infrequently come to the conclusion that they do not yet know what makes a *good* teacher, much less how to *make* one. At the same time, the country faces the urgent challenge of developing extensive in-service programs to prepare teachers to face the new demands of the school reform now in progress, which places great emphasis on self-learning strategies and school projects, and thus requires new roles for students and teachers. And so the focus shifted from initial to in-service teacher education. As one of our educational analyst points out:

> In the course of the 80s, we saw the institutionalization process of pre-service teacher education reach its highest point. Throughout the 1990s, in-service teacher education must give great attention to the dynamics of participant self-education of teachers, in close relationship with the educational projects of the schools (Nóvoa, 1991b:68).

Socio-Political Changes Affecting Teacher Education

To better grasp the present situation, one needs to consider it in the context of two events: the democratization process following the 1974 revolution and the integration of Portugal in the European Community in 1986. The revolution brought about profound changes in the country, not the least of all in education, which was revalued as a way of introducing new democratic attitudes and developing human, social, scientific and technological fields. In the 1980s the government passed several laws concerning education, the most influential being the National Educational Act in 1986. In this official paper, which defines the general framework for the educational system, the role of teacher education is stressed as essential in the changing Portuguese educational process. The document highlights the general principles that should serve as guidelines for the development of teacher education programs and activities. Issues such as excellence of initial training, flexibility and modular organization of instructional components, emphasis on experiential, active and critical learning processes intended to promote positive attitudes towards research, innovation, intervention, and self-learning are all here to be found. In-service education, viewed in the framework of a continuous learning process, appears as a new, important issue. Because of its relevance, Paragraph 1 in Article 30 of the Educational Act is quoted:

The following principles underlie teacher education:

(a) initial training at tertiary level in order to make it possible for teachers at all gràdes to have access to basic information, academic and pedagogical methods and techniques as well as to personal and social education appropriate to the functions they will fulfill;

(b) in-service education to complement and up-date initial training in the light of education as a continuous process;

(c) flexible education to enable teachers to change from one grade to another and to acquire complementary, specialized professional education;

(d) integration of academic and professional studies as well as articulation of theory and practice;

(e) experience of teaching/learning methods similar to the ones the teachers-to-be are expected to employ in their professional lives;

(f) development of a critical, interventionist attitude in relation to social reality;

(g) development of positive attitudes towards research and innovation, particularly as regards educational practice; and

(h) active involvement of prospective teachers in teaching/learning methods intended to foster reflective self-learning strategies.

This fundamental piece of legislation established some general principles which have subsequently been defined by other legal documents. So, a law passed in 1989 specified the criteria to which initial teacher education programs should adhere, but left the training institutions with some degree of freedom to develop their own curricula. The document reinforced the principles issued in the National Educational Act, stressed some features and advanced more precise guidelines. It highlighted the personal, social, cultural, academic (technological or artistic) and pedagogical components which should be included in teacher education, mentioned critical analysis, research strategies and innovation processes as relevant skills and values to be developed; emphasized the need for teachers' involvement in school and community activities; and stressed practice teaching as a substantial part in the development of professional skills. Although not thoroughly considered in this document, in-service education clearly emerged as a teacher's right as well as an obligation. I shall return to this later.

Another document, Decree 139–A/90 which defined the laddered nature of the teaching career of elementary and secondary school teachers and stated the rules for promotion which were to be followed, also had a great impact on changes in teacher education. An interesting innovatory aspect of this unifying statute was that it made the salaries of pre-elementary, elementary and secondary school teachers dependent on teachers' qualifications and grades obtained rather than on grades taught. The document established graduation from an initial training course as a *sine qua non* condition to becoming a teacher and determined the physical and psychological prerequisites for the teaching function. A probationary year after the student has completed his or her course is compulsory before the teacher can apply for tenure.

As Formosinho (1991) remarked, the structure of the teaching profession based on promotion derived from further qualification and merit implies in-service facilities (p. 238). No wonder then that another decree regulating in-service education came out some time afterwards. According to this legislation (249/92) in-service education aims at the personal and professional development of teachers and has as its final goal the improvement of the quality of teaching. It was also intended to foster applied research and spread educational change and innovation. This change was felt to be necessary because the country was undergoing profound educational reform which required a fundamental reconceptualization of the role of teachers and students and more dynamic representations of what school must be. Qualifications obtained in in-service courses now make it possible for teachers to move up the career ladder or across disciplines or go into specialized areas such as supervision, school administration, special education, etc. The document specifies the agencies that can promote in-service courses and activities, namely higher education institutions, (e.g. Education Departments in Universities, Colleges of Education), professional associations and teachers' centers based on networks of associated schools. The fact that teachers can gather to promote their own further education is an innovation and reflects the recognition of teachers' power and professionalism.

In-service activities may assume different modalities (post-graduation courses, short-term courses, training modules, specialized courses, workshops, action-research projects). If compulsory, they are financed by the Ministry of Education and are free for teachers.

Because of its relevance to the present context, I quote the principles underlying the document as expressed in section 4 of the aforementioned decree:

(a) freedom of initiative for the institutions vocationed [i.e. legally entitled] for training;

(b) scientific and pedagogic autonomy in the design and implementation of training models;

(c) progressiveness in training courses;

(d) adequacy to the needs of the educational system;

(e) functional and territorial decentralization of the in-service educational system;

(f) institutional cooperation between public, private and cooperative institutions;

(g)   association between schools and community integration as a means of establishing their autonomy;
(h)   improvement of the educational community;
(i)   promotion of teacher association in the pedagogic, scientific and professional fields.

This most recent piece of legislation shows evidence of a trend towards giving voice to teachers by moving responsibility for teacher development from Government to teachers' communities or to the institutions where they were initially trained. One-day sessions intended to train teachers to work with new curricula are now being replaced by extended periods of reflective learning on an experiential and co-operative basis, but more theoretical courses are not to be excluded. It is worth noting that a recent funding scheme established priorities for analysis of educational issues rather than the recycling of subject matter knowledge.

The Impact of Educational Discourse on Political Decisions

In this chapter I attempt to posit a personal interpretation of changes which occurred in contexts with which I am familiar. This point notwithstanding, I contend that the legislation which came into existence in Portugal in recent years has been influenced by educationalists' discourse. By discourse I mean language representative of theories, beliefs, and patterns of action emanating from a professional community and embodied in books, journal papers, newspaper commentaries, seminars, and conferences. In order to confront my personal opinion with some objective information, I perused Portuguese titles in the last twenty years in search of the emergence of key notions. In the first ten years or so I found titles justifying the role of foundation studies in teacher education programs and defining assumptions for the integration of academic and professional studies, as if the educational community were looking for a knowledge base for learning teaching. In this search models and paradigms of teacher education were extensively scrutinized and efforts were made to find the most efficient. Faced with several discourses rather than one single scientific language, educationists complained of the lack of consensus and rigour in the field. The lack of consensus at this time is not surprising given that scholars did their post-graduate courses in several different countries, mainly Belgium, France, the United Kingdom, the USA and took leading positions as soon as they returned home to Portugal.

As time passed, people grew progressively less interested in finding the best training model and started paying more attention to the effects of the teaching/learning contexts. Issues like teachers' thinking and pupils' representations, interpersonal relationships, personal knowledge acquisition, training for uncertainty, moral development, new information technologies and reflection as a learning strategy came to light. The discourse moved from giving credit to disciplines in foundations of education to emphasizing the personal construction of knowledge and the analysis of professional knowledge as exhibited by expert teachers. Titles related to child psychology, sociological studies in education, and models and paradigms in preservice teacher education were replaced by articles and books addressing questions such as the value of experiential learning as a prerequisite to teaching (*Self-education: A Step to Educating Others*, and *Experience Education, Construct Change*). Personal involvement in educational changes can also be seen in such titles as, *Continuous Self-education, Renovation, Innovation*, and *Innovation, Change and Education: Elements for an Intervention Praxis*. Reflection as a strategy for development can be seen in titles concerning the education of reflective teachers and evidenced in action-research school-based projects as suggested by such titles as, *ECO-A Project for Change with Teachers*. Education and research underlying innovation in schools appear united like two faces of the same coin. *Changing Schools: The Role of Education and Research* is such an example.

In these new trends one could suspect a dichotomy between two poles: individual self-learning and collaborative project work intended to change schools, but this apparent dichotomy vanishes on consideration of a title like *In-service Education: Between the Teacher as a Person and the School as an Organization*, thus giving credit to the idea of the substantial role of teachers in the reconceptualization of school life.

When we look back at what took place in Portugal, we find evidence of what could be called an ecological process. New contexts in the post-revolutionary era favoured the emergence of new concerns, knowledge and skills, and most of all the building of a research community. At the same time the newly developed expertise exerted influence on political decisions and gave origin to changes in the educational contexts including the field of teacher education. Changes in teacher education corresponded with changes in schools. And, as change brought about new challenges and new research interests, more researchers were attracted and more investigation undertaken. Initially subject to foreign influences, Portugal is now elaborating its own framework for action and analysis of national problems, but at the same time it maintains contacts with the countries where most of its researchers graduated. We might say the country finds itself in a process of professional growth as if it had developed confidence in its own resources. Side-by-side with bibliographic references to well-known names of foreign scholars such as Mialaret, Schön, Stones, Zeichner, le Boudec, Ferry, Perrenoud, Huberman, Popkewitz, we now find leading Portuguese figures in the field, two of whom are referred to in this paper. Moreover, the legislation to be passed was discussed by the educational community and some suggestions were taken into consideration. Behind the above legislation in preservice and in-service teacher education and as evidence for this spiraling interactive process, I can recognize the influence of groups of educationists and consultants in educational departments.

Restructuring or Reconceptualization?

I have used the term *change* throughout this chapter. A question about the nature of the changes in teacher education is now in order. The educational historian António Nóvoa (1992) commented that:

> The '70s are . . . the starting point in the present debate on teacher education. The essence at the theoretical, curricular and methodological references which have inspired the recent construction of teacher education programs date from this period. One can argue for several reasons that the reflection surrounding teacher education stabilized at this time, shortly followed by a very limited renewal of approaches and issues (p. 21).

In the period under consideration Portuguese educators made an attempt to look for a theoretical body of knowledge on teacher education and tried to identify the areas that could contribute to the education of teachers. They thought they had been able to bridge the gap between theory and practice when they started integrated teacher education courses. They believed they had found a rationale when they advocated a paradigm of technical rationality. In the 1970s they thought they had managed a steady conceptualization for initial teacher education programs; in the 1990s they realize they had dreamed too high. Unable to reconceptualize them, they stopped at restructuring them. Presently Portuguese education suffers the influence of trends which emphasize uncertainty, change, new roles for teachers and learners, and valuing attitudes like autonomy and self-evaluation as the only possible way to a personal construction of knowledge appropriate to deal with the uncertain complexity of professional situations. We now believe future teachers are in great need of being equipped with thinking and decision skills to cope with ever novel problems. In the current literature, reflection emerges as the magic solution. But, to my thinking, the application of this discovery carries further concerns. Even assuming it is possible to reflect when one is involved in practise teaching, I find it very difficult to relate theory and practice in most preservice education environments. Focused on learning, teaching without immersion in teaching situations, first-year students do not see the point of decontextualized inquiry activities, neither do they have the theoretical framework to which they can anchor possible thoughts they may derive from observation or action.

Moreover, whereas the theoretical discourse emphasizes a constructivist model, circumstances force a traditional academic pattern based on large groups and lecture-type teaching. We wonder then how to develop reflection on practice strategies with big classes of student teachers who have not yet practised teaching and the best we can do is to make attempts to be creative in developing virtual worlds of practice through the presentation of teaching cases (Alarcão and Moreira, 1993).

The gap between theory and practice is not the only difficulty, however.

Another, still unsolved problem in preservice education lies in the tension between the emphasis on student teachers' knowledge of subject matter and of educational studies. In a recent restructuring of teacher education programs in my own institution, what Zeichner and Liston (1990) term the *academic tradition* has taken the form of cuts on educational courses. Specific didactics (also called teaching methodologies), a field of study which has been given great attention in some universities in Portugal since the 1970s, aims at integrating knowledge of subject matter and pedagogical knowledge in a way similar to the proposal implied in Shulman's (1986) concept of 'pedagogic content knowledge', i.e. active knowledge of subject matter in its application to the teaching context. In my view, specific didactics provide a constructive learning context for reflective analysis of the ecological adjustments required in teaching a given subject matter to a certain group of students. But, although some scholars share my belief in the integrative and conceptualizing nature of this field of study, others view it as restrictive, prescriptive, and conservative.

Teaching practice, it seems to me, remains as much a major problem as ever. As in other countries, supervision of teachers is undervalued in terms of academic careers and a trend is currently underway in some sectors to make it once more the schools' responsibility and leave it unrelated to the university. There are, however, those who argue that teaching practice is the essential point of integration between theoretical studies and practice of teaching and claim that this should be implemented in such a way as to involve higher institutions and schools in inter-institutional partnerships.

In preservice teacher education we face problems for which we have no conclusive answers at present. This may justify Nóvoa's (1991a) opinion when he writes that at present, as opposed to the 1970s, 'there is a diffuse circulation of ideas without any theoretical coherence or its own scientific consistency' (p. 28). I do not entirely agree with Nóvoa's opinion, although I concede that my positive attitude may be related to issues in in-service rather than in preservice education. My partial disagreement may also be associated to the period of time elapsed between his paper and my own. In the last two years there has been a plethora of writing on education. As stressed earlier in this chapter, some leading figures in the Portuguese arena are being given more and more credit and, after what I would call an incubation period, I think we are in the process of merging the theoretical thinking of the research community to the expert knowledge of teachers. My opinion is that this marriage is likely to be brought about in the context of in-service programs which will be developed if we are able to overcome some of the problems still looming on the horizon.

So far I have considered initial teacher training. Let me now move to in-service teacher education which has become a national priority as stated earlier. A great number of in-service programs and activities are on the way. Some are university-based; some are based on clusters of schools. Some point to inter-institutional collaboration between schools and universities or colleges of education. Because of the novelty of these initiatives, we still wonder what the nature of these activities will be. Will the university-based ones follow the traditional, lecture and theory-based pattern? Will the school-based ones be able to surpass Day (1993) calls the 'practical level' of reflection? We are all aware that the development of reflection to deeper levels of ethical interpretation requires time and energy, but Formosinho (1991) fears the risk of 'an education which adheres to existing practices and thus is not a source of innovation, and an education which contains more elements of socialization (focus on what is) than of renovation (focus on what could be)' (p. 250).

Again, I think that inter-institutional collaboration could help in solving the dichotomy between theory and practice, technical rationality and epistemology of practice, but I also fear institutional constraints at the tertiary level make it difficult for this to happen. The most obvious constraints leave these institutions facing a financial crisis that forces teaching staff to see their teaching load increased and leaves them with very little time for involvement in out-of-institution activities.

A promising trend can be seen in the growing emergence of post-graduation courses in education (Skilbeck, 1992). Because career promotion is based on credits obtained, post-graduation courses are flourishing in higher institutions with a great enrollment of teachers. This new reality in turn impacts and influences the school culture where educational research discourse is now being shared by a growing number of schoolteachers. Interaction with this new public makes some of us realise that studies in education have much more relevance after teaching has been practised and the consciousness of this fact, together with the issue of reflection raised above, brings us back to the queries about the nature of educational studies in preservice education – a point in need of reconceptualization.

Final Remarks

In Portugal, as in other countries, we live with problems for which we seek solutions. Teaching is an extremely complex task. No doubt we still have a long way to go before we can map out and identify the central core of knowledge, skills and values in the field of teacher education as well as the contributing areas from which we should derive answers to the problems of curriculum design of initial training courses. Much research so far has been diffuse and inconclusive. Some questions have to be answered in a systematic way. Is there a scientific field of study that can be called teacher education? If so, then teacher educators should identify it, show how it relates to other fields, outline what agencies are involved, as well as suggest roles student teachers and teachers should play.

But my main concern is that this lack of a consistent theoretical body of knowledge in the field seems not to be the crucial problem. Cost is one of the problems. Preservice education of teachers is very money-consuming and I doubt whether politicians and nations all over the world are really aware of the real value of initial education for teaching. Yet, interestingly, governments

Isabel Alarcão

seem to recognize that highly motivated teachers depend on the quality of
teachers' continuous professional development.

Still another source of difficulties seems to lie in the nature of higher
education institutions. In a recent colloquium on teacher education, Vieira
(1992) referred to the constraints in the university milieu and raised several
questions: Is this (teacher education) possible within a system that emphasizes
status and power over competence?

- where academic degrees are preferred to pedagogical excellence?
- where disciplines grow in isolation?
- where pedagogical knowledge is still looked upon as something vague
  and useless?
- where positivistic thinking prevails over other epistemological approaches?
- where knowledge tends to be seen in its regulatory function rather
  than as a means to empowerment and emancipation?
- where research is broadly separated from teaching and schools?

Reflecting on these questions, one is prone to think that institutions are also
in great need of reconstruction. Or is it reconceptualization?

References

ALARCÃO, I. and MOREIRA, A. (1993) 'Technical rationality and learning by reflecting on
action in teacher education: Dichotomy or complement?', *Journal of Education for
Teaching*, **19**(1), 31–40.

DAY, C. (1993) 'Reflection: A necessary but not sufficient condition for professional
development', *British Educational Research Journal*, **19**(1), 83–94.

FORMOSINHO, J. (1991) 'Modelos organizacionais de formação contínua de professores', in
Formação Contínua: Realidades e Perspectivas, Universidade de Aveiro, 237–57.

NÓVOA, A. (1991a) 'Concepções e práticas de formação contínua de professores', in
Formação Contínua de Professores: Realidades e Perspectivas, Universidade de
Aveiro, 15–38.

NÓVOA, A. (1991b) 'A formação contínua entre a pessoa-professor e a organização-
escola', *Inovação*, **4**(1), 63–76.

NÓVOA, A. (1992) 'Formação de Professores e Profissão Docente', in NÓVOA, A. (Ed.) *Os
Professores e a sua Profissão*, Lisboa. Publicações Dom Quixote e Instituto de
Inovação Educacional, 15–33.

SHULMAN, L.S. (1986) 'Those who understand: Knowledge growth in teaching', *Educational Research*, **4**(1), 63–76.

SKILBECK, M. (1992) 'The role of research in teacher education', *European Journal of
Teacher Education*, **15**(1/2), 23–31.

VIEIRA, F. (1992) *The Training Institutions*, Paper presented at the 1992 JET Colloquium,
Curia, Portugal.

ZEICHNER, K.M. and LISTON, D.P. (1990) 'Traditions of reform in US teacher education',
Journal of Teacher Education, **41**(2), 3–20.

Chapter 7

Teacher Education in Canada: A Case Study of British Columbia and Ontario

Nancy Sheehan and Michael Fullan

Introduction

Teacher education is largely seen as an irrelevant or hopeless player in educational reform. In this chapter we have two main themes. First, that teacher education has failed to achieve the place it deserves in the improvement of education. Second, that there are several myths which continue to present major barriers to achieving needed breakthroughs. Despite this, there are growing pressure points which represent great potential.

One of us in a recent review called teacher education 'society's missed opportunity'. Despite the rhetoric about teacher education in today's society, there does not seem to be a real belief or confidence that investing in teacher education will yield results. Perhaps deep down many leaders believe that teaching is not all that difficult. After all, most leaders have spent thousands of hours in the classroom and are at least armchair experts. And they know that scores of unqualified teachers are placed in classrooms every year and required to learn on the job. In addition, investing in teacher education is not a short-term strategy. With all the problems facing us demanding immediate solution it is easy to overlook a preventative strategy that would take several years to have an impact (Fullan, 1993:104).

The first sentence in Tyson's (1994) book, *Who Will Teach the Children*, reads: 'It would be hard to find a highly educated adult in the United States today who lacks an opinion, nearly always a negative one, about the education of American teachers' (p. ix). Goodlad (1990; 1994) has hammered home the dual message that teacher education is badly in need of radical overhaul, and that many of the critics themselves represent the biggest obstacles to reform. Nikiforuk, in both his *Globe* and *Mail* columns and his book, *School's Out: The Disaster in Canadian Public Education*, is equally critical of Canadian teacher education institutions.

One result of these critics is powerful negative myths that persist despite the fact that they are partially, largely and in some cases completely untrue. To say that 'faculties of education are intransigent', 'teacher education candidates are weak', 'not enough time is spent in the practicum', 'schools and teachers are not interested in collaboration', is to be out of touch with current reality. And yet faculties of education do not seem to be able to get their message across. There has been significant movement especially at the ground level (as distinct from the policy level) which is virtually not recognized in these larger debates. These movements represent preconditions and potential searching for major improvements, perhaps even a breakthrough. So far that breakthrough has not occurred, and there is no assurance that it will. If we fail to capitalize on these new directions we remain mired in the mythology of past teacher education. We run the risk of ensuring a self-fulfilling prophecy. And we allow our history to dictate our future.

Background to Teacher Education Reform

Reform of teacher education in Canada is fraught with problems, not the least of these is the decentralized nature of education in Canada and the fact that schools, the curriculum and teacher certification are controlled provincially. Faculties of education suffer from the certification practices of ministries/departments of education which are not uniform across the country. Certification requirements specific to individual provinces have been in existence since the turn of the century with only a few reciprocal agreements on certification between provinces and none involving British Columbia. One result of this control by provincial governments is that faculties of education have produced no permanent, durable models for teacher education. We have not worked together to share ideas, learn from one another or pilot new approaches. We have tended to be reactive, particularly when changes to our programs have to be approved, not only by the bureaucracy of the university but also by the bureaucracy of the government.

The second difficulty is the location of all teacher education in the universities – places where theory and research appear to be more important than practice. Teacher education in Canada has been firmly located in faculties of education in universities for the last quarter of a century. Although the universities had programs suitable for secondary teachers early in the century, the transfer of elementary teacher education from the normal schools to the universities began in Alberta in 1945 and was completed across the country by 1970; most elementary teachers were by then receiving two years of university education, and the goal of a BA or a B.Ed for all teachers was within sight.

However, the normal school curriculum and the educational qualifications of their instructors did not meet university standards. Universities believed that academic qualifications with no attention to pedagogy were the only requirements necessary to teach in the university. Therefore, the transfer of teacher education to the universities was hampered both by its history in the normal schools and by the attitude commonly found in universities that anybody could teach, that only a knowledge of subject matter was necessary to be a good teacher – whether in the school system or at the post-secondary level. The emphasis on practice in the normal school versus the interest in research in the university did not facilitate a smooth transfer.

Another difficulty with reform of teacher education is the notion prevalent over time and still existing among many in the society today, that teaching requires no special knowledge or skill, the belief that has dogged us for years that teacher education has no knowledge base: that is, that anyone can teach. The development of normal schools was an affirmation that more than subject matter knowledge was necessary. However, the knowledge base that normal schools concentrated on was one of knowledge and practice of textbook and blackboard use. Lax admission policies, devotion to the content of textbooks, mechanics of classroom operation, very short programs and lack of a theoretical backdrop to teaching, were found in most normal schools. On the other hand, control by the ministry, instructors who were experienced school teachers, and emphasis on practice endeared these schools to many.

A fourth problem is the lack of agreement in the teacher education community about either the quality of the existing program or the kinds of reforms which are necessary. Teacher education programs across the country vary in their admission practices, the number of courses in the teaching subject content area vs. courses in pedagogy, the length of the practicum, whether the programs are concurrent or consecutive, whether the student receives a bachelor's degree as a first degree or whether the B.Ed degree is the second degree. There is agreement that there is no one best way to prepare a teacher. Individual faculties of education are wont to think that their own programs are successful and they point to the number of graduates who find teaching positions as an indication of successful programs.

A fifth concern has to do with the fact that schools are not viewed as learning institutions where the accumulated wisdom of practice is appreciated and disseminated. Schools are still characterized as places with closed classroom doors. There are very few induction programs in schools in Canada and often new teachers are saddled with the worst assignments. Furthermore, there is no link between the graduates in their first teaching assignments and the programs where they have done their preservice teacher education.

Another problem which has dogged the history of faculties of education in universities has to do with both historical and contemporary attitudes towards social issues. For example, there is ample evidence to suggest that schools today are classic cases of the division of labour by gender, and so are universities. Administrative structure and practices which favoured males, curriculum and resource materials which ignored females, and teachers and professors who consciously or unconsciously paid more attention to males and their needs, have been factors in this inequality. The language, course content, and atmosphere of both the school and the university have delivered different messages. Both messages reflect societal practice. There are numerous other social issues, such as multiculturalism, mainstreaming, English-as-a-second-language, and native awareness, all of which put demands on teachers and teacher education programs. Universities, and therefore their faculties of education, have been slow to come to grips with some of these issues.

With this kind of history, faculties of education have had a difficult time reaching maturity as both good teacher education institutions and good university faculties. Both are critical if we are to have a well-defined public education system in the hands of competent, responsible professionals for the twenty-first century. There is some evidence that change is underway with some faculties looking toward the professional community while remaining securely anchored as research/teaching units within the university. British Columbia and Ontario are two such provinces and there are similarities and differences in their approaches to reform. Both have had recent major studies on teacher education. Both have deans who are exerting some leadership in the professional community. Both have faculties of education which are developing teacher education research centres, professional partnerships and revising teacher education programs. The transfer of teacher certification from the Ministry to a College of Teachers and the decentralization of teacher education to university colleges has the potential to shape reform in British Columbia. In Ontario the Teacher Education Council has commissioned a number of reports on topics ranging from admissions to support for beginning teachers.

British Columbia

In British Columbia the establishment of a Royal Commission on Education in 1987, the promulgation of Bill 20, creating the BC College of Teachers (also in 1987), and the creation of university colleges under the 1988 Government Access Program, are the major events which have both pressured faculties of education to change and have acted as catalysts for change in teacher education programs. The timing of these developments has created an atmosphere conducive to some reform and in which there is some trust developing among the education partners.

The British Columbia College of Teachers

Of these changes probably the most dramatic has been Bill 20, *The Teaching Profession Act*, which established the British Columbia College of Teachers (BCCT). This was dramatic because it gave teachers, not the government, control over certification, discipline and professional development. Teachers throughout North America and world-wide have talked about professional autonomy and control over their own affairs for years. Although it would appear that teachers in BC had won the long-sought right to professional autonomy there has been a fair amount of disagreement over this development. The legislation was created without consultation with teachers, the universities, or other members of the education community. The BC Teachers'

Federation (BCTF) which has existed since 1919 and which had compulsory membership for all teachers in the public schools of British Columbia was not happy with the notion that a second and, in some ways, rival association was being established by the government. The enabling legislation established the college as a professional body of teachers with jurisdiction over membership and a college council of twenty individuals as the governing body. Membership on the council was composed of fifteen teachers elected by teachers in each of the fifteen zones of the province, two members appointed by Cabinet, two appointed by the Minister of Education, and the last appointee a representative of the Deans of the Faculties of Education. Control over certification, discipline and professional development was in the hands of the teaching profession. To teach in the public schools of British Columbia membership in the college became mandatory. The college has exercised its right of control over certification and discipline but has decided that professional development belongs with the BCTF.

The creation of a College of Teachers has produced a number of issues affecting teacher education in the province. The certification process and the approval of programs for initial teacher certification at the three universities have proved interesting challenges for the college and for the institutions. In the initial months of its operation the college adopted the certification practices of the Ministry and gave interim approval to the three universities' teacher education programs. Over time it has developed certification policy, by-laws, and appeals procedures. A major effort of the college was a review of Teacher Education in British Columbia, specifically of the three universities' pre-certification programs. The Review produced a report, *Teacher Education in British Columbia* (Bowman, 1991), which was circulated for discussion and considered at a number of forums on teacher education. From these forums, documents and material collected in the course of the review, the college has approved on an ongoing basis the programs currently in existence at the three universities and has established criteria for approval of new teacher education programs. It has also established a process for working collaboratively with the faculties and other education partners for the improvement of teacher education in the province. It is in this last area – the area of working collaboratively with the faculties – that the college has the opportunity to make the greatest impact.

There are difficulties with both the report, *Teacher Education in British Columbia*, and the on-going collaboration between the college and the faculties of education and these may challenge educational reform. Vested interests in both schools and universities, a lack of respect for one another by the players involved, the problem of defining and implementing a knowledge base whose vision and framework are accepted by faculty members and teachers, and the tendency to count courses and numbers of weeks of practicum rather than to concentrate on distinctive qualities and abilities of teacher candidates have been reflected in the report and/or in the ongoing collaboration and have hampered the move to true reform. Since the college had requested and received a legislative change eliminating their control over professional development, the notion of teacher education as a continuum, with life-long learning an important aspect, may be down-played. Although the creation of the college has the potential for encouraging major improvements, it has taken a conservative, traditional approach to teacher education.

The Access Program

The government also introduced legislation which gave four of the colleges in the province the opportunity to work with universities and offer degree-completion programs. The government's Access Program, as it is known, was developed in 1988 with a goal of creating 15,000 new places for university students. In association with a university these colleges are granting university degrees and over time hope to become autonomous degree-granting institutions. The faculties of education have responded to the interest in the colleges for teacher education programs and are currently working with several colleges in the province offering teacher education programs on site.

Along with these opportunities for collaboration with the colleges, the Ministry of Education also developed a rural consortium model for offering off-site teacher education programs. Simon Fraser University (SFU) has had a long tradition of offering programs off-site; the one best known is the Alaska Highway Consortium Project, and SFU has a number of other projects at various locations around BC. The University of Victoria is offering a program in Cranbrook and the University of British Columbia (UBC) is offering one in Castlegar under this consortium arrangement. These programs offer both challenges and opportunities to the faculties and the profession.

There is concern that there are too many small programs developing in a province with a sparse population. Teacher educators and members of the Council of the College of Teachers worry about this trend to small programs destroying what, until now, have been teacher education programs on university campuses using the resources of the university in terms of libraries, audio-visual and computer resources, and with subject matter content courses available from other faculties. Small, off-site programs have more difficulty with both the above-mentioned resources and with the ability to offer teaching subject specializations. Some of the consortia have become semi-permanent and an emphasis on practice without the accompanying theory and reflection may not be the reform impetus that will prepare teachers for continuous learning in schools or help schools become learning institutions.

Curriculum Reform

In response to the Report of the Royal Commission on Education the Ministry of Education developed a set of initiatives known as *Year 2000*. Year 2000 and the working papers and program documents associated with it outlined major changes. Ungraded primary classrooms, continuous progress, integration of subject areas, a common curriculum, changes in approaches to assessment and more emphasis on various social issues such as gender equity, multiculturalism, mainstreaming and the education of First Nations (Native Canadians) students, were some of the elements outlined.

Responses to these changes were varied: enthusiastic support was evident for the primary program as it was seen to advocate practice in primary classrooms. On the other hand, the intermediate program, which was aimed at grades 4 through 10, met with considerable resistance. Teachers of the grades affected were dubious about the benefits of instructional assessment techniques which integrate subject areas and ignore grading norms. Overt rejection was the case for the graduation program draft which suggested a series of pathways for students to elect, incorporated work experience into all programs, and required all students to take an integrated course called *general studies*. With such mixed responses from teachers, parents and the universities, the intermediate and graduation program drafts were redrawn in 1994, the government changed reporting structures, deemphasized integration, introduced specific core content, and accepted skill development and career preparation as a strong component of the secondary school curriculum.

The role of faculties of education in these ever-changing reforms has fluctuated. A number of faculty were instrumental in the work of the Royal Commission and its recommendations. The policy and curriculum reforms which followed saw little faculty input except as critics to some of the draft documents. Generally, faculty who are experts in educational policy have had little influence on policy formation. On the other hand, as the Ministry moves to develop curriculum to fit the new (1994) policy, faculty involvement has been encouraged through ministry/school district/faculty of education partnerships.

The triangulation of these three developments, BC College of Teachers, the Government Access Program, and attempts at curriculum reform, is beneficial to achieving change. The dialogue encouraged by the college, the opportunity to pilot curriculum/program reform in small off-campus programs, and the need for teachers in the field to adapt their classroom practice has created an atmosphere in which alternate ways of doing things can be attempted. The three universities in the province have a history of collaboration with the field, e.g. Simon Fraser's university/faculty associate program, the University of Victoria's internship project, and UBC's numerous off-campus teacher education programs of the late 1970s and early 1980s. The current emphasis on working in partnership with the university colleges and rural teacher education consortia, and the College of Teachers' focus on collaboration has meant that it is easier for the faculties of education to propose, react to, and develop a variety of collaborative projects with school districts. There are a large number of these under way sponsored by universities, school districts, teachers, and local teachers' associations. They emphasize the practicum, create opportunity for dialogue and research, and foster understanding of the problems of teaching. They operate at both the elementary and secondary level and each of the projects has its own team of faculty which works with a team from the field. Although these may not be major improvements, they do hold promise for a creative approach to the preparation of teachers.

Ontario

At about the same time as the British Columbia Royal Commission was reviewing all of education in that province, the Ontario government established a Teacher Education Review Steering Committee (TERC). It's mandate was 'to examine all aspects of the education of teachers, including admission procedures to teacher education institutions, preservice programs, entrance to the profession, and ongoing professional development' (Ontario Teacher Education Review Committee, 1988:1). TERC commissioned a report, *Teacher Education in Ontario, Current Practice and Options for the Future* (Fullan, Connelly and Watson, 1987) that provided a brief history of teacher education in Ontario, analyzed the current scene (in the late 1980s) and made a series of recommendations.

Teacher education is less intensive in duration in Ontario than in the western provinces. The normal schools and teachers' colleges for elementary teachers were not incorporated into universities until the end of the 1960s. To this day, the official requirements to become certified as a teacher in Ontario are comparatively minimal – an undergraduate degree, followed by a one-year Bachelor of Education, which is actually an eight-month program requiring only 40 days of practice teaching. We will see later that many faculties have gone beyond the policy requirements, but by and large the vast majority of the 4000 to 5500 graduates per year in the 1987–94 years from the ten faculties of education in the province take the post-baccalaureate route.

The Fullan, Connelly and Watson report made a total of thirty-three recommendations to TERC which include:

- Establishing a constituency-based Teacher Education Council;
- Identify undergraduate prerequisites and experiences in cooperation with Arts and Science faculties;
- Lengthening and strengthening teacher preparation through a mandatory preservice-induction continuum in collaboration with local school boards;
- A variety of admission and inservice recommendations.

All of these new developments were to be overseen by the Teacher Education Council as advisory to the government.

TERC, in turn, made thirty-three recommendations in its Final Report to the Minister. The core of its recommendations was to establish the aforementioned

Teacher Education Council, and to channel virtually all of the other recommendations through the Council for consideration or action. For example, as part of teacher preparation and certification, Recommendation 21 stated:

> It is recommended that, by September, 1995, an induction phase be mandatory as part of the teacher education program. [The Council] be responsible for development, selection, and evaluation criteria (Ontario TERC, 1988:40).

In February 1989 the government accepted the main enabling recommendation of the report by announcing that a Teacher Education Council of Ontario (TECO) would be established to advise 'on ways of shaping a quality teacher education process.' The 16-member council would represent four major stakeholders: universities, teachers, school boards and the government. The official announcement emphasized that future directions would be guided by an important principle stated by TERC: 'that teacher education should be viewed as a continuum which begins in the undergraduate years and spans the full extent of a teacher's career' (p. 40).

The newly formed TECO proceeded to establish – mistakenly in our view – several task forces on each of the major topics: admissions and undergraduate requirements, teacher preservice, induction, in-service, program review, etc. From 1989 to 1992, TECO produced well over one thousand pages of analysis and further recommendations. By 1992, TECO's initial team had elapsed and the newly formed New Democrat Party conducted the required *sunset review*. No decision was made, but TECO was discontinued until further notice. In short, although TECO's reports contained a number of recommendations about reforming teacher education, none of these saw the light of day. The policy pertaining to teacher education remained unchanged.

In mid-1993, the Ontario government established a Royal Commission on Education with a mandate to review all of education including teacher education. Its recommendations are due in December, 1995. Again, these will be recommendations not necessarily policy actions.

TERC was established in 1985; the Royal Commission will be reporting ten years later. It has been a decade of ever-increasing calls for educational reform. To say that teacher education has been studied to death is only an exaggeration if you believe that study should be accompanied by action. In the change literature we have a saying 'Ready, Fire, Aim'. So far, teacher education in Ontario is a classic example of 'Ready, Ready, Ready' (Fullan, 1993).

In the meantime, on the ground there have been a number of developments and changes within exciting parameters (see Watson and Allison, 1992). The applicant pool of teacher education candidates is exceedingly strong, virtually all faculties combine academic and experience criteria for admission, the ethnic composition of preservice cohorts has substantially changed, time spent in schools by teacher preparation candidates has increased dramatically, partnerships with schools for both preservice and in-service purposes have been established, research has expanded in faculties of education, large numbers of new faculty members have been hired, and so on.

To take two related examples, The Learning Consortium (1994) in Toronto which includes six partners – four school boards and two higher education institutions – has been working since 1988 on teacher development, and school development and their linkage. Thousands of educators have been involved in designing and implementing educational improvements through the Learning Consortium.

The Faculty of Education, University of Toronto (FEUT), as with other faculties in the province has been redesigning its teacher education program with the following design features:

- cohorts of student teachers;
- teams of faculty and field-based staff;
- clustered, designated partner schools;
- educational reform focus;
- research and inquiry embeddedness.

The Faculty's proposed newly designed two-year Bachelor's/Master's program builds on previous pilot projects. The curriculum has been revamped, on campus and field-based work is carefully coordinated through the cohort/ cluster design. Students will spend over 150 days of the 300+ total days in focused field placements and internships (FEUT, 1994).

Both the Learning Consortium and the FEUT proposal are examples of the new trends toward teacher education reform in Ontario. They focus on the teacher education continuum, the linkage of teacher development and school development, changes in the teacher education curriculum, and new leadership at both the school and faculty levels focusing on lengthening and strengthening teacher preparation and continuous learning throughout the career. They represent examples of substantial change on the ground.

At the policy level, however, little has happened beyond the initial transfer of teachers' colleges in the 1960s into universities. Immediately on the heels of the transfer, the school system, and consequently the numbers of teachers needed, grew dramatically in the period 1965–73. In effect, this rapid quantitative expansion precluded quality control. There followed a period of stagnation from about 1974–84 where teachers and teacher educators grew old together in a climate of economic and educational decline or stagnation. Since 1985, there has been a renewed assault on the educational system with ever-increasing pressure for reform. For a variety of reasons, reform in teacher education, rhetoric notwithstanding, is not seen as an instrument of reform. At the same time, pressure points, both negative (dissatisfaction with teacher education), and positive (example of redesigned programs) have been mounting.

The optimist might say that these developments represent necessary preconditions for an inevitable breakthrough; the pessimist might observe that the more things change, the more they remain the same. The Royal Commission's report and its immediate aftermath in 1995 will be one litmus test worth observing closely.

Conclusion

This look at British Columbia and Ontario emphasizes the political arena in which educational change occurs. It also discusses the variety of ideas, the interest among partners and the possibilities for collaboration. The danger with numerous and small ventures, such as the off-campus programs, pilots and partnerships, at a time of fluctuating political decisions may be one of a lack of coherence. We need to ask how many teachers and faculty beyond those directly involved benefit from consortia, professional development schools and other collaborative ventures? Do numerous and varied collaborations change the learning environment of either the schools or the education faculties? The difficulty is that each program develops its own culture and does not easily transfer to another institution, especially to a large faculty with its own structures, traditions and bureaucracies. Even pilots within large programs have some difficulty sustaining enthusiasm over time and expanding beyond the confines of the original pilot boundaries. In addition, the socialization of beginning teachers sees them quickly adapt to the traditional school culture. If teacher education is going to experience major improvements, even a breakthrough, then attention must centre on the experiences and evaluations of partnerships like The Learning Consortium and Professional Development Schools. The development of teacher education as a field of research may provide answers to these and other questions over time. There is a momentum for change in schools and educational institutions and in such a climate teacher education programs should be encouraged to question long-held assumptions, evaluate objectives and explore alternatives and improvements in collaboration with the professional community. At the present time then, there is not a close link between changes in practice and changes in policy in teacher education. The preconditions for convergence, however, appear to be in place: namely, innovative examples of redesign 'on the ground', combined with policy discourses at the level of the province which could lead to new policies that propel incipient reforms forward.

The developments in British Columbia and Ontario are similar to what is happening in other parts of Canada, i.e., there is considerable debate and some action, but no major breakthroughs. Nova Scotia, for example, just completed a province-wide review of teacher education which resulted in a government decision to close down four of its eight teacher education programs and increase the length of the program from one to two years (post-baccalaureate). This consolidation is aimed as well at redesigning teacher education programs in the direction of reforms discussed in this chapter.

Looked at from the perspective of time, the history of development of teacher education in Canada has been remarkably short – some thirty years from about 1965 to 1995 – and it has evolved through unique periods. In other words, teacher education has not come of age. We expect that the next decade will result in major new developments in which teacher education will increasingly become a major player in educational reform. If so, this will represent a sea change in how teacher education has been seen in Canada.

To do this, however, we must begin to work together, learn from one another and identify individual institutional success, even if that success suggests that some teacher education programs are inadequate. Our location in universities should be our strength. We can learn from other professional faculties – law, medicine, business – to understand how they have gained respect from both the university and their professional communities. Teaching hospitals, clinical and adjunct instructors, co-op programs and field-based courses have had some success for these other faculties.

At the same time faculties of education can help universities redefine their missions with strong foci on quality teaching at the post-secondary level, and the development of new knowledge through field-based collaboration and enquiry as new models are developed and tested. Teams that include faculty, teachers, administrators and students working on a problem, suggesting solutions, monitoring progress, and communicating results, should be formed.

To begin to find this success we must accept responsibility for our graduates, understand the changing society and its schools, teachers and children, reflect that society in our instructors and programs and do the necessary interdisciplinary, local and national research to find out what works best, when and with whom. None of this will be easy. Change is difficult, research dollars are scarce, work in schools and with teachers takes time (for both teachers and faculty) and there is little agreement on what will make a difference. However, to not attempt change is unacceptable. At issue is not only the viability of teacher education institutions but the long term health of our teachers and our schools.

References

BOWMAN, J. (1991) *A Report to the College of Teachers on Teacher Education in British Columbia*, Vancouver, BC: BC College of Teachers.

FACULTY OF EDUCATION, UNIVERSITY OF TORONTO (1994) *B.Ed/M.Ed in Teaching and Learning: A Program Proposal*, Toronto, Ontario: Faculty of Education.

FULLAN, M. (1993) *Change Forces*, London: Falmer Press.

FULLAN, M., CONNELLY, F.M. and WATSON, N. (1987) *Teacher Education in Ontario: Current Practice and Options for the Future*, Toronto, Ontario: Ministry of Colleges and Universities, Ontario.

GOODLAD, J.I. (1990) *Teachers for our Nation's Schools*, San Francisco, CA: Jossey-Bass Publishers.

GOODLAD, J.I. (1994) *Educational Renewal*, San Francisco, CA: Jossey-Bass Publishers.

NIKIFORUK, A. (1993) *School's Out: The Catastrophe in Public Education and What We Can Do About It*, Toronto: MacFarlane Walter and Ross.

ONTARIO TEACHER EDUCATION REVIEW COMMITTEE (1988) *Final Report of the Teacher Education Review Steering Committee*, Ministry of Education, Ontario, and Ministry of Colleges and Universities, Ontario.

TYSON, H. (1994) *Who will Teach the Children?* San Francisco, CA: Jossey Bass Publishers.

WATSON, N. and ALLISON, P. (1992) *Ontario Faculties of Education: Responding to Change. A Report prepared for the Ontario Association of Deans of Education*, Ontario, St Catharines.

Part Two

Policy Directions for Change in Teacher Education

The case studies in Part One set out a broad spectrum of restructuring efforts in the six Western countries they represent. It is quite conceivable, however, that such efforts to restructure may come to nought if teacher educators are not clear on the directions that teacher education should take. Lengthening teacher education will mean nothing if current practices are simply extended. The question then becomes, if we were to have the opportunity to change, where would we begin?

The two chapters by Tuinman and Tom focus at the policy level. They set out general directions for change that represent significant reconceptualizations of how teacher education can be organized and carried out. Tuinman reflects on his experience as having been a Dean of a Faculty of Education for eight years and comes up with a series of propositions for university teacher educators to take seriously into account. Tom draws on his many years of experience as a teacher educator. He finds the activity much the same as when he graduated in 1963. He attacks four structural assumptions in teacher education and offers radical counter proposals. Though these two authors take different approaches to their task, their views about how teacher education could be reformed at the ground level are remarkably similar.

Chapter 8

Rescuing Teacher Education: A View from the Hut with the Bananas

Jaap Tuinman

Introduction

The Cambridge sociologist Anthony Giddens repeatedly focused on *reflexivity*: the capacity of knowledgeable human beings to reflect on their experience and so transform structures and institutions to influence the terms of social reproduction. I presume that the editors of this volume were mindful of his work when they asked me to comment on teacher education from the specific perspective of an (ex)-dean of a faculty of education.

> In a Kuranko village there is no one main path leading to a privileged vantage point where one can take up the position of spectator or observer. On the contrary, the structure of the village enforces participation . . . one is part of the ongoings in the village, immersed in its sights and smells and sounds: the feel of cracked mud against the palm of one's hands, the pungent odor of cassava leaf and fried fish sauce, the fetid smell of bodies, the cries of children, the rhythmic thud of mortars pounding rice, the crowing of a rooster, the raised voices of men debating some vexed issue in the court yard (Jackson, 1991:7, 8).

In my years as Dean of the Faculty of Education at Simon Fraser University I may have had few opportunities to smack my hand against mud walls, or to smell dried fish sauce, but I seem to remember the crowing of the odd rooster. I do have memories of the thud of mortars aimed at the obliteration of academic opposition and I recall most vividly men and women indefatigably debating vexed issues not only in the courtyard, but in the university's lounges as well. And for me, there distinctly was no objective vantage point, no perch above it all.

The view of teacher education I will set forth here is a very personal view, informed by the intimacy that sharing space with individuals who work and live in the same small village brings. If that view owes anything at all to my years as an administrator it is mostly a consequence of the fact that my somewhat larger hut served as the storage place for bananas and other good things and hence, may have attracted more than the average amount of traffic and interaction.

The View From My Village

Simon Fraser University's Faculty of Education, is, I think, among the best in North America. It is located in a relatively young university and the faculty's architects in the middle-sixties took advantage of their opportunities. They designed the faculty keeping in mind two basic principles: it is hard to get along with, and have the respect of, the rest of the university and at the same time be accorded the benediction of the field, i.e. the teaching profession. Hence, a faculty was created in which in effect half of the full-time positions were allotted to regular, tenure track professors, and half to seconded members of the profession, i.e. teachers. Many faculties of education employ teachers from time to time. The difference at Simon Fraser University was, and is, that these individuals are numerous, that they are assigned major teaching responsibilities, and that they will normally remain for a very strictly enforced period of two years, and finally, that they generally represent the very best the teaching profession has to offer. Three consequences, easily anticipated, follow from this staffing design. First, the faculty's relations with the profession are excellent. In effect, I cannot think of an environment where the profession has a larger influence on a university curriculum. Second, the tenure track professorate finds itself by and large relieved from preoccupation with practical professional matters; that is, professors can escape all the 'down to earth stuff' if they wish. Not surprisingly, the faculty has been very productive in that area of scholarship traditionally valued by the universities. Not only does SFU's Faculty of Education hold its own with any other social science department on campus, it has often bested all other faculties of education in the country when it comes to traditional measures of research and scholarship. Third, if ever there was a perfect arena where the classical conflicts between professor and practitioner, whether the latter are teachers, lawyers, engineers, or family physicians, could be played out creatively, the Faculty of Education at SFU is it.

So, this was my village, and I lived in it, and eventually departed from it as a Dean contented. In the process, I did form some generalizations about the business of teacher education. The purpose of this chapter is to pass those on. As I do so, and make some rather critical comments in the process, it is not my intention to antagonize my former colleagues. I think that teachers, and *ipso facto* teacher educators, often are held to standards very difficult to meet. However, I also believe that universities and faculties of education are not taking their mandate or their public seriously enough.

It is my belief that teacher education is the joint property of the university and the profession. The two major points that spring from this observation are that teacher education should not be owned exclusively by the university and that the area of responsibility for teacher education that does properly belong to the university is co-owned by the faculties of arts, science and education; this should be a given. Much has been written about this assertion in one way or the other. The collective writings have had little practical impact, however, except for isolated pockets of action. From my view from the hut, I saw how this assertion could be realized.

Professions such engineering, law, and medicine tend to exert considerable formal influence over the education of aspiring novice members. Education, perhaps because it is seen as a weak profession, is an exception. Practical measures are required and feasible, as Simon Fraser University has shown in its Alaska Highway Teacher Education Project (AHCOTE) and other similar consortia.

In the mid 1980s SFU's Faculty of Education signed the first such agreement in British Columbia (and presumably Canada) with three northern BC school boards and the Northern Lights College. In essence, it was agreed that consensus among partners was required for all decisions affecting budget, staffing, and curriculum, 'respecting the various restrictions, inherent in law and university senate regulation'. Together they planned and offered a program to prepare teachers for schools in that community.

SFU's AHCOTE and similar consortia worked well from the perspective of the creation of new teachers. However, over time, the responsibility and the control fell too much toward the field partners. The major reason for this shift in control was that the majority of tenure track faculty members were a) not sufficiently interested in the practicalities of teacher education and b) not sufficiently prepared or knowledgeable. Hence, they tended to absent themselves from the process, though, of course, there were many excellent exceptions to this rule. This experience from the hut lead me to six propositions about teacher education. I begin with the first here.

Proposition A
Formal agreements must be made between the university, its faculty of education, local school authorities and, where appropriate, local colleges, to operate jointly teacher education programs designed to meet local needs.
Proposition B
Faculties of Education must make a public acknowledgement that they are professional schools.

Some History

Given a choice, many professors of education would identify themselves more with their colleagues in arts and science than with those in business, medicine, engineering or law. This is somewhat surprising, and the correlate of much incompetence in teacher education. One can, of course, point to reasons for this state of affairs: if teaching is not a profession, and there are those who would argue the point, then *ipso facto*, teacher education cannot be a professional enterprise. That, however, is a bit of sophistry; if we were to accept, for argument's sake that teaching is a semi-profession, then teacher education faculties could be rightly called semi-professional schools and it should still follow that their faculty might feel at least more aligned with those in the professional schools than is currently the case. But this is not so.

On my current campus, to illustrate the issue from another venue, there existed for a long time a Vice-President (Professional Schools). Typically, education was excluded from his or her mandate. Among the reasons for this state of affairs is the historic self-enforced self-sufficiency of teacher education programs. Generally, they were imported into the university, managed as a separate unit, and their curriculum for a large part resembled a watered-down arts and science curriculum. The autonomy of Schools of Education in universities in Canada and the US, an autonomy ironically deriving from both their status as lepers and their attraction to large numbers of students, allowed (or forced) these schools to appoint their own professors of English, math, history, and so forth. Hence, the identification with the non-professional faculties. In fact, of course, the major mandate of faculties of education is not the study of history for its own sake, not the study of mathematics for the purpose of learning mathematics, but the formation of teachers. If, to fulfill that purpose, students must learn mathematics, or history, or English, so much the better, but these studies need not necessarily take place within the faculty of education.

A minor mandate of these faculties, it must be conceded, is the study of education *per se*. But that task does not, by any stretch of the imagination, require the huge numbers of education faculty attached to our universities. The only reason faculties of education are so large is that many students want to become teachers; hence, most of the faculty appointments should be justified on the grounds of that professional requirement. But often they are not. Often education faculty find the professional work boring, academically unchallenging and not rewarded. Not unreasonably, given the context of their own training and early work expectations, rather than being a professor of methods of teaching history, they prefer to concentrate on the justification of teaching history; rather than working on the difficulties of teaching mathematics, they prefer to study the different levels of achievement in mathematics around the globe; rather than improving the way English is taught in high schools, they prefer to join the debate on the limits of interpretation in understanding texts. With very unfortunate consequences, concern with practical professional matters has become identified as a low-level academic, non-scholarly activity.

Teacher Education and the Medical Model

Faculties of Medicine are run by practitioners, with doctors doubling up as clinical professors. There often is a department of basic sciences which houses more traditional academic scientists. But, the clinical faculty are in charge – they take care of the professional formation. The high professional status of medicine makes that possible. In education, however, it appears that the equivalent of medicine's basic scientists have taken over and defined the work of the faculty. The practitioners are on the outside. The tenured or tenure-track faculty resent references to the necessity of practical knowledge. Education's equivalent of the teaching of the art of straight incisions or of reading CAT scans, skills well valued in medical schools, is beneath the dignity of the typical professor of education.

The argument is made that teachers either do not possess an arsenal of professional techniques analogous to those of a physician or lawyer, or accountant, or that these are so rudimentary that they should not soil a university curriculum or calendar. But then, where should they be taught; why do we have large faculties of education, and what things of value to the profession do the members of these faculties teach? It is, in this context, of great interest to see how the emphasis on the basic sciences is disappearing from the curriculum of future physicians.

Proposition C
Education faculty must be held accountable for an up-to-date knowledge of the profession.

Reflecting on the dual-track model of staffing in SFU's Faculty of Education, I see as its major strengths: i) the freedom which tenure track faculty members are accorded for research, reflection and scholarship; ii) the presence, through seconded faculty associates, of an up-to-date knowledge of teaching practices; and iii) the ever-renewing creative dialogue between the two faculty groups. Its weaknesses included, however: i) frequent lack of knowledge of today's schools and their problems on the side of the tenure track faculty (there was no requirement that faculty members ever visited schools or ever spoke to the children they wrote about); and ii) an unresolved tension between professional education as a passing on of *status quo* and legitimate challenges of that very state of being.

I do not believe that it will be easy to mirror the medical model of professional training, where clinicians can arrange their own practice so they can find time and opportunity to teach, or professors can arrange their university lives so they can practice medicine on a regular and continuing basis. Different professions have different constraints when it comes to ensuring that the professorate has current practical expertise. Engineers, for instance, frequently use consulting as a vehicle to achieve that end. I think that universities must become far more aggressive in requiring that their education faculty know what they are talking about. If there is understanding of the need to act in this respect, and a will to do so, there are many possible models. I cannot, for instance, see any reason why three faculty members, through a contract with a local school, could not agree to be responsible for teaching a particular class.

It also should be possible to require that a proportion of sabbatical time be used for the upgrading of professional skill and knowledge. And finally, joint appointments of tenure-track faculty between the university and educational authorities are, in my view, not out of the question. For an individual university to make major changes may be difficult, however, in the absence of a national consensus on these matters.

I believe that measures such as these are essential for the survival of faculties of education. (Those skeptical of the validity of this comment should take note of recent events in Britain, described by Pimm and Selinger in Chapter 4, where teacher education has been taken out of universities and placed in the schools.) The interest in and preparation for academic analysis, so important to the lives of university faculty, is of great importance. Teacher preparation must not be turned over to those only interested in practical issues. However, I have observed that even my colleagues in philosophy, could benefit greatly from more exposure to the real world. It is hard to make a convincing argument of any kind to students who know, through your examples, that your knowledge of what is going on in schools is outdated by twenty or forty years. This claim reduces the argument for the need to be up-to-date to the domain of effective communication. A stronger argument is that life's perennial questions – so favoured by philosophers – are only intelligible in the language of the day. Those philosophers of education who do not know what today's education means in practice, do have, I maintain, a very difficult time getting the questions right.

Proposition D
Faculties of Education Must Become Models.

This point is more or less directly related to the preceding one. Above I mentioned that I left my faculty as a contented dean. I thought, and still think, I could be justifiably proud of the faculty's achievements: an excellent reputation within the university, often cited as a centre of excellence; an international presence in the circle of educational scholarship, well beyond the faculty's numbers; a very good rapport with the profession; a seven-year program of consortia in which the task of and the authority over our teacher education programs was formally shared with local school boards and colleges. Even so, I was less than impressed with our achievements in at least two areas: the quality of teaching environment we created for our students and the lack of research on teacher education. In this segment I will focus only on the first of these shortcomings.

The Teacher Education Environment

The times one walks into a faculty of education and feels compelled to exclaim: 'Behold, here we see a model school environment' are rare indeed. I have not had the pleasure in thirty years in the business, years of direct experience with six schools or faculties of education. We teach students the value of a pleasant classroom, of exhibiting the work of students, of functional arrangements for instruction in classrooms that are the absolute opposite of our message. 'Don't look around you, just listen to my words of wisdom' is the order of the day.

I'm sure that there are colleagues reading this who can't even understand why I would bother making such a trivial point. Indeed. It is of course related to my previous one: education faculties are not, by and large, professional environments. Many faculty members will probably be quick to point out that the right conditions simply were not provided. I think this is a cop-out. The real issue, I believe, is that those of us studying for Ph.Ds in education believe that we are leaving the mundane matters of classroom teaching behind us in our march to advanced scholarship. Hence, making sure that the environment in which we form future teachers exemplifies the values we pronounce is simply not a priority. It is a matter of too low an order. In this regard, our education Ph.Ds are no different from those in other disciplines. Their doctoral programs, in fact, are focused entirely on matters of narrow scholarship, not on their roles as university faculty members, and not on their roles as professional educators.

Lest there be any doubt, I am not simply speaking about the physical environment. Universities often neglect the supervision of graduate students; professors are not available, they don't always keep their office hours, and so forth. Faculties of Education, where posters adorn the walls proclaiming caring teachers have, in my judgment, no better record of graduate supervision than any other department in most universities. Similarly, I truly doubt that the quality of teaching in education faculties is any better than elsewhere in the university. During inservice instruction we advocate visits to other schools and classrooms, to see how your colleagues teach poetry, or social studies, or logos. However, university professors, those in education included, tend to shy away from peer visits. Faculties of education are simply not modeling in a sufficient manner good teaching, or good education for that matter. A change will only follow a thorough realignment of values and a rededication to the primary mandate of education faculties: the formation of teaching professionals.

Research on Teacher Education – Where Is It?

Research on teacher education is scarce when compared to the body of work, valuable or not, devoted to learning and to teaching. As I indicated above, the Faculty of Education at Simon Fraser can point to a prolific record of scholarship and, as well, lay claim to some fundamental innovations in teacher education. The record shows in many ways that the SFU faculty of education during its twenty-five year history has been home for a relatively large number of good education scholars. At the same time, SFU introduced the concept of faculty associates and the related differential staffing model, put in practice teacher education consortia, and pioneered the long practica. The remarkable thing was, and I guess still is, that the faculty basically did not do research on itself, its programs, its successes and the reasons for those. Why?

First, I think that teacher education never was considered a preoccupation quite *de rigueur* for those who see themselves as the intellectual elite in the faculties of education. There is a long history, for instance, in the US Colleges of Education of separate student teaching divisions, staffed by marginal academics or retired school administrators. This attitude is changing, but ever so slowly. Second, most educational researchers have strong disciplinary roots: they are historians, or philosophers, or psychologists or sociologists. Their work usually takes place within their discipline. Studies on teacher education, however, more often than not, cross disciplinary boundaries. New and unfamiliar conceptual frameworks are required; teams of investigators must cooperate. All that takes work and, generally, the work is not rewarded. It is more comfortable, and definitely at least equally rewarding, to pursue a subject in an established discipline in a familiar vein. Third, program evaluation studies in naturalistic environments take relatively large investments – in dollars, in time, in energy. It is much easier to set up brief, controlled interventions featuring a well-understood, artificially isolated variable. Publications come faster that way; methodologies meet easier with the approval of reviewers, and life is generally less complicated. Fourth, too many professors of education graduate from graduate programs where training in research methodologies is marginal at best. Hence, the more complex problems are not really accessible to them.

What I am saying in effect is that faculties of education have not discharged, in terms of their research programs, a major responsibility, i.e. applied and not so applied research for the single-minded purpose of improving their own educational practices.

Changes are underway, but a number of practical measures would speed those up:

Proposition E
Graduate education must include much tougher requirements for methodology, of whatever kind. The one-or two-course programs in quantitative or qualitative methods are simply inadequate. For far too many graduate students their thesis research is the only research they have been or will be ever involved in.

Proposition F
Universities must direct their scarce internal support for research specific to the major mandate of each of their faculties. Such a policy would probably have little differential effect in faculties of arts and science, but might foster the kinds of research on teacher education necessary in faculties of education.

The area of responsibility for teacher education that does properly belong to the university is co-owned by the faculties of arts, science and education. Among the foremost critics of teacher education are the members of other university faculties, particularly those in arts and science. Generally these faculties deplore the low level of intellectual ability of prospective teachers and their low level of academic preparation. The first point is most easily answered. In times of great demand for teachers, or in environments where there is no direct relationship between supply and demand, the academic qualifications of teacher education students tend to be low. When these conditions do not hold, however, it is not unusual for prospective teacher to perform as well or better than the average university student. This was the case, for instance, in the late 1980s in British Columbia when the education faculties could admit only the most able; this resulted often in admission criteria well above those of other professional schools. Even so, the general point is correct: students in teacher education programs in North America tend to have less academic ability than the average university student. There are, however, a great many exceptions, and the trend appears to be upward.

The matter of academic preparation is of a different nature. In North America teacher education generally is integrated into the universities. That is, sort of. What really has happened more often than not is that universities have incorporated teacher education, but shielded the rest of their operations from the dirty work. Educators, in an effort to avoid having to compete with the presumed academic rigor of other university faculties and departments, gladly co-operated in this charade. Thus developed a system where the university put all the responsibility and blame for the education of prospective teachers on their faculties of education, whether or not these had control over the programs of these students, or indeed, should have had such control. If one believes, as I do, that the average teacher should have a better general education than the average university graduate, it is difficult to understand why a university would choose to relegate all the control over a student teacher's education to a faculty of education (not particularly concerned with the arts or the sciences), or alternatively, why faculties of arts and science would feel no responsibility for teacher formation. The Zeitgeist pervading the Holmes' report foreshadows the demise of the self-sufficient faculty of education. What no one says in clear terms, however, is that teacher education within a university is not in the first place the responsibility of the faculties of education but of the university at large. This means, quite simply, that no teacher education curriculum should be solely put forward by the faculty of education, but that any such curriculum should be the product of an all-university concern. It makes no more sense for education professors to teach English without being challenged by the English department than professors of English teaching their specialty to prospective teachers without being challenged by those who should be knowledgeable about pedagogy and its real world contexts. I am not alone in thinking, for instance, that one of the great impediments to the preparation of first rate science teachers is the way they are taught science in the university in the first place. Good models (and I am aware of the vicious circle implied here) are too scarce.

The case I am making for the true integration of teacher education in the university is a special case of the more general argument that universities have balkanized their educational curriculum as a consequence of ill-considered governance practices. Academic freedom is a precious good and essential to the function of the university as we know it. The corollary is that abuse of academic freedom is a grave threat to the well-being of that very same university. I take academic freedom to mean that professors are protected from negative consequences when they utter opinions not pleasing to others. I do not take academic freedom to mean that a professor does not have an obligation to teach an agreed-upon curriculum. A professor of chemistry, for instance, should be subject to discipline when he uses Chemistry 205, Inorganic Chemistry, to deliver daily lectures on the value of religion, or to cover the contents of a course in organic chemistry. Of course this professor is entitled to his or her opinions on religion; of course he can speak on the topic of organic chemistry. He or she must, however, teach inorganic chemistry in Chemistry 205. To use claims of academic freedom in order to escape what is in effect an implicit contract to teach a certain segment of the university curriculum is not acceptable.

Yet, this is what happens with regularity in teacher education courses, and of course, in other university courses as well. Faculty spend enormous amounts of time to get course details correct as far as paper outlines are concerned. In fact, much professorial blood is spilled over such matters. But when these very same professors close the door of their lecture hall or their classroom they proceed to ignore these details and teach what they want. As often as not, two sections of the same education course taught by different individuals are likely to differ so much that they might not be recognizable as the same course.

The unwillingness of education faculty members to agree on content and approach to a particular course makes a shambles of the concept of a university curriculum and a mockery of the idea that teacher education entails the preparation for a profession. Of course, one encounters the odd romantic who maintains that universities don't have curricula; that students merely come to sit at the feet of this professor or the other. Blessed is the student who is so motivated, and blessed is the university with large numbers of professors of such reputation. The fact is that much university education has, per force, become mass education. The fact is that society has rather specific ideas about the benefits of that education. The fact is that even a substantial segment of the professoriate, through the medium of accreditation, have not only acknowledged, but even promoted, the validity of university curricula negotiated among many internal and external partners. This is particularly true for the professional faculties.

In other quarters, faculty often proceed from the assumption that they own the curriculum. What the university teaches is what faculty, collectively and indeed individually, wish to teach. There is some limited merit in this view. Professors are hired because of their special and up-to-date knowledge in a specific field. Subject knowledge, however, is only one credential when it comes to formulating curricula. There are many individuals who have mastered a discipline, without any special qualification for how to teach it, or indeed without understanding its pedagogical structure or its relationship to other subject matter. In one sense faculty are the most qualified to make curriculum decisions, particularly in the collective; in another sense, however, they bring many disqualifying features to curriculum decisions, particularly when acting as individuals. What professor would ever make the decision that what he or she knows has become of less importance as time has gone on? Taxonomy was once a dominant subdiscipline in biology. Now it is a minor element in most science programs. Should taxonomists keep their power to define the biology curriculum? Should the university not assure that other players have a say?[1]

Conclusion

Teaching was always more difficult than the lay public imagined. Tremendous social shifts have made the teacher's job ever so much more complex in recent decades. Schools have been left behind in terms of the technological advances capitalized on by the entertainment industry to provide an alternative education. Parents and the public have become ever more divided over the goals of public education. Teaching today is a very complex profession – a profession asked to meet what may be unrealistic and even impossible demands.

By inference, one might conclude that teacher education, too, is asked to do things it cannot deliver. That may be so to a degree, but much more can be done than is accomplished now. It cannot be achieved, however, without very fundamental shifts in the way we view the collaboration between universities and the profession, without recasting teacher education as professional education, and without serious changes in our concept of how university curricula should come about and be implemented.

At the end of a 300 page essay, Anthony J. Cascardi (1992) concludes an argument on the integration of public and private interests as follows:

> As I have interpreted it, aesthetic liberalism does not ask that we attempt to hold the ideals of self-creation and justice simultaneously in place, but rather derives its force from our inability to do just that (p. 309).

I like Cascardi's analysis of the possibility of reducing the tension between the needs of the individual and the demands of the community because it recognizes in the end the transformative power of individuals over their identity, so that it can at the same time be grounded in 'the terms of recognition promised by the community and to distinguish it therefrom' (Cascardi, 1992, p. 309).

To me this means that just as Umberto Ecco (1990) found it necessary at a late hour to correct 'some intemperance' of so-called reader – response criticism, so has the time arrived for faculty to limit the intemperate individualism which I see as one of the roots of the university's inability to respond decisively to a call for improved teacher education.

Note

I neither assume that all teaching in faculties of education represent good models and all teaching outside of education represents bad modeling. My earlier comment on this issue should be clear. However the powerful influence of the *expert* discipline professor must be understood and acknowledged. Most secondary teachers of my acquaintance teach literature as if they were junior professors. Sadly, few professors of literature ever were tutored in teaching their subject.

1   In defense of taxonomists, but not at all contrary to my thesis, I note some recent expressions of concerns regarding the effect on science of systematic biology.

References

CASCARDI, ANTHONY J. (1992) *The Subject of Modernity*, Cambridge: Cambridge University Press.

ECCO, U. (1990) *Intentio Lectoris: The State of the Art: The Limits of Interpretation*, Bloomington, IN: Indiana University Press.

HOLMES GROUP (1990) *Tomorrow's Schools: Principles for the Design of Professional Development Schools*, East Lansing MI: The Holmes Group.

JACKSON, MICHAEL (1991) *Paths toward a clearing – Radical Empiricism and Ethnographic Enquiry*, Bloomington, IN: Indiana University Press.

Chapter 9

Stirring the Embers: Reconsidering the Structure of Teacher Education Programs[1]

Alan R. Tom

Teacher education in the United States looks fundamentally the same as it did when I completed my certification in 1963, and this programmatic stability has persisted for at least a half century (Cogan, 1958; Conant, 1963; Counts, 1935; Monroe, 1952). Then, as now, the professional preparation for teachers began with several foundational courses followed by so-called *methods* courses, and was capped by a few weeks or months of apprentice or student teaching. This course and content structure, organized and delivered by campus-based professors of education and their graduate students, has been amazingly resilient to attempted structural and curricular reforms.[2]

During my thirty-year career as a teacher educator, I have witnessed such structural 'innovations' as competency-based teacher education, clinical professorships, the Master of Arts in Teaching degree, field-based teacher education, paid internships, joint appointments across the faculties of arts and sciences and education, the Teacher Corps, and others. A few of these attempted structural reforms did leave lingering vestiges in the teacher education enterprise, but none of them has had the substantial and enduring effect anticipated by its proponents. I suspect that the minimal impact of these reforms is because they concentrate on changing surface patterns rather than deep structures.

In the following pages I discuss and question four structural assumptions that typically underlie our thinking about teacher education. These assumptions focus on four aspects of conventional programming: its intensity (the assumption that new content and experiences must be introduced gradually); its sequencing (the presumption that pedagogical knowledge should come before teaching practice); its staffing (the supposition that programs are composed of detailed and segmented content taught by disciplinary specialists); and its grouping of students (the assumption that students can be continually regrouped as they move through a program). After critiquing these four assumptions and concurrently presenting an inverse set of assumptions, I conclude with a brief analysis of the barriers to acting upon the four inverse assumptions.

While many argue, as I do, that the substance of the curriculum ought to be a prior question to any consideration of structural issues (Tom, 1989), I have come to believe that structural issues merit independent attention, though the results of such consideration must also be related to a concept of teaching. What is needed is simultaneous attention to structural and substantive issues so that programs represent not only a vision of good teaching but also thoughtful regard for the practical and organizational arrangements through which such a vision is to be pursued.

Gradualism vs. Compression

No assumption is more revered than the idea that prospective teachers ought to be introduced to professional content and teaching experience in a carefully planned and gradual way. Thus a high school cooperating teacher may be admonished by campus-based professors to turn over teaching responsibility to the student teacher one course at a time, and then only after a period of observation helps the novice become familiar with the classroom situation. Another variant of the gradualist assumption is the belief that professional course work ought to be distributed over several years and that the content in these courses needs to be introduced in small chunks, with frequent opportunity for related clinical experiences. With this reasoning in mind, many teacher educators who favor extending teacher preparation beyond four years draw a sharp distinction between a five-year program (in which professional study is intermingled over several years with both field experiences and academic study) and a fifth-year program similar to the Master of Arts in Teaching model (in which all of the professional study and related field work is viewed as inappropriately jammed into the last year of preservice preparation).

The difficulty with gradualism in professional preparation, as in life, is that step-by-step experiences are not particularly exciting, and may even be boring, since the ultimate goal of becoming a *real* teacher is invariably just over the horizon. Two more theories, three more reading assignments, one more clinical experience, a partridge in a pear tree, and the prospective teacher might finally arrive at teaching, or at least the pretend teaching commonly referred to as student teaching. The teacher-in-training often lacks the patience to proceed through the typical multiple-year professional curriculum since this curriculum is frequently perceived as being impractical and vapid (Tom, 1991).

Many of the most powerful learning experiences of our lives are compressed and thus are all-encompassing and even transformative events or episodes, e.g., falling in love, taking a new job, defending a dissertation, witnessing the death of a parent. These are experiences that grab us, rivet our attention, and literally force us to respond to new and largely unforeseen demands. The typical multi-year professional program – with the possible exception of student teaching – generally fails to capture the undivided attention of the novice and may well account for the oft-noted observation that professional teacher education tends to be a relatively weak educational intervention.

How might we overturn the premise of gradualism and take advantage of the potential of compressed training in which the professional program is short and intense? The beginning of a preparation program, where teachers' judgments about the potential value of their overall program are formed, would be the perfect place for a compressed experience, rather than through a survey course that includes general information about the schools and about the teaching profession. However, prospective teachers rarely do anything more than take just another course, much like the dozens they have sat through for the prior fifteen years.

One possible approach is to break abruptly with the standard university practice of defining a course as something that occurs on an intermittent and extended basis. Instead, the first course in professional education could be designed as a short and intense episode, for example, a full-time experience conducted either for a few weeks or for several consecutive weekends. Using 'continuous time blocks' fosters such advantages as the 'deliberate building of group consciousness, emphasis on both conceptual and experiential learning, [and] a learning environment that involves both intellect and emotion' (Lasker, Donnelly and Weathersby, 1975:8). One disadvantage, according to three experienced instructors of compressed courses, is that the intensive format can be 'disorienting' for the student due to the 'high degree of student involvement' (p. 9), a characterization of student involvement that seems odd unless we consider how infrequently schooling experiences really engage students.

Compression can also be thought of in programmatic as well as in course terms. Instead of relying on a two- or three-year professional program, I suggest that a single year of professional study would lead to a more involving experience in which conceptual, affective and skill components could be better integrated. Another possibility for compressing a portion of a teacher education program is the professional semester, a format in which methods instruction can be combined with student teaching at either the elementary (Cohn, 1980) or secondary (Cohn, Gellman and Tom, 1987; Tom, 1984:165–70) levels.

In addition to their educational advantages, compressed programs also have a significant cost advantage in that compressed programs are characterized by: more natural opportunities for interaction among faculty members; an overall reduction in the number of field experiences; less attention required for the advising of students; increased faculty knowledge of the prospective teachers; reduced need for developing data systems to track students; and other economies that occur when faculty and students are brought into closer proximity with one another.

There are, however, some trade-offs involved in relying on the principle of compression, especially when this principle is applied to a full semester or to the entire program. Integration of subject matter study and professional study can be a casualty of compressed professional study if this professional study occupies literally all of the time of the prospective teacher. Yet real cooperation between the faculty responsible for academic and professional study is rare and generally is dependent on the interests and goodwill of individual faculty members rather than being built into the structure of the university. Therefore, losing the opportunity for such cooperation is not a real loss on most campuses. A more serious problem is the tendency for the faculty who have key roles in compressed programming to show signs of strain over time and even to burn out; untenured faculty may also opt out of such programming due to career-building considerations since compressed programming is often labor intensive. Thus, what is good for the teacher-in-training may be a mixed blessing for the professional faculty in the contemporary university. Plans for compressed programming ought to take into account the needs of the faculty as well as the advantages to students.

Knowledge–Practice vs. Practice–Knowledge

Teacher educators routinely believe that teaching, usually construed as student teaching, is a forbidden activity until the teacher-in-training has mastered certain prerequisite professional knowledge. So the prospective teacher begins professional study by examining the relationship of school to society, theories of learning and development, approaches to classroom management, varied ways of representing complex subject matters to students, one or more models for planning a lesson, and other forms of professional knowledge. While a few clinical experiences may be tossed in with this professional content, often in conjunction with methods courses, substantial teaching responsibility is typically withheld until the very end of the professional program.

Professional knowledge, therefore, tends to be introduced prior to, and often separated from, teaching practice, and student teaching is seen as the capstone course in which the student takes the accumulated professional knowledge and relates or applies this knowledge to the problems of teaching practice. Interestingly, the student teacher is left largely alone to work out the teaching implications of the body of professional knowledge learned prior to student teaching, as neither the university supervisor nor the cooperating teacher is likely to know precisely what professional knowledge was taught by the campus-based professors of education. Staffing the student teaching portion of the program with supervisors unfamiliar with the professional curriculum – usually lowly graduate students or part-time adjuncts – reveals, if nothing else, that education professors attach considerable value to campus-based knowledge and concurrently desire to distance themselves from teaching practice.

A variety of justifications are offered by education professors for delaying significant teaching experience until the end of the program, ranging from the practical argument that cooperating teachers expect student teachers to have some rudimentary pedagogical knowledge (and do not have time to teach this knowledge to novices) to the claim that student teachers will be reduced to imitating their host teachers if these beginners lack the knowledge on which to construct a personal view of teaching. Novices, however, have great difficulty stockpiling this knowledge for subsequent application to practice (due to the context-bound nature of most of this knowledge), and the application process itself is enormously complicated for any teacher, particularly a beginner (Shulman, 1987; Sigel, 1990; Tom, 1984).

The belief that professional knowledge can be stockpiled for later use in teaching situations is a particularly suspect idea since this knowledge does not come in the form of principles which can be easily applied to varied situations. Early in the twentieth century, researchers did aspire, in the words of E.L. Thorndike, to discover 'laws in terms of rigid, unambiguous equations' in the belief that they were on the verge of developing a 'science of education' (quoted in Tom, 1984:13), but this goal subsequently was disavowed by those interested in the scientific study of education in favor of the more modest enterprise of developing what Gage calls a scientific basis for the art of teaching. Gage (1978:18) argued that effective teaching requires a knowledge of 'concepts, or variables, and their interrelationships in the form of strong or weak laws, generalizations, or trends'. In recent years, leading researchers on effective teaching have further moderated their claims, and the findings of educational research are no longer portrayed as 'the solution to educational problems' but rather as 'findings and concepts that teachers must apply flexibly to particular contexts' (Good, 1990:61).

Even in those limited cases when professional knowledge might be in the form of a generalization and perhaps borders on being a principle, the issue of applying this knowledge to a specific context is still an extremely complicated issue. For example, Sigel (1990:89) argues that while Piaget's work on the stages of cognitive development is one of the few comprehensive theories in this area and thus really does have distinctive curricular and instructional implications, the nature of these implications is quite complex since prospective teachers have 'neither the background nor the sophistication to do this [application] on their own'. Prospective teachers, therefore, need help, but the educational psychology instructor, the person likely to be responsible for teaching about Piaget and other developmental content, 'is not even in the classroom with the student teacher to see how he or she applies the principles acquired in the course'. The fact that instruction in such human development content as Piagetian theory is routinely separated from issues of application to practice is considered by Sigel to be 'irresponsible behavior on the part of [the] teacher training faculty'.

Sigel (1990:91) closes his discussion of teacher education by lamenting the way in which knowledge in human development is 'fragmented and isolated from the context in which it should be used,' and argues that serious attention to relating human development knowledge to the process of designing curricula for youngsters 'would require reorganization of teacher education programs by breaking down some of the barriers that exist between departments and even within colleges of education' (p. 91). By implication from his earlier argument, he would have instructors of educational psychology directly involved with student teachers to help these beginners work out the curricular implications of Piaget's stage theory of cognitive development. Sigel, however, does not speculate about how this reorganization of education faculties might occur.

The knowledge-stockpiled-before-practice assumption can be altered by reorganizing programs in one of two ways: employing situational teaching to link knowledge and practice, or using teaching practice as an introduction to professional study. The more modest of the two structural changes entails what Cohn (1981) calls 'situational teaching' in which the professional knowledge introduced earlier in the program is retaught, when situationally relevant, during student teaching. If, for example, a particular approach to lesson planning was taught during methods course(s), then the university supervisor can follow-through during classroom observations and subsequent conferences to make sure that such principles of lesson planning as *set induction* or 'linking one day's teaching to prior instruction' are being appropriately implemented by the student teacher. Through such a process 'the supervisor was *reintroducing* recently taught general principles in relation to the ongoing classroom situation' (Cohn, 1981:28). Thus professional knowledge essentially gets taught twice to the novice, once by the teacher education faculty through didactic or case-based instruction and a second time by the university supervisor as that person watches how well the novice employs that knowledge during teaching practice.

Cohn and her colleagues (Cohn, 1981; Cohn and Gellman, 1988; Cohn, Gellman and Tom, 1987) have found two adaptations that facilitate the use of situational teaching for purposes of integrating educational theory and practice. First, they have sequenced the methods courses to occur at the same time as student teaching (so-called *professional semesters*) so that relating ideas from these courses to the student teaching experience does not require the student to stockpile this knowledge for one or more semesters. Second, the professional semesters are team-taught, with a small group of faculty taking responsibility for both the methods instruction and the supervision of the student teaching experience of twenty to thirty prospective teachers. Playing the dual roles of methods instructors and university supervisors, in the same semester, greatly facilitates the faculty team's use of situational teaching with professional semester students. Moreover, members of the professional semester faculty also have occasionally taught the educational psychology and philosophy of education courses taken by students in prior semesters so that linkages between the ideas in these courses and teaching practice are easier to make than if faculty unconnected to the professional semesters were responsible for foundational instruction (Liston and Zeichner, 1991:163–6).

A structurally more radical attempt to integrate professional knowledge and teaching practice occurs when teaching practice is part of the introduction to the professional curriculum. A now largely-forgotten experiment of the late 1950s and early 1960s, the Harvard–Newton Summer Program, was created to induct beginning Master's degree students into professional education. The newly admitted elementary interns began their studies by apprentice teaching in a Newton elementary school which housed a morning summer program for elementary students. Recent liberal arts graduates, these interns were assigned, in groups of four, to a master teacher, and each team of five became responsible for a classroom of elementary students. In the morning, the five teachers took turns teaching the elementary students; in the afternoon, the master teacher conducted a group evaluation of the morning's teaching experience and led a planning session to prepare for teaching the class the following morning. Along with this intensive teaching experience, the interns also took courses in methodology and language arts (Emlaw, Mosher, Sprinthall and Whiteley, 1993).

The decision to begin a professional program with teaching experience is a high-risk strategy. The enormous pressure of introducing the demands of teaching practice concurrently with educational ideas can lead the novice to revert to survival techniques. Fortunately, in an early teaching experience format similar to the Harvard–Newton Summer Program, the beginner is working under the daily supervision of a master teacher who is both skilled in teaching technique and should be able to foster an analytical cast of mind within the novice – as opposed to the imitation-of-a-model approach that frequently occurs in conventional student teaching. At the same time, however, the master teacher – being fully occupied with teaching, observing the instruction of novices, and leading the afternoon analysis and planning sessions – is unlikely to be well-informed about the educational content being concurrently presented to the novices by the methodology instructor(s).

Yet the summer school teaching model is a powerful intervention that can facilitate the integration of educational knowledge and practice. In abandoning the conventional assumption of having knowledge before practice a structural change is established with great potential for reenergizing the preparation of teachers.

Horizontal vs. Vertical Staffing

In conventional teacher education programs, prospective teachers proceed from course-to-course, as if on an elevator moving slowly from floor-to-floor; professors stand at the elevator doors and dispense knowledge to the students who methodically stop at each floor on the way to student teaching on the top floor. Each professor is presumed to be giving some valuable piece of knowledge to the teacher-in-training whose task it is to accept this bit of professional knowledge and trust it will have some utility when the elevator finally arrives at student teaching.

This inert and piecemeal curricular approach is a logical outcome of the predominant staffing pattern that is horizontally structured, with each floor representing individual professors' particular forms of expertise, i.e., social foundations, educational pychology, etc. It has real appeal to faculty members since it enables them to maximize contact with faculty peers who share their specialized intellectual interests. Moreover, this teaching is not particularly demanding since these faculty members are specialists in the area to be taught, and the prospective teachers are usually naive about the content and can be rather easily dazzled. In all but the smallest programs, preservice teacher education is only one part of the typical faculty member's work so that this person often has substantial time to pursue specialized research and graduate-oriented interests.

While horizontal staffing minimizes the intellectual and practical demands made upon the faculty member and fits right in with the contemporary university's penchant for favoring specialized knowledge, this form of staffing has substantial negative consequences. Significant faculty interaction concerning the substance and rationale for the overall teacher education program is unlikely to occur among professors in differing areas of specialization, for example, between educational psychologists and social foundations professors or between instructors in special methods and ones in special education. Moreover, while extensive contact with one's horizontal peers is a source of pleasure and stimulation for teacher education faculty members, the teacher-in-training inherits the difficult task of integrating the diverse forms of knowledge and skill that are sequentially introduced over the four to six 'floors' of the conventional professional program. In addition, our traditional reliance on horizontal staffing has usually led to constructing a professional curriculum that covers much more material than the typical novice can absorb and covers this material in a superficial and often disorganized way.

The bias in teacher education for breadth without depth is frequently the consequence of falling back on horizontal staffing by specialists, specialists who, if asked to identify what teachers need to know about their area, tend to develop detailed and complex statements (see, for example, the chapters in Reynolds, 1989, and Houston, 1990). Such an outcome can be resisted since some specialists do argue that 'a small number of core, organizing ideas should be the basis of the teacher education curriculum' (Anderson, 1989:101). However, the more normal approach of specialists is to expand the range of content covered in their courses, press for increasing the credit hours devoted to their specialization, and so forth.

When we add together the conclusion that novices really do not need huge amounts of specialized professional knowledge (but rather need a few core ideas from each area of study) with the earlier argument that the critically difficult issue for novices is working out the implications in practice of these core ideas (Sigel, 1990), we can now make the case for vertical staffing. By vertical staffing I mean a situation in which faculty members assume responsibility for a greater portion of the professional program than a single course or experience. Thus, for example, a faculty member could teach courses at more than one point in a program that follows a traditional approach to course sequencing; this situation often occurs by necessity, as for instance, in programs offered by small professional faculties in liberal arts institutions, or by design, as in the case of programs offered in large institutions by a small group of interdisciplinary faculty. Another way to develop vertical staffing is to combine, in one or two semesters, several elements of a program that are typically separated and have a team of faculty become responsible for the resulting programmatic whole.

This teaming of teacher education faculty members can be a particularly powerful mechanism for bringing about vertical staffing. For example, one form of teaming occurs when four or five of the elementary curriculum and methods courses are blocked together in one semester, usually just before the student teaching semester. Typically the four or five faculty members in the elementary methods block team plan the overall effort in order to coordinate the content of assignments and the schedule of due dates for papers and projects, as well as to prevent overlap through such mechanisms as agreeing on a single lesson plan format (e.g., Hart, 1990; Lasley, 1990). A wide variety of other forms of course blocking and concomitant teaming have been attempted, including social and psychological foundations with associated tutoring and participant observation in schools (e.g., Duell and Yeotis, 1981). Teaming is also central to the earlier mentioned elementary and secondary professional semesters at Washington University (Cohn, 1980; Cohn, Gellman and Tom, 1987).

One of the powerful aspects of the Harvard–Newton Summer Program was that this effort eliminated the division of responsibility between cooperating teacher and university supervisor. In the summer program, the master teacher could, and often did, play both the cooperating teacher and the supervisor roles, as this person was in charge of the class of students being taught by the interns in the morning as well being the person primarily responsible for the afternoon supervision of the interns' teaching.

Vertical staffing can be used either to foster communication across layers of the teacher education curriculum or even to eliminate these layers in cases where substantial segments of the program are conducted concurrently. At the same time, vertical staffing can help overcome situations in which depth of content treatment has been sacrificed to breadth of coverage, as bits and pieces of professional knowledge have been stuffed into the curriculum. Of course, it is also important to remember that teaming – one of the main mechanisms for vertical staffing – requires more effort from a teacher education faculty, effort for which there may well be no institutional reward. It also involves designing interpersonally and theoretically compatible teaching teams, an issue that has frustrated more than one administrator of a teacher education program.

Continual Student Regrouping vs. Cohorts

With some historical exceptions,[3] teacher educators have treated prospective teachers as if these novices were nothing more than individuals learning to teach through the personal mastery of professional content. Teacher educators generally have ignored the social aspect of teaching in which individuals have relationships with one another and collective obligations to the overall profession. Admission to teacher education, for example, is often on a rolling basis in which individuals apply whenever they meet such admission requirements as 60 units of general education or the completion of a mandatory introductory course experience in education. In fact, students often take three to five education courses before seeking admission (Goodlad, 1990), leading Goodlad to note that there was no 'clear point at which the class of 1992, say, came together and began its journey' (p. 205). This finding confirms the longtime teacher educator presumption that teachers-in-training are individuals who ought to be able to choose freely from among the section offerings for any particular course, proceeding through the program at a rate they determine, continually regrouping themselves, course-by-course, according to their personal schedules and desires.[4]

In contrast, graduate students aspiring to be college professors typically enter their chosen graduate department as a cohort and usually remain, at least for the first two years, with their peers until the completion of residence requirements or doctoral examinations. On the other hand, entry into elementary and secondary teacher education programs is typically made relatively easy, progress through these programs is designed to fit in with student schedules and choices, and completion of these programs is dependent on a student finishing courses and doing student teaching, with no shared 'tension point similar to the general exam for the doctorate' (Lortie, 1968:257). The only hint of an ordeal in teacher education is student teaching, which few students fail, and which, in any case, is typically experienced privately. This absence of any ordeal – shared or otherwise – is reinforced by the finding that only half of a sample of experienced teachers said that there was a turning point when they knew they had become 'real teachers' (p. 258).

Lortie (1968:259) argues that the 'shared ordeal' involved in the preparation experience of college teachers accounts for some significant differences between the beginning professor and the beginning public school teacher. In particular, the novice professor almost immediately assumes an 'adult' status, with a concomitant sense that this person is supposed to carry out assigned duties 'with a minimum of intervention from others'. At the same time, a schoolteacher, who often receives no more supervision than a beginning professor, is subject to the public school rhetoric that affirms 'the subordination of the teacher within a formal authority system,' thus extending the adolescentlike status of the schoolteacher. Lortie concludes that for the prospective academic a 'shared ordeal and other rites of passage signal an incipient status change of some consequence' while 'that is not the case for the beginning teacher', a development that is consistent with school systems that are 'unwilling to gamble on the trustworthiness of new teachers' (p. 260).

How might we take advantage of Lortie's analysis of the value of shared ordeals in professional training and concurrently solve some of the administrative problems associated with giving students free reign to schedule themselves? While each teacher education program operates in a differing institutional and social context, certain general approaches for developing the shared nature of programmatic experience are likely to be adaptable to a variety of settings. Several of the ideas already mentioned as instances of vertical staffing also have the effect of increasing the shared nature of the student experience by converting prospective teachers into a temporary cohort. For example, the blocking of elementary methods courses for perhaps twenty to thirty students (increasing the size much beyond thirty converts a potentially meaningful group into a mass) makes it relatively easy to develop a feeling of group spirit and a sense of mutual support. While the blocking of elementary methods usually constitutes a full semester of work, other forms of combining course and field work involved only a portion of a semester's course of study, e.g., merging generic strategies and educational psychology or combining child development and learning theories.

While the above examples establish the basis for participating in shared events, the intensity of these events and intellectual and practical demands embedded in them may not be demanding enough to create and sustain an ordeal. In fact, many teacher educators consciously attempt to prevent their students from experiencing an ordeal on the rationale that such situations are too stressful to be productive learning environments, except perhaps in the case of student teaching. Even with student teaching, however, the notion of gradual and systematic introduction to responsibility remains the conventional wisdom of university-based teacher educators.

Earlier I discussed the elementary and secondary professional semesters at Washington University as an instance of compression and a means of integrating knowledge and practice as well as an example of vertical staffing. These professional semesters also create a semester-long faculty and student cohort as a small group of faculty assume responsibility for both the methods instruction and the supervision of student teaching for a group of prospective teachers. Not only is the professional semester experience shared by faculty and students, but in addition, it also tends to be an ordeal for students as they must cope with new methods content as well as with being student teachers. While the student cohort for a Washington University professional semester lasts only a single semester, other cases exist in which the student cohort stays together for the entire teacher education program (Ayers, 1988; Denst, 1979; Singleton, Hakes and Kerr, 1989).

In the end, student cohorts, especially long-term ones or full-time semester-long ones, have several advantages. They can become an opportunity for monitoring student progress, in a caring and non-bureaucratic environment. These cohorts also help bring a social dimension to a teacher education program, establishing a norm for the group as a source of personal support and for an overall collegial approach to the work of the teacher. And, lastly, they can become the source not only of shared experiences but also of shared ordeals that help mold the developing teacher into a professional ready to assume substantial responsibility with a sense of self-confidence.[5]

Alan R. Tom

Barriers to Considering the Inverse Assumptions

Some of the barriers to acting upon the four inverse assumptions reside within teacher educators themselves. Due to the long history of gradual change in teacher education and the frequent initiation of change by accrediting agencies and other external forces, teacher educators are used to reacting to the proposals of others and, at most, to making modest changes in existing structures. Teaching educators rarely even consider challenging the validity of the deep structures which undergird conventional programming. At the same time, teacher educators, under the influence of university culture, tend to have excessive faith in the power of ideas. This faith encourages teacher educators to see the stockpiling of knowledge as a natural approach and also leads them to underestimate the enormous problems novices have in integrating theory with practice. A third problem for teacher educators is their propensity to see professional preparation primarily in terms of the cognitive and curricular tasks of teaching as opposed to such sociological ideas as peer support, socialization, shared ordeal, and colleagueship, among others. The passiveness of teacher educators, their essential optimism, and their psychological and curricular orientation all serve to inhibit their ability to move beyond existing deep structures.

By no means, however, are all of the barriers to experimenting with the four inverse assumptions attributable to particular characteristics of teacher educators. A second category of barriers are institutional in nature. One of these barriers has already been discussed: the supremacy of specialized knowledge within the modern university. This high status of specialized knowledge supports several forms of established deep structure, especially horizontal staffing but also gradualism and knowledge-before-practice.

Another institutional barrier is the low status of teacher education within colleges of education. Ironically, while most academics in other colleges within the university see teacher preparation as the major calling for the faculty in the college of education, the education faculty often has bigger fish to fry. Status within the college of education tends to be inversely related with one's distance from the enterprise of teacher education. Many senior people within teacher education specialize in the study of teaching rather than in the preparation of teachers. Money follows status so that practising teacher educators are frequently left with neither the clout nor the resources to engage in major, long-term experimental efforts.

All these barriers within teacher educators and within institutions can easily make one cynical about the chances of reconsidering the deep structures that underlie teacher education programming. Causes for optimism, however, do exist in that the generation of faculty recruited to teacher education appointments in the last ten years is more intellectually diverse and apparently more willing to challenge past practices than were preceding generations of teacher educators. Moreover, in the last few years a number of institutions have attempted cohort grouping of students, although other forms of deep structure remain largely unchallenged. Future progress depends heavily on whether teacher preparation can attain higher status within colleges of education and the resources and self-confidence that should accompany such increased status.

We ought not wait for that status to be given to us. Let us not maintain our tradition of being passive. While none of us really knows whether we can alter our own status, we can make real attempts to rethink the deep structures which ground the programs in which we work. Whether we can pull ourselves up by our sociological bootstraps is unclear, but I do not see many school-based practitioners, state department personnel, state legislators, and members of the general public who have much confidence in our current efforts. By suspending belief in the old structures and experimenting with new ones, we have precious little to lose.

Notes

1 This chapter is adapted from my forthcoming book, *Redesigning Teacher Education*, to be published by State University of New York Press.

2 I have taught and administered in two major public research universities and in a teacher education program lodged in a similarly oriented private university. However, my experience is limited to the United Sates, and my analysis of underlying structural assumptions should not necessarily be taken to be applicable to teacher education in other countries.

3 While Master of Arts in Teaching programs have received mixed evaluations since their professional curriculum differed little from traditional undergraduate programs and since their graduates rarely taught in inner city schools (Coley and Thrope, 1985), these programs did, upon occasion, develop a sense of group identity among program participants. When this group identity did occur, it was promoted by such cohort-inducing factors as: a common programmatic beginning point for all MAT students; full-time study, usually made possible by financial aid; special MAT sections of certain professional classes; and special social events for MAT students. Group identity and *esprit de corps* were even more likely to develop in the field-based teacher education efforts of the 1970s, especially those programs in which students were clustered in a very small number of schools (e.g., Cohn, 1980; Denst, 1979).

4 Some may challenge my critique of our casual way of socializing teachers into the profession and argue – on equity grounds – that we must sustain part-time and/or evening study, as well as self-selection of courses and other forms of student accommodation, in order to maintain access to teaching careers to career-change students, to low-income students who need to hold a job while studying, or to single parents with multiple responsibilities.

On the one hand, I concur with these equity considerations, and I have administered with enthusiasm an evening post-baccalaureate program designed for career-change and other people who were occupied with conflicting responsibilities during the day. But the post-baccalaureate program was run as a separate entity, with an attempt to build into that program some of the advantages of cohort programming. On the other hand, our overall willingness to compromise on student grouping issues indicates that we teacher educators really do not take ourselves and our work seriously and are prepared to accept, as the norm, program designs that verge on being impotent.

5   We cannot, however, expect a change in the training process for teachers to automatically alter their subsequent status on the job. Instead, as Lortie (1968:260) suggests: 'Role conflict for the beginner would be heightened by socialization processes which implied that adulthood was imminent.' Thus we have an instance of Goodlad's (1990) claim that reform of teacher education cannot be considered apart from school reform.

References

ANDERSON, L.M. (1989) 'Learners and learning. Classroom instruction', in REYNOLDS, M.C. (Ed.) *Knowledge Base for the Beginning Teacher*, Oxford: Pergamon Press, 85–99; 101–15.

AYERS, W. (1988) 'Problems and possibilities of radical reform: A teacher educator reflects on making change', *Peabody Journal of Education*, **65**(2), 35–50.

COGAN, M.L. (1958) 'Professional requirements in programs for the preparation of high school teachers', *Journal of Teacher Education*, **9**, 270–9.

COHN, M. (1980) 'The interrelationship of theory and practice in teacher education: A description and analysis of the LITE program' (Doctoral dissertation, Washington University, 1979) *Dissertation Abstracts International*, **40**, 3965A.

COHN, M. (1981) 'A new supervision model for linking theory to practice', *Journal of Teacher Education*, **32**(3), 26–30.

COHN, M.M. and GELLMAN, V.C. (1988) 'Supervision: A developmental approach for fostering inquiry in preservice teacher education', *Journal of Teacher Education*, **39**(2), 2–8.

COHN, M.M, GELLMAN, V. and TOM, A.R. (1987) 'The secondary professional semester', *Teaching Education*, **1**(2), 31–7.

COLEY, R.J. and THORPE, M.E. (1985) *A Look at the MAT Model of Teacher Education and its Graduates; Lessons for Today*, Princeton, NJ: Educational Testing Service, Division of Education Policy Research and Services.

CONANT, J.B. (1963) *The Education of American Teachers*, New York: McGraw-Hill.

COUNTS, G.S. (1935) 'Break the teacher training lockstep', *The Social Frontier*, **1**, 6–7.

DEMBO, M.H. and HICKERSON, N. (1971) 'An integrated approach to foundation courses in teacher education', *Education*, **92**(1), 96–100.

DENST, K.A. (1979) 'Shared decision making in teacher education: A case study' (Doctoral dissertation, Washington University, 1979). *Dissertation Abstracts International*, **40**, 550A–551A.

DREEBEN, R. (1970) *The Nature of Teaching: Schools and the Work of Teachers*, Glenview, IL: Scott, Foresman.

DUELL, O.K. and YEOTIS, C. (1981) *Integrating Methods and Educational Psychology in Teacher Preparation*, Paper presented at the annual meeting of the Association of Teacher Educators, Dallas, TX. (ERIC Document Reproduction Service No. ED 204 260), February.

EMLAW, R., MOSHER, R., SPRINTHALL, N.A. and WHITELEY, J.M. (1963) 'Teacher effectiveness: A method for prediction and evaluation', *National Elementary Principal*, **43**(2), 38–49.

GAGE, N.L. (1978) *The Scientific Basis of the Art of Teaching*, New York: Teachers College Press.

GOOD, T.L. (1990) 'Building the knowledge base of teaching', in DILL, D.D. and ASSOCIATES (Eds) *What Teachers Need to Know: The Knowledge, Skills, and Values Essential to Good Teaching*, San Francisco, CA: Jossey-Bass Publishers, 17–75.

GOODLAD, J.I. (1990) *Teachers for our Nation's Schools*, San Francisco, CA: Jossey-Bass.

HART, P. (1990) *The Block Elementary Methods Experience: A Developmental Model*, Paper presented at the annual meeting of the Association of Teacher Educators, Las Vegas, NV, February.

HOUSTON, W.R. (Ed.) (1990) *Handbook of Research on Teacher Education*, New York: Macmillan Publishing.

LASKER, H., DONNELLY, J. and WEATHERSBY, R. (1975) 'Even on Sunday: An approach to teaching intensive courses for adults', *Harvard Graduate School of Education Bulletin*, 6–11, Spring/Summer.

LASLEY, T.J. (1990) *Designing a Curriculum that uses the Knowledge Base*, Paper presented at the annual meeting of the Association of Teacher Educators, Las Vegas, NV. (ERIC Document Reproduction Service No. ED 318 697), February.

LISTON, D.P. and ZEICHNER, K.M. (1991) *Teacher Education and the Social Conditions of Schooling*, New York: Routledge.

LORTIE, D.C. (1968) 'Shared ordeal and induction to work', in BECKER, H.S. GEER, B. RIESMAN, D. and WEISS, R.S. (Eds) *Institutions and the Person*, Chicago, IL: Aldine, 252–64.

MONROE, W.S. (1952) *Teaching-learning Theory and Teacher Education, 1890–1950*, Urbana, IL: University of Illinois Press.

REYNOLDS, M.C. (Ed.) (1989) *Knowledge Base for the Beginning Teacher*, Oxford: Pergamon Press.

SHULMAN, L.S. (1987) 'Knowledge and teaching: Foundations of the new reform', *Harvard Educational Review*, **57**, 1–22.

SIGEL, I.E. (1990) 'What teachers need to know about human development', in DILL, D.D. and ASSOCIATES (Eds) *What Teachers Need to Know: The Knowledge, Skills, and Values Essential to Good Teaching*, San Francisco, CA: Jossey-Bass, 76–93.

SINGLETON, H.W., HAKES, B.T. and KERR, M. (1989) *An Analysis of an Undergraduate Teacher Education Experiment*, Paper presented at the annual meeting of the Association of Teacher Educators, St Louis, MO, February.

TOM, A.R. (1984) *Teaching as a Moral Craft*, New York: Longman.

TOM, A.R. (1989) 'A critique of the rationale for extended teacher preparation', in WEIS, L., ALTBACH, P.G., KELLY, G.P., PETRIE, H.G. and SLAUGHTER, S. (Eds) *Crisis in Teaching*, Albany, NY: State University of New York Press, 55–68.

TOM, A.R. (1991) *Restructuring Teacher Education*, Bloomington, IN: Phi Delta Kappa.

Part Three

Changes at the Ground Level: The Wedge of Progressive Practice

The five chapters in Part Three illustrate the broad-brush strokes of reform in teacher education at the policy level set out by Tuinman and Tom. As such they represent changes at the ground level – to use a term that Sheehan and Fullan propose. The chapters by Wassermann, Carson, and Dittmer and Fichetti focus on improving teaching at the post secondary level – an important feature of any reform in teacher education. Wassermann's case teaching, Carson's practice of reflection, and the application of Foxfire principles in teacher preparation used by Dittmer and Fichetti represent approaches that these authors have developed and pioneered in their respective institutions. They illustrate some of the possibilities that could be considered by those making changes in the preparation of beginning teachers.

The chapters by Dawson and by Scott and Burke illustrate principles enunciated in earlier chapters by Tuinman and Tom. Dawson's chapter reframes the clinical professor's role and shows how teacher preparation can become a joint venture between the university and the field. Scott and Burke's chapter on collaboration not only emphasizes the connection to schools but also provides an exemplar of the concepts of vertical staffing and student cohorts that Tom describes. Both chapters speak to the importance of respecting the knowledge inherent in practice and illustrate the power of a model designed to be responsive to both the university and the field.

Chapter 10

Teaching with Cases: Teacher Educators and Preservice Teachers in Professional Preparation

Selma Wassermann

Scene 1

When Professor Ecks received his first teaching assignment – a course in Social Issues in Education – he spent over a hundred hours in the library reading background material and reviewing old course outlines and half as much time again preparing his lecture notes. Throughout his preparation, his prevailing concern was how he would cover all the relevant material in the twelve-week semester. Programmed to teach in the style of his own professors, Ecks sees teaching as information dispensing, and he will spend virtually the entire course time in lecturing to his students.

A visitor to Professor Ecks's class observes that his lectures are well pre-pared. He refers repeatedly to his notes, his way of insuring that he keeps on track. It is easy, he knows, to become diverted by students' questions. He has learned to pace himself in the lectures, thereby getting all the important points across by the end of each period. The observer also notes that while Professor Ecks has been diligent about his preparation, his manner of presentation lacks the power and the polish of an accomplished lecturer. Ecks believes, however, that this is not a major concern for him. It is enough to present the information, to address the key points, to cover the curriculum. He is not required to make his presentation entertaining. It's the students' job to listen and to do the work of comprehending what he says.

There are thirty-five students in Professor Ecks's class, seated in a small lecture auditorium. None of them sits in the first three rows and more than 80 per cent of them sit in the rear section of the room. Some are looking at the teacher, appearing to be listening. Some are writing in notebooks. A few, in the rear of the hall, are dozing. Some are reading material and doing assign-ments for other classes. The visitor chats informally with a group of students after the class. They tell her that the lectures are boring; that Professor Ecks's presentations are difficult to follow and to comprehend. They see the lectures as a waste of time. They are able to find the material they need in their textbooks, where the presentations are clearer, better organized and where they can study at their own pace. They are unable, they say, to process the information the teacher is presenting. But, they claim, that is what it is like in most lectures, isn't it? Sometimes, but only rarely, there is that one professor whose lectures are gripping, full of rich ideas, presented with pizzazz – but that, they say, is less than one in a hundred.

To pass the final exam, they will need to know specific pieces of information which are easily memorized from their textbooks. The lectures are largely irrelevant. What would happen, the observer asks, if the students were given the very same final exam two months after the course was finished? The students laugh, as if they had just been treated to the latest light bulb joke. 'You're not serious!' one guffaws. 'Who remembers?' she says. 'Who even remembers anything two weeks after the exam, let alone two months?'

'It's all part of the game,' another student offers. 'Sit in the lecture hall, be there, pretend you're interested; memorize the information from the text; give this back on the exam, then forget all about it – or, should I say clean out your brain so that it is ready for the new semester's input.'

Some call it teaching.

Scene 2

Professor Wye's assignment in the university across town also includes a course in Social Issues in Education. She spends a hundred hours in the library collecting materials about social issues in education from books and professional journals, local and national newspapers, magazines and other primary sources which bring life to the complex aspects of social issues in education. She also reviews old course outlines from which she is able to extract what she considers to be the *big ideas* of the content to be examined in the course. These big ideas become the areas of inquiry around which she will prepare cases for the students to study. Professor Wye believes that teaching requires students' active involvement in learning. Learning about social issues from studying cases involves students actively. Instead of lecturing, Professor Wye will use her in-class time for *discussion teaching* – an interactive process in which her questioning strategies will involve students in critical examination of the big ideas, in order that they may comprehend the complexities of the issues.

A visitor to Professor Wye's class observes that the students have been examining the issue of inequalities of educational opportunity – one of the social issues included in the curriculum. In preparation for this class, these thirty-five students have read the case, 'How Can I Make A Difference?' (Wassermann, 1993) about a teacher's poignant struggle in an urban ghetto school which is short of supplies and services, and long on inner-city violence, drugs, and social disintegration. Students are assigned to small study groups in which the study questions appended to the case are examined in serious, thoughtful discourse. In the initial class session on this case, the first forty-five minutes are spent in small group discussions. During this time, the teacher observes and keeps aware of how the groups are functioning, but does not insinuate herself into the discussions.

The final half of the period is spent in *debriefing the case*. Following the format of discussion teaching developed at the Harvard Business School (Christensen, Garvin and Sweet, 1991) the teacher uses certain questioning and responding strategies that require students to bring intelligent analysis to bear on the critical issues under examination (Wassermann, 1992b). Forty-five minutes pass like butter on a hot griddle; under the teacher's artful orchestration, the discussion is electric. There are always more than a dozen students' hands in the air, and at the end of the session, the issues have only just begun to be examined. Professor Wye announces that the discussion will continue next day. She recommends several books and articles for the students to read as preparation for further discussion on the case. The students leave the class and gather in the corridor – the discussion about the issues still very much alive.

The visitor engages a small group of students and asks them about this class. They tell her of their excitement and enthusiasm for learning with cases. Classes are interesting, relevant; learning with cases gives the issues more significance. In this class students' ideas are listened to; 'you have to think about what you say.'

One student says

I really understand what it means when they say that there is inequality of educational opportunity. The case helps me to see that, to know how it feels for those who have been shortchanged. Cases involve us; they make the issues real.

Another student offers

Even after the class is over, we are still discussing the issues. We talk about them during lunch, in the car driving to and from the university, with our families. I want to read more, know more. I'm constantly challenged to think more, to find out more. I know I'll be thinking about these issues ten years from now.

This, too, is called teaching.

Teaching by the Case Method: A Historical Perspective

While some of us in teacher education are viewing case-method teaching as a new and innovative methodology – promising, but suspect (let's be very cautious before embracing these innovative ways; let's make sure we have the research to back up the claims) – those who have spawned and used teaching with cases are quietly going about their work, preparing students in schools of business, law, medicine, as they have done for over fifty years. Far from new, far from innovative, and having successfully demonstrated its promise in graduate programs and professional schools in some of the best universities in the land, case-method teaching has been the primary instructional mode at the Harvard Business School since 1930.

> Harvard Business School conceived and refined the business case method, which has revolutionized management education all over the globe . . . The School places enormous emphasis on excellence in teaching; its quality control of instruction has no equal and has become a gospel to educators elsewhere (Ewing, 1990:7).

As one wag put it, 'There are two reasons that a tenured professor can get fired from HBS. One is for gross immorality. The other is for lecturing' (Ewing, 1990).

Those who would doubt the power of teaching with cases to influence students need only to look to Harvard and its history in the preparation of business leaders. David Ewing writes,

> you need only compare what comes in with what goes out . . . The incoming students, bright, energetic, talented, exhibit a naiveté about business and about their own powers that is 'colossal'. Two years later, these same students possessed a remarkable understanding of profit and nonprofit organizations large and small, had an astonishing ability to put their arms about complex management problems and analyze them, were able to make decisions with imperfect information with great skill, possessed penetrating insights into their own strengths, weaknesses, and aims in life (Ewing, 10).

Professors at Harvard Business School as well as graduates of the program claim that

> Harvard does one thing better than any other school: it *changes* students . . . From dealing with data in an amateurish way, missing significant points, pontificating, applying glib solutions to complex problems, making every other mistake that a group of bright, but wet-behind-the-ears people might be expected to make, and being so sure of themselves that it was frightening, students change profoundly in their ability to undertake critical analysis and discuss issues intelligently, coming to greater understanding of the complexity of doing business (Ewing, 10).

The power of case-method teaching is also realized in other graduate schools, where it has been systematically used in the preparation of professionals in other fields. Both MacMaster University, in Ontario, Canada, as well as the Pathway Program in Harvard's medical school have used the case method in medical training successfully for many years. To the claims that case teaching does not adequately 'teach content', C.R. Christensen, Professor Emeritus at Harvard, points to the graduating physicians at Harvard, 'who are held in the highest regard' in the profession. 'So,' Christensen teases, 'we must be doing something right.'

It has only been in the last few years that the issue of teaching with cases has begun to receive wide forum as an instructional methodology in teacher education. Ironically, a search of the literature reveals a small surge in case-method advocacy in the early 1950s, (Andrews, 1954; Lloyd-Jones, 1956; Millard, 1958; Sargent and Belisle, 1955) but for whatever reason, the methodology did not take, and teacher education programs remained largely entrenched in the showing-and-telling format that has given the training of teachers such a bad press (Goodlad, Soder and Sirotnik, 1990). Goodlad's (1990) recently completed five-year study of teacher education programs in the United States is a clarion call to educators to 'clean up their own houses, citing the low prestige of education departments in colleges and universities, the explicit and implicit valuing of scholarly publishing over teaching in education faculties, the low regard of education courses among those students enrolled, and the limited effects of teacher training courses on graduates who emerge as unprepared to teach as before they entered the training programs. Perhaps this 'hanging out of the dirty laundry' for all to see is one way of explaining the current interest in case-method teaching in education. Perhaps it is because faculties of education are ready to put good teaching first in their priority list for teacher education in the twenty-first century. Whatever it is that is moving case-method teaching forward, it is a welcome and opportune occasion.

Teaching by the Case Method: A Pedagogy for all Seasons

'Case study teaching?' queries the social studies instructor. 'I do that all the time.' In closer examination, the instructor describes how he injects current events, taken from newspaper accounts, into his classroom discourse, which he calls *cases*. For example, when the teacher taught about the case of the Exxon Valdez, students read several newspaper articles about the breaking up of the oil tanker and its disastrous consequences on the environment. After the students had read the articles, the instructor discussed with them the implications of the spill. As the teacher described his role in presenting the case it was clear that he was the one who did the discussing, while the students listened to what he had to say. This may seem to this teacher case teaching, but it is about as far from case-teaching methodology as the moon from Miami in the use of curriculum materials, instructional strategies, and learning outcomes.

It is certainly possible to embellish what one does by putting a label on it borrowed from another pedagogy that is quite different in form, style and consequence. The label, however, is not enough to transform frogs into princes.

While there is room for variation in case-method teaching, certain basic components must be operative if what is happening in the classroom may go under the name case-method teaching. This is not just nit-picking; if the essential features of case method are ignored, there is no reason to expect that the pedagogy will be successful in delivering the promised goals.

Cases

One obvious feature of teaching by the case method, is the use of an instructional tool called a case. A case is a complex educational instrument that appears in the form of a narrative. The content of a case includes information and data, psychological, sociological and anthropological observations and technical material. Cases are drawn from specific curriculum areas (e.g. history, economics, government, bioethics, education, human relations, administration, etc.), but, by their nature, are interdisciplinary. Cases are rooted in big ideas – the significant issues of the content that call for serious and in-depth examination. The narratives are so constructed that they appear as real-life problems confronting humans.

> A good case is the vehicle by which a chunk of reality is brought into the classroom to be worked over by the class and the instructor. A good case keeps the class discussion grounded upon some of the stubborn facts that must be faced in real-life situations. It is the anchor on academic flights of speculation. It is the record of complex situations that must be literally pulled apart and put together again for the expression of attitudes or ways of thinking brought into the classroom (Lawrence, 1953:215).

There are hundreds of cases that already exist for use in different disciplines and professional schools and upon which teachers may draw for their classroom work. In education, four recent texts add to the existing case repertoire (Greenwood and Parkay, 1989; Kowalski, Weaver and Henson, 1990; Silverman, Welty and Lyon, 1992; Wassermann, 1993). Teachers have also been known to write their own case narratives that are more appropriate to singular issues related to their own courses (see particularly, Kleinfeld's *Teaching Cases in Cross Cultural Education* series, 1989; and Bickerton *et al. Cases for Teaching in the Secondary School*, 1990).

Not every narrative is a case, and cases themselves have distinct characteristics. Teachers who have studied and written their own cases identify these attributes of cases:

- a case uses narrative writing techniques;
- a case is based on a meaningful knowledge base;
- a case is interesting to read;

- a case emphasizes *showing* rather than *telling*;
- a case invites the reader to become immersed in the experience;
- a case is built on single events that are generalizable;
- a case contains the big ideas or the important concepts that are to be taught as part of the curriculum;
- a case ends with a kicker – that is, instead of ending with a resolution, or leading students to the correct answer, the ending raises a question or dilemma that creates considerable cognitive dissonance (Wassermann, 1992b).

The quality of a case depends very much on the quality of the writing. Good cases *drive the need to know*; if cases fail to motivate that need, they are worse than useless.

Study Questions

Appended to each case is a list of study questions – higher order questions that require students to examine important ideas, concepts, and issues relevant to the case, to think more intelligently about the important issues. The writing of good study questions calls for skills equal to those of writing good narratives. The purpose of study questions is not to lead students to know certain bits and pieces of information, or certain answers. They are, instead, intended to allow for examination of ideas, which, in turn, leads to increased understanding. The teacher who writes study questions knows the difference between framing questions that call for students merely to *know*; and those that call for students *to use what they know to further their understanding*.

Good study questions may not be too abstract, lest they lead to shallow or unproductive responses. They may not be ambiguous, lest they be misunderstood by the students, resulting in discussion of unrelated issues. Neither may they be leading, so that students know in advance what the 'correct responses' are, and tilt their thinking in the direction of what the teacher wants. Teachers who have written study questions have identified what they see as their characteristics:

- they are open-ended, rooted in the higher order mental operations;
- they must be answered in many words;
- they have particular relevance to the students;
- they are sequenced according to a pattern that allows for moving from analysis to generation of new ideas, to action;
- they are clearly focused on the big ideas;
- they call for examination of broad, cognitive issues – those issues that warrant thoughtful examination in the area of inquiry – as well as personal and affective dimensions of issues being studied (Wassermann, 1992b).

Selma Wassermann

Good study questions make the mind buzz. Some are so provocative that they continue to dwell in the mind for years. These questions keep students thinking, searching for understanding. They are questions of magnitude, provoking examination of ideas worth knowing and thinking about. They are particularly nettlesome because they are rarely rooted in certainty. It is the very reason they make students think. Good study questions add vigor and breadth to case-method teaching; poor study questions diminish even a good case, and bog the discussion down in the land of the trivial and irrelevant.

Small Group Work

Another feature of case-method teaching is seen in opportunities for students to discuss, in small study groups, their responses to the study questions that the case raises. These small group sessions may be arranged by out-of-class assignments. Or, small group sessions may take place within the class. There are benefits and limitations to each format; in the balance, it does not seem to matter whether the small group sessions take place inside the class or out, but only that students do, in fact, have such opportunities to discuss the cases with each other prior to the whole-class discussion. The small group discussions give students their first chances at examining the issues; ideas are tried out with each other in the safest of environments. Small group discussions begin the ball rolling in the court of intelligent thinking about the issues in the case; they ready the students for the whole-class discussion on issues to follow.

Teachers who have adequate in-class time to allow small group discussions within class sessions will benefit from observing how the study groups function, and how individual students function within groups. Which students seem to take the initiative most of the time? Which students feel inhibited about speaking, even in the small group forum? Which students tend to dominate the discussions? Which seem too eager to go along with what others have said, reluctant to voice their own views? Which groups seem to race through the questions, touching each only briefly, and with minimum of in-depth analysis? Which groups tend to go off topic, meandering about personal history fields? Data from observing groups at work yield high returns for teachers who want to know their students better, and who are able to use that knowledge in providing individual help. Yet, teachers may understandably balk at devoting too much in-class time to small group work.

An alternative is to insure that small group work is assigned outside of class. To what extent the students take such assignments seriously will soon be clear from the ways in which they respond in the whole-class discussion. While outside-of-class study groups do not allow for teacher observation of individual and small group functioning, the additional time available for whole-class discussion may be worth it.

Teachers who have never used case-method teaching sometimes point to the possibility that small group sessions will result in 'exchanges of ignorance';

that students will never evolve from their more primitive and naive views of issues to more sophisticated understandings. While such primitivism in students' thinking may be observed in their very first discussions, the strong emphasis on critical analysis and reasoning from the data that is demanded in the whole-class session eventually accounts for students' progression to more thoughtful, intelligent discourse. For the small group discussions to be elevated to thoughtful inquiry, students must have increased experiences in building habits of thinking. This is served through the whole-class discussions.

Debriefing the Case

If the quality of a case is critical to generating student interest in the issues, it is the teacher's ability to use discussion teaching to enable students to reach for deeper meanings within the material that determines whether the instructional process of case method teaching stands or falls (Christensen and Hansen, 1987:40–4). Known as *discussion teaching* at the Harvard Business School, and also called *debriefing a case*, this type of discussion is at the very heart of case-method teaching (Wassermann, 1994:86–117).

For some teachers, the word *discussion* implies teacher-dominated discourse injected with information-type questions thrown at students to keep them attentive. Such a discussion may give the illusion of active student involvement, but in fact, it is the teacher who is actively engaged. It is the teacher who is doing most of the thinking. The students, for the most part, are passive listeners.

This is in contrast to the picture of discussion teaching seen in a case-method classroom: Thirty-five students sit in a semi-circle, with the teacher standing in the open part of the arc. They have just come from their study group sessions, prepared for the whole-class discussion on the case of How Can I Make A Difference? The teacher, notes on the table in front of her to help her keep the discussion on track, begins with an invitation to students to respond: 'What do you see as the significant issues in this case? Who would like to start?'

There is an understandable delay, a shuffling of papers, an air of tension, as students wait to see who will break the silence. The teacher also waits, until a student's hand signals a volunteer. She acknowledges Betsy, who will open the case.

> To me, this is a case in which a teacher wrestles with his own values, about making a difference to the lives of the children he teaches. He also wrestles with the poor conditions in the school – meagre supplies, broken equipment, and, of course, the dismal socio-economic conditions in which the children live. He feels he is working hard, but that the gains he can make are only minimal. He doesn't know if he is wasting his time. I find it a very sad and disheartening case.

Betsy sighs, and looks at her classmates, as if for affirmation. Several nod and smile.

The teacher leaves the open area of the arc, and moves closer to Betsy, the response and question already forming in her mind. 'As you see it, Betsy,' Professor Wye looks directly at her, 'this is a case of a teacher whose values and whose day-to-day life in the classroom are in conflict. He wants to make a difference in these children's lives, but the operating conditions in the school are formidable obstacles.'

Betsy nods, as the teacher's response provokes new material. 'You know,' she says softly, 'it isn't easy to teach in a school like that. It's enough to break your heart, if you are a dedicated teacher.'

The teacher moves closer and smiles encouragement. 'So, dedicated teachers would have a very difficult time teaching in schools where the conditions are so heartbreaking. They might not be likely to remain in those positions for long. I wonder what the implications of these statements are?'

Several other hands are raised. The teacher acknowledges Betsy's initial contribution and shifts to another student. In the ninety-minute debriefing time, the teacher's questioning and responding skills call forth students' examination of issues surrounding socio-economic conditions at slum and suburban schools, lives of children in disintegrating neighbourhoods, and the overwhelming odds faced by teachers who try to make a difference in children's lives. The discussion is intense, and the teacher knows how to keep it focused on the issues of significance, elevating the complexities and the conflicts, while at the same time extracting students' thinking, and challenging them to think more clearly. At the end of the debriefing time the issues are far from resolved; students will leave class with the knowledge that issues of consequence do not lend themselves to tidy solutions; these are not TV sitcoms with trite and simplistic answers to larger-than-life problems. In real life, people wrestle with social issues and have to make their own meanings and find their own resolutions.

This kind of teaching demands the very best that teachers can give; it demands the very best that students can give as well. No one is spared from doing his or her very best thinking about the issues in the case. A successful debriefing is electric; it leaves the students buzzing for hours afterward, their minds turning the ideas this way and that, trying to find their own resolutions in the web of dilemmas. One student told her professor, 'I always have a sleepless night after this class. I can't get the case out of my mind. Each time I turn it around, I see new perspectives, new angles.' Effectively done, debriefing shifts students' mindworks from seeing only simplistic solutions to vast and complex problems, to recognizing complexities, reasoning from the data, suspending judgment. Debriefing builds habits of thinking.

Orchestrating a debriefing session is as difficult for a teacher as it is demanding for students. Teachers are required, first and foremost, to be intimately knowledgeable about the content behind the case, to have read widely about the issues. The more knowledgeable the teacher, the better he or she is able to use questions that probe for the deeper meanings. Teachers are required to suspend their need to tell students what the students should be thinking; they must refrain from judgment during the debriefing session, since passing judgment on students' ideas is the very death of spirited inquiry on the issues. Teachers are required to listen thoughtfully and attentively to students ideas, to hear and apprehend what is being said, and to remember what is being said, and by whom. Teachers are required to be able to use students' ideas as working material, formulating appropriate responses and questions that allow for discovery of deeper meanings. Discussion teaching does not mean the teacher discusses; it is the teacher's prodding and asking and inviting and probing that demands the students do the discussing. The word *orchestrate* is used deliberately to describe how the debriefing session is conducted. To play in tune, to keep the rhythm, to observe the musical nuances, to hear the different instruments take the melody, to make beautiful music – that's the art of discussion teaching.

The secret of successful debriefing lies in the way the teacher interacts with students, and observing an effective debriefing reveals the essential components of that interactive process. No matter how 'tough' the professor is, demanding students' best thinking at all times, he or she always treats students and their ideas respectfully, which makes it safe for students to voice their ideas. Teacher responses and questions give students something more to work with, taking them to new levels of understanding, and keeping their attention riveted on the issues being examined. As the big ideas are examined in their complexity, as the teacher works to extract meaning, students come to a richer appreciation of the complexities and ambiguities of the case and of life in classrooms. In this kind of discussion teaching, it is primarily the students who are doing the discussing.

Learning to debrief a case is not done in a day. Such skills are not learned from reading about them, or from listening to lectures, however good. For teachers to learn the skills of debriefing, they must first perceive differences between questions and responses that call for examination of issues, and those that call for answers. They must come to value the former as more important. This is only the beginning. What follows is the commitment and the inclination to do this kind of teaching in their classrooms – to try it – and to be consistently alert to improving one's own skills, until they are elevated to art. While professional development sessions can introduce teachers to these interactive skills, the continued fine-tuning of the process must take place in a lifetime of actual classroom practice.

In sharpening one's debriefing skills, it may be helpful to reflect on the following discussion-teaching guidelines:

1   Questions that ask students to think more generatively about issues of substance are drawn from the higher-order mental operations. These include asking for comparisons to be made, for observations, for classifications, for hypotheses, for interpreting data, for evaluating

and identifying criteria for those evaluations, for imagining, for choosing actions, for applying principles to new situations.

2   The clearly-stated question makes it easier for the students to understand what is being asked of them.

3   A question that has a clear focus enables students to respond more productively.

4   The question that invites, rather than intimidates, makes it safe for students to give their best thoughts.

5   Productive questions make a demand on students to think about important issues, rather than come up with specific pieces of information.

6   Questions that are respectful of students' feelings and opinions create a climate of trust in which they feel safe in offering their own ideas.

7   Questions that require students to show how they reason from the data allow them to use what they know in order to understand important concepts.

8   The challenge of *why* questions can be reduced by narrowing their focus. Rather than 'why do you think so,' try instead, 'Tell me a bit more about what you mean.'

9   Tough questions are made *softer* by turning them into declarative statements. Rather than, 'What examples can you give?' try instead, 'You may have some examples to support your statements.'

10   Evaluative and judgmental responses are death to the spirit of open inquiry. They should be avoided.

11   The three little words, 'Tell me more' can unleash a veritable torrent of ideas as well as communicate interest in and respect for what the student has to say (Wassermann, 1992b:22–8).

Follow-up

If the case drives the need to know, debriefing escalates that need. The students are motivated; they want to know how this could have happened. They want to find the data. Because answers have not been given, because ambiguities have been elevated, tension is increased and the need to know is urgent. Motivation is high to read more, to find out more, to discover more. Students are primed for further reading. This is one means by which knowledge building occurs. Information is not dispensed by some ordered schedule, but is now singularly relevant to students' needs. Acquisition of content is thus insured.

Teachers will, of course, have lists of readings: textbooks, journal articles, newspaper and magazine articles, research abstracts, and other written information to suggest or to distribute to students for further reading. Novels are another good source of gathering perspective on issues and should be included as powerful resources. Films, both commercial and documentary are a vital source of information. Follow-up activities may be carried out individually, or in small groups, may be incorporated in subsequent classes as follow-up to case discussions. Whatever subsequent activities are used, it is helpful to follow these up with further debriefing-like discussions, in that way providing for the examination of new and different perspectives, and examining the issues from the vantage point of new data. The process of students' thoughtful, critical examination continually evolves.

Teaching with Cases: Challenges for Teacher Education

The past decade has been a time of great unrest for public schools and the fallout has understandably spread into the ivy halls of schools of education. Problems in public school systems abound and educators are knee-deep in proposals for reform. Will children be prepared to live productive and satisfying lives in the twenty-first century? And how should schools prepare children for what is to come? The issue of what it is like to live in a world of increasing and accelerating change, to become part of the information age, has shifted from rhetoric to reality; and the implications for what schools will do impact vigorously on the preparation of teachers.

For those of us who have been around the educational establishment for a while, none of these calls for change will sound like news. They seem to come, in cycles of foment, about every ten years. Should teacher educators heed such calls this time around? Or should we just sit back and wait for the new wave? Goodlad believes that teacher educators no longer have any choice.

> Schools grown accustomed to a humbler task cannot meet the challenge of today simply by doing better what they have always done. Educators must rethink what education is, what schools are for; and they must examine and rework the structures and practices that have always been out of sync for some students and are now revealed to be inappropriate for many (Goodlad, 1990:2).

> Teachers must be driven by a clear and careful conception of the educating we expect our schools to do, the conditions most conducive to this educating (as well as the conditions that get in the way) and the kinds of expectations that teachers must be prepared to meet ... The problem is one of preparing teachers to confront and deal with the daily circumstances of schooling while redesigning their schools. They are not now prepared for this ... (p. 11)

'Teacher education' Goodlad concludes, 'is at a critical juncture. Virtually every element common to a profession and necessary to that profession's impact on the common welfare is out of kilter.' The data from Goodlad's study are unequivocal: Schools of education are already moribund.

> Recorded in our field notes are countless incidents of indifference and neglect on the part of individuals who have it in their power to make a difference, and of thoughtlessness among individuals casually perpetuating tired practices of yesterday that should never have been resorted to in the first place (p. 67).

Unless teacher education responds positively to the call for significant and profound change in what they do, and in how they do it, they are likely to have to close shop, since no college or university will have the means or the inclination to support a system that is grossly ineffective.

Will case method teaching make a difference in the education of teachers? Will such methodology do for the preparation of teachers what it has done in the education of business school graduates and doctors? What are the promises of case-method teaching, and what are some of the obstacles that lie in wait for the intrepid teacher-educator/case teacher? And what is the prognosis for case-method teaching in teacher education?

Those of us in teacher education who have used case-method teaching as their primary instructional mode note learning outcomes similar to what has been seen at the Harvard Business School. Students are more actively involved in learning. They are more motivated to learn more, to seek information they need to understand the issues better. They become more self-initiating. They develop better habits of thinking; become less satisfied with simple and simplistic solutions to complex educational problems. They learn to use good judgment and to reason from data, in working out case-related dilemmas. They learn to see the world of the classroom in its complexity, and they have increased tolerance for ambiguity. They become problem solvers, instead of lesson learners. They grow more confident in themselves as problem solvers, and they learn more about the values and beliefs they hold that guide and inform their educational decisions. Their communication skills are increased; they appreciate others' points of view and learn to listen respectfully to others' ideas. Data from Adam's study on case teaching with Grade 11 high school students revealed similar findings (Adam, 1992). Case-method teaching brings these goals into realization, no matter what the grade level, the subject area, the context. These are the kinds of goals we can expect. Is this what we, in teacher education, want for our graduates?

For the professor of education who invests time, energy and commitment to case-method teaching, there are also powerful, personal rewards. Student interest generates increased teacher enthusiasm; teachers feel good about what they are doing when they see that the learning goals they had hoped for are realized. There is an increased emphasis on, and awareness of, *good teaching* and that generates a spirit among teachers that is palpable. As Rich Chambers put it,

You just have to watch and see what's happening to the students – the amount of participation, of preparation, of interest, of involvement – it's never been quite like this for me before . . . You know, on some mornings, you're tired, bored with what you are doing, going into your class thinking, 'Oh, no. Not Social Studies 11. Ho hum!' Well, this never happens with cases. *I'm* excited! The variety of responses from the students, their enthusiasm – it's always fresh and new for me. I look forward to these classes each day, and it's great to be able to feel that excitement after eleven years of teaching (Wassermann, 1992a).

But life on the path of learning to teach with cases is not exactly a rose garden. Teachers will, of course, have to learn the skills of debriefing a case – about as easy as learning to play a Bach fugue. Teachers will have to learn to give up classroom control – a frightening and intimidating thought for those professors for whom control is everything in teaching. Teachers will have to take a good, long, hard look at what they do, and give up any illusions that what they might have labeled as teaching with cases is in fact the real thing. Cases will have to be found, or even written, that are appropriate to the needs of a particular course. Teachers will have to be patient in waiting for the study groups to evolve in their discussions from primitive and naive thinking, to more sophisticated ways of dealing with the issues. Teachers will, in effect, have to undergo a 'paradigm shift' in their conceptions of what teaching actually is. Such changes are not easily made; but all are accessible for those teachers who wish to embark on such a teaching pathway.

Preservice and in-service education students who are given their first experiences with case-method teaching will likely not, at first, be willing participants. They want answers! 'Tell us what to do,' they will cry, feverish in their quest for certainty. Cases, far from giving answers, elevate ambiguity. Students will have to be encouraged to move from their dependency needs, to positions of autonomous functioning. And this must be done respectfully, and with every sensitivity for students' needs to know. Students will have to learn that responsibility for learning is theirs; that there is no one 'out there' who will be able to tell them; that they must find the ways to knowing and understanding for themselves. This, too, is a scary notion. But the sooner students accept their professional roles, the more likely they are to behave as professionals in their own classroom functioning.

Will case-method teaching take root in teacher education? What is the prognosis for professors of education making shifts of such magnitude in what they do? Without a crystal ball, it is impossible to say for sure; but who would have believed, as we entered the ninth decade of the twentieth century, that Communism would fall in the USSR, and that Russia would wish to embrace a democratic form of life? If wonders never cease, perhaps it raises hope for the future of teacher education.

Selma Wassermann

References

ADAM, M. (1992) 'The response of eleventh graders to the use of the case method of instruction in social studies', Unpublished MA thesis, Faculty of Education, Simon Fraser University.

ANDREWS, K.R. (1954) *The Case Method of Teaching Human Relations*, Cambridge, MA: Harvard University Press.

BICKERTON, L., CHAMBERS, R., DART, G., FUKUI, S., GLUSKA, J., MCNEILL, B., ODERMATT, P. and WASSERMANN, S. (1991) *Cases for Teaching in the Secondary School*, Coquitlam, BC: CaseWorks.

CHRISTENSEN, C.R. and HANSEN, A. (1987) *Teaching and the Case Method*, Boston, MA: Harvard Business School Press.

CHRISTENSEN, C.R., GARVIN, D. and SWEET, A. (1991) *Education for Judgment: The Artistry of Discussion Leadership*, Boston, MA: Harvard Business School Press.

EWING, D.W. (1990) *Inside the Harvard Business School*, New York: Random House.

GOODLAD, J. (1990) *Teachers for our Nations Schools*, San Francisco, CA: Jossey-Bass.

GOODLAD, J., SODER, R. and SIROTNIK, K. (Eds) (1990) *Places where Teachers are Taught*, San Francisco, CA: Jossey-Bass.

GREENWOOD, G.E. and PARKAY, F.W. (1989) *Case Studies for Teacher Decision Making*, New York: Random House.

KLEINFELD, J. (1989) *Teaching Cases in Cross Cultural Education Series*, Fairbanks, AK: University of Alaska.

KOWALSKI, T.J., WEAVER, R.A. and HENSON, K.T. (1990) *Case Studies on Teaching*, New York: Longman.

LAWRENCE, P. (1953) 'The preparation of case material', in ANDREWS, K.R. *The Case Method of Teaching Human Relations and Administration*, Cambridge, MA: Harvard University Press.

LLOYD-JONES, E. (Ed.) (1956) *Human Relationships in Secondary Schools*, New York: Teachers College Press series in Guidance and Student Personnel Administration.

MILLARD, C.V. (1958) *Case Inventory for the Study of Child Development*, Minneapolis, MN: Burgess.

SARGENT, C.F. and BELISLE, E.L. (1955) *Educational Administration: Cases and Concepts*, Boston, MA: Houghton Mifflin.

SILVERMAN, R. WELTY, W.M. and LYON, S. (1992) *Case Studies for Teacher Problem Solving*, New York: McGraw Hill.

WASSERMANN, S. (1992a June) 'A case for social studies', *Phi Delta Kappan*, **73**(10), 793–801.

WASSERMANN, S. (1992b). *Asking the Right Question: The Essence of Teaching*, Bloomington, IN: Phi Delta Kappa Fastback series.

WASSERMANN, S. (1993) *Getting Down to Cases: Learning about Teaching from Studying Cases*, New York: Teachers College Press.

WASSERMANN, S. (1994) *Introduction to Case Method Teaching: A Guide to the Galaxy*, New York: Teachers College Press.

Chapter 11

Reflective Practice and a Reconceptualization of Teacher Education

Terrance R. Carson

The phrase *reflective practice* has been abroad in the land. So much so, that student teachers will roll their eyes at the very mention of 'the "R" word'. Surely, the term has become overused in teacher education and students are right to object to its endless and often empty repetition. But reflective practice does signal an attitude of thoughtfulness that is necessary for teaching in these uncertain and changing times.

Reflective practice is not necessarily new. Reflection has always been part of good teaching. This is because, despite the importance of good planning, teaching is always an uncertain enterprise in which teachers are called upon to respond pedagogically to unanticipated events. Lately reflective practice has taken on a greater significance because of its relevance to teachers' involvement in processes of educational reform. Reform in teacher education is part of a widespread rethinking of the role of public education in Western societies. As in the past, much of this reform has been legislated. Reflective practice tries to reposition the teacher as having an active voice in educational decision-making. It suggests that rather than just being the conduit for change (the person who delivers someone else's mail), teachers, as thinking and acting subjects, can and will bring about what is educationally appropriate through their thoughtful, reflective practice.

In teacher education it has not been difficult gaining assent to the value of reflective practice (Clift, Houston and Pugach, 1990; Grimmett and Erickson, 1988). The difficulty for teacher education has been trying to deal with the ambiguities of reflective practice as a concept. The first impulse is to want to clear up these ambiguities and give reflective practice definitional shape so it can be molded into a teacher education curriculum. Such an impulse is to be resisted[1], for if we are to understand reflective practice in a way that is consistent with the idea, then its meaning will continue to unfold through our own thoughtful work as teacher educators. To promote reflection in the education of teachers we will need to become more reflective ourselves.

Rather than beginning with definitions and descriptions of a program in reflective practice, spaces need to be cleared for reflection in the teacher education program. This is difficult to do, because, as teacher educators, we are driven to hyperactivity. Our busy world is already more than fully occupied by many things to do: covering subject matter in the discipline and the school curriculum, conveying information and strategies for instruction and evaluation, and so forth. Aspiring teachers, who are our students, are anxious to acquire the requisite skills in teaching, evaluation, and classroom management, because each knows full well that their mettle as a *real teacher* will be assessed on their performance in these areas of teaching practice.

Such demands compel us to live on the surface of things in teaching. Guided by these demands for a performative excellence, we are discouraged from digging beneath the surface for fear of wasting time and turning up difficult matters that lie beyond our control. The turn toward reflectivity in teacher education requires courage to set aside demands to deal with the performance aspects of teaching, convinced of the need to cultivate reflection.

The Call to Reflect

What is it that calls for reflection? As the editors of this volume suggest, we live in changing times where the answers are no longer clear. Some years ago Martin Heidegger (1968) characterized the modern age as a 'thought-provoking time'. In making this characterization, Heidegger noted our proclivity for not thinking:

> most thought-provoking for our thought-provoking time is that we are still not thinking. The reason is never exclusively or primarily that we men [sic] do not sufficiently reach out and turn toward what properly gives food for thought; the reason is that this most thought provoking thing turns away from us (p. 17).

'Not thinking' in Heidegger's terms happens not for the want of effort, but from a misunderstanding of our place in the world. It is the conceit of modern consciousness that places human beings at the centre of the world as creators and controllers of what is. Such a homocentric view forgets that all of this depends on our more essential belongingness as beings in the world, not the masters of it. By operating from an essential misunderstanding of our place we have come to create an ever expanding representational world of ideas and concepts which close us off from experiencing the actual world as it is.

The tendency to construct a representational world of teaching is reflected in the volumes of research that have been generated since teacher education came to be housed as one of the professional schools in the university. Much of this research has emanated from education psychology and follows the paradigm of behavioural science. These investigations assume that teaching is something that can be torn from a communal context to allow aspects of it to be objectified and examined by social science. Lost in these representations is an appreciation of teaching as a way of life, as a particular kind of responsibility that one accepts, as a 'vocation' in the words of Dwayne Huebner (1987: 20) where one accepts a call to be transformed by children, and to be a trustee watching over the 'recollection and hopes of communities that give structure, meaning, and value to individual and collective life'.

Reflective practice, therefore, is not really an alternative paradigm of teacher education. Rather it consists of clearing spaces and opening up places for thinking, allowing that which turns away from us to show itself. It means trying to lay aside preconceptions about teaching and teacher preparation in order to listen more attentively to how we live together pedagogically in teacher education classrooms and in the schools we serve.

Developing Reflective Practice: An Action Research Project

What follows is a description of our attempt to become more reflective in our teacher education practice at the University of Alberta. In 1989 a task force on teacher education recommended that reflective practice become the philosophy undergirding the program (Faculty of Education, 1989). This report outlined various interpretations of reflective practice, resting most heavily on Donald Schön's writings and the work of Zeichner and his colleagues at the University of Wisconsin (Schön, 1987; Zeichner and Liston, 1987). Wishing to be edified by these two versions of reflective practice, rather than simply replicating their approaches, we began an extended action research project on our teaching secondary education social studies majors. The purpose of the action research project was twofold: to implement the processes of reflective practice in our teaching and to better understand the questions facing social education at the end of the twentieth century. The participants in the action research project included two instructors (Hans and I), two faculty consultants, two doctoral students (who acted as researchers and critical friends for the project) and four different classes of secondary education social studies student teachers that we taught over a two year period.

We embraced the idea of reflective practice in social studies teacher education, because in our judgment this is a particularly thought-provoking time to be a teacher of social education. It is these new teachers who will be educating the youth who, in the words of Maxine Greene (1988), 'have been raised in a consumerist world, and a world dominated by electronic media' (p. 759). They are responsible for civic education in a society that has grown cynical about politicians and bureaucrats, they are trying to teach international understanding in a world where the threat of nuclear war has receded only to reveal a multitude of virulent ethnic hatreds that have surfaced in many quarters, and they are trying to teach for social justice in a world where the gap between rich and poor continues to grow. Such are the perplexing times facing the aspiring social studies teacher who is still usually white and middle class, but who will probably be teaching in an urban classroom where many of the students will be of different cultures and family backgrounds. This new teacher will be joining a profession that has come under increasing scrutiny from a worried public that is itself uneasy about the quality of education for the future.

Narratives From the Teacher Education Classroom

A record of our attempt to teach teachers reflectively, is told as a narrative. Aoki comments that teachers' stories are neither 'merely representational, nor merely a critical praxis . . . [they are] a reflective theming more concerned with what we might call a hermeneutic returning to the lived ground of human experience' (Aoki, 1990:2). He goes on to say that such a reflective theming 'may allow us to come to know how sufficiently as humans we inhabit where we already are as teachers'.

The narratives are based on dialogue journals kept by the students and by the two instructors (Hans Smits and me) during a fourteen-week *integrated term*. The integrated term consists of eight weeks of practicum, teaching social studies interspersed with a total of six weeks of campus-based curriculum and instruction work. During this term, the two instructors tried consciously to encourage a reflective approach to social studies teacher education. Student teachers were invited to actively consider alternative ways that social studies teachers might relate students, subject matter and milieu. For example, student teachers were asked to consider the problem of the outdated textbook in the post-Cold War world. At the same time they also worked with strategics for cooperative learning.

During their explorations two kinds of journals were kept, a dialogue journal and a teaching log. The dialogue journal was used to explore issues and questions. These were shared with fellow student teachers and with the course instructors. The teaching log was used to record and reflect on teaching strategies they used themselves and observed being used in the university class and in the secondary school classrooms they visited. The student teachers continued to use the two journals during their practicum. The instructors also kept dialogue journals and teaching logs which they shared among themselves and, from time to time, with their students.

Three narratives are constructed from the dialogue journals. These are entitled, 'teaching techniques and the authority of experience', 'theory, practice and the self' and 'constructing an identify of the person who teaches'.

Story #1 – Teaching Techniques and the Authority Experience

A student grows frustrated with our constant emphasis on reflection in the curriculum and instruction class. In his journal he writes,

I know critical reflection is important to teaching, but if you have no
ideas regarding the strategies to be used in teaching, the reflection
becomes almost useless. We have no actual teaching experience, so
we are desperate for strategies. So, I'm confused about the purpose of
this course for my future teaching career!

Hans and I had both taught the course in previous years, giving emphasis
to teaching strategies and techniques. We knew that students appreciated this,
but we had hoped that they would now learn to develop and trust some of
their own 'practitioner derived knowledge' as suggested in the reflective practice literature (Smyth, 1987). But now, in attempting to implement a reflective
practice approach, we found ourselves caught in a conundrum of still wanting
to be helpful to our students and yet trying to encourage them to trust themselves. The conundrum had a particular urgency because we knew that students depended upon this term as the only time that there would be focused
attention on social studies curriculum and instruction. Hans wrote about the
conundrum in his journal, saying,

I haven't escaped the trap of 'giving' and 'telling' . . . there is still a
certain dependency built into the class (and probably conditioned in
all of us). On the one hand students always want the comfort of more
guidance. On the other hand they are frustrated for not overcoming
their own dependency. I'm not sure how much students are aware of
this and how it is related to their lack of confidence.

This tension of help and autonomy pertains to many pedagogical situations. Parents wonder when to step in and when to let children learn on their
own. The same is true of a teaching relationship. In calling upon us to share
the benefits of our experience, we came to better understand that there is also
a quality of apprenticeship in the student teacher/teacher educator relationship. In this relationship the expectation of being shown strategies and techniques was not simply a demand for technical know-how. Student teachers
understand that these strategies have been learned on the job by experienced
teachers. In this way, sharing techniques provides novice teachers with vicari-
ous experiences of teaching, helping them to orient their own teaching identities. The student became frustrated when he felt that the insights we had
gathered from our experiences of teaching were being withheld.

The tension of help and autonomy was not resolved, but upon reflection
Hans and I begin to realize the dangers of positioning reflective practice as a
binary to technicism. Unable to think about reflection except in terms of binary
oppositions had caused us to misunderstand the authority of experience and
the place of the older person in inducting the novice into the traditions of
teaching.

Terrance R. Carson

Story #2 – Theory and the Uncertainties of Practice

Reflective practice re-positions us as instructors which creates uncertainties. In my journal I wrote to Hans about this saying,

> there is a troublesome side to critical reflection, it makes you doubt yourself. For me this raises a question about the relationship of critical reflection to the self. Can self-doubt be a positive impetus for change? Are we not, in critical reflection, questioning something very basic about ourselves as teacher educators?

As teacher educators our subjectivities are structured in large part by the place we work – the university. Expert knowledge is expected and valued by the institution and anticipated by student teachers based on their previous university experience. Our subjectivities as experts are de-stabilized as we encourage students to critically reflect, and as we learn to hold our own experience and expertise in check. It is an unfamiliar pedagogy for ourselves and for the students and the image they hold of professors.

In discourses on theory and practice it has been relatively easy to describe the different epistemologies of technical and critically-reflective practice. A technical practice assumes the existence of a proven and generalizable body of knowledge about teaching which will reliably inform practice. A critically-reflective practice makes such generalizable knowledge problematic, since it suggests that a critical analysis of the particular situation by and for the participants informs thoughtful action. Decisions in critically-reflective practice are the responsibility of the participants. Decisions in technical practice are based upon the authoritative application of validated generalizations. While the theoretical distinctions had been convincing – they had indeed been a large part of our motivation for implementing a reflective practice – we were surprised by how the practice of reflection unsettled us as teacher educators.

The students, too, found an 'unsettled self' disconcerting. One student teacher wrote,

> I was so engrossed in reflection that it nearly drove me bonkers. A cooperating teacher told me one day it would be the end of me if I didn't learn to relax and accept my mistakes or what I considered to be 'failures'. I constantly felt I was to blame for my shortcomings. My problem was over-analyzing – one should be critically reflective, not critically destructive.

Student teachers are normally self-absorbed. But, we noticed, somewhat perversely, that reflective practice brought about an even greater-than-usual focus on personal performance. Even the most self-assured seemed unable to remove themselves from the centre of their reflections. Realizing this forced us to again question the pedagogy of our own planning. How open was our

156

teaching to the students' voices? Were we ourselves guilty of pushing a conception of reflective practice so much that little place was left for the students in our plans? In my journal I wrote,

> We impress the importance of planning upon student teachers. We tell them that planning shows a pedagogical care to prepare oneself with the students in mind. So how do we make plans that allow a meaningful place for our students? How can our plans show care for them rather than having an undue preoccupation with our own performance in teaching reflective practice?

Story #3 – Constructing an Identity of the Person who Teaches

Opening ourselves to the students' voices enabled us to hear them speak of the difficult processes of forming their identities as teachers. This involved a destabilization of old identities and reconstitution of new ones. One of the students, Wanda, wrote about this destabilization as having a 'much less glamorized view of teaching'. She went on to say,

> I mark for hours, plan in my sleep and in the shower, with creative ideas refining themselves as I consider the angles . . . I really do not think you can be a social studies teacher without reading the newspapers, listening to the news and following special reports.

The hard work inside the teaching profession comes as a surprise to many student teachers. As Deborah Britzman (1991) remarks, teaching is the 'most familiar of professions'. Most people carry images of teachers that they form as students and that the culture continually reproduces. Most of these have to do with the custodial functions of teaching that seem to come 'naturally' to teachers. Wanda's 'less glamorized view of teaching' prefigures a personal identification with pedagogic sensibility of a teacher. She begins to think of subject matter in a teacherly way, feeling responsible for staying current about news and public affairs, thinking of how to draw this to the attention of her students. Thoughts of teaching begin to preoccupy her, not so much in terms of how to perform effectively for others, but out of concern for students.

The pain of destabilization and reconstitution is described vividly by another student, Kerri, as she recalled encountering her personal and received theories of teaching at the end of her first four-week round of student teaching. In her journal Kerri wrote,

> I feel I am beginning to locate myself realistically as a teacher. I build on a few positive points and have a little more patience with my 'weaknesses'. I try not to allow them to overwhelm me and to erode my self-confidence and self-respect. More and more, I am becoming

attuned to the kids and their real needs versus my idea of what their needs ought to be. I am beginning to let go of this compulsion to feel responsible for everyone and everything and to do all the work. I am perhaps feeling out a role and an understanding of the structure of roles set out in a school for the teacher, students, administrator, counselor and how each functions best within their parameters. I have a better realization of the limits and potentials of myself, my students, and the school's ability to accomplish what it sets out to do.

There are signs of struggle and pain as Kerri speaks of not allowing her 'weaknesses' to erode her self-confidence and self-respect, but comments about 'locating herself', show an unfolding identity that is beginning to open itself to others and that does not feel so responsible for doing everything. She tells of how, over the course of the term, she becomes able to 'let go of this compulsion' and to become 'attuned' to the students. Attunement hears the actual voices of young people with whom she works as a teacher, not the universal child of the developmental theorist, or the university methods class. To be attuned to young people signals a pedagogic responsibility for the way they are and for the way we are too. This is not the abstracted critical reflection based upon universal ideals of justice and emancipation, but a seeing of our values and the conditions of our culture as they are embodied in the children who are actually in our classrooms. It is this which allows her to put aside the preconceived notions and plans about what is good for them.

Both students would claim that they have become more modest and realistic about what they can do as teachers. This is a hard-won realization as Kerri writes in her final journal entry,

Anyway I hope to survive and learn from this experience. I feel battered and exhausted from constant self-bereavement and self-doubt and from this exhaustive focus on 'self'. I can't wait (no I can wait, let's not rush things) until I emerge from this intense worry and fear of failure/future perfection, and appreciate the experience for the present. And know how each experience is a learning one, and to make that connection with at least some of the special people I am working with that we call students and staff.

In somewhat the same way Hans and I, as the course instructors, were also reconstituting ourselves as teacher educators. Because we were doing action research on reflective practice, it was like becoming aware of ourselves as teacher educators for the first time. Our journals spoke of our thoughts and our struggles to understand the pedagogy of teacher education. The tension between providing the certainty of techniques and confronting the ambiguity of teaching is one example of this destabilization of a teaching identity, so is making room for the students' voices in our planning. As a class of students left us I reflect on the difficulty of letting go in my journal,

It is hard not to regard the performance of my students as either a vindication or a condemnation of my own teaching. It's hard to know what one has done. So much of how they turn out will depend upon the students they will face, the milieu of the school, and how they will choose to become teachers in their own right.

Reflections on the Narratives from the Teacher Education Classroom

The collaborative action research inquiry into reflection began with the intention of implementing critical reflection in a teacher education program. The mode of implementation was itself intended to be critically reflective, with participants following a spiral of action, research cycles, each cycle consisting of moments of planning, action and reflection. We also felt that action research was appropriate because of the perplexing nature of the question of reflective practice, which could be best illuminated through an inquiry into our own practices as teacher educators.

As instructors we begin by initially siding with the critically-reflective objection to the reified knowledge and skills in a technicist representation of effective teaching. However, our action research revealed that the oppositional program of reflective practice carried its own 'epistemic grammar' (Bowers, 1987:8) with it. We remained caught within the web of two alternative discourses, both of which speak in some sense to teacher education, but neither of which hears the voice of teaching.

One way of breaking out of the binary opposition of technicism and critical reflection is by privileging the ear over the eye. In her essay 'Derrida and the Ethics of the Ear', Diane Michelfelder (1989) calls this, giving priority to *saying* over the *said*. By attentively listening to what student teachers and we as teacher educators are saying about critical reflection and how it relates to learning to teach, we better understand teaching and teacher education. This saying speaks of learning to teach as a process of constitution and reconstitution of identify.

Rejecting the limitations of the binary opposition of technicism and reflective practice as the discourses, teacher education does not necessarily mean that we can design a new model that somehow captures the nature of teacher education as the development of professional identities. John Caputo (1987:270) suggests that the notion of conceptual capturing is a modernist illusion 'that we have managed to close our conceptual fists around the nerve of things, that we have grasped the world round about [and have] circumscribed and encompassed it.' Following Caputo, we understand that teaching is not essentially something we have grasped in its essence, rather teaching is something that we *are* and *do*. Teaching means, in the words of Heubner (1987), to accept the transformative possibilities of 'our inherent openness to otherness and to the newness in the world'. This makes teaching always fragile and insecure.

Heubner suggests that 'those of us who teach know it in the pit of our stomach every time we start a new class' (p. 24).

With these thoughts in mind I return again to what action research inquiry into critical reflection has said about teacher education. What we hear in the narratives is a tension between making oneself vulnerable and being skilled and competent as a teacher. Competency covers a wide range of skills, background knowledge and organizational abilities necessary to be an *effective* teacher. Students legitimately expect that in a curriculum and instruction course they should minimally become familiar with techniques for planning, classroom organization and management, student evaluation, and be introduced to specific teaching ideas. These are regarded as practical tools because they hold possibilities for themselves in their classrooms. Such practicalities are also important surrogate experiences, and experience is what the student teachers chiefly lack. Becoming competent in the skills and the knowledges of teaching means more than simply having technical effectiveness. Showing skill is an important aspect of building an identity as a teacher. As well, a certain level of skill is necessary for one to have an openness to one's students.

Openness to the Other signifies the other part of the tension. It means accepting one's vulnerability. To encounter the face of the Other is to face the ambiguity and the responsibility of teaching. This is the continuing source of vulnerability in teaching. Whatever the organizational ability, background knowledge, or teaching skills one might possess, these are secondary when meeting actual children in the classroom. As Levinas (Peperzak, 1989) notes, 'finding myself facing another awakens me to the infinite responsibility for the other who is in need of everything that is necessary for human life.' To be committed to teaching really means to take responsibility for children in this way. Even the most knowledgeable and experienced teacher knows the insecurity that comes when first facing a class. The children, our students, come to us as strangers. And even after one gets to know them better, they can still surprise, delight, and puzzle the experienced teacher.

Teaching means to live in the flux of the newness of the world and in the play of competence and vulnerability. Part of the objection to overly technical teacher effectiveness programs is that they want to deny the flux. They see methods as a protective armour to ward off the unexpected and to control the engagement with students. If being armed with this armour is a student teacher's idea of good preparation, then it is probably a good thing that our students are never prepared well enough to meet classroom 'realities'. It is in the places where the armour wears thin, and in the naked places, that the openness to the Other and an openness to the relationship, that is teaching, enters in.

If teaching means to live in the tension of vulnerability and competence, what are our responsibilities as teacher educators? We understand first that teacher education is not discontinuous with teaching itself. It, too, is exposed to the same flux of vulnerability and competency. We must be prepared, at times, to set aside our own answers and solutions to listen to the stories the student teachers tell about their journey to becoming teachers. By positioning the student teachers as reflective practitioners we did open up a potential for them to critically reflect on their personal investments and social responsibilities as social studies teachers. But missing from this identification of the social studies teacher as a reflective practitioner is an appreciation of the teacher as a self in transition.

In his recently completed doctoral study, Smits (1994) points out that the question of identity is central to becoming a teacher. The reflections of the student teachers in the action research were primarily about understanding what teaching is and what it means for them to be a teacher, it is not primarily an engagement in socially-critical reflective practice. Intervening appropriately in the process of professional identity formation points to pedagogical responsibility of teacher educators as they provide support for students' explorations of teaching identities.

Note

1   This is not to deny the usefulness of analyzing the various meanings given to the phrase reflective practice, such as that provided by Zeichner and Liston (1987) in 'Teaching student teachers to reflect', *Harvard Educational Review*, **57**(1), 23–48, which employs Habermas's taxonomy of technical, practical and critical reflection.

References

AOKI, T. (1990) *Voices of Teaching*, Vancouver, BC: British Columbia Teachers Federation.

BOWERS, C. (1987) *Elements of a Post Liberal Theory of Education*, New York: Teachers College Press.

BRITZMAN, D. (1991) *Practice makes Practice: A Critical Study of Learning to Teach*, Albany, NY: SUNY Press.

CAPUTO, J. (1987) *Radical Hermeneutics: Repetition, Deconstruction and the Hermeneutic Project*, Bloomington, IN: Indiana University Press.

CLIFT, R.T., HOUSTON, W.R. and PUGACH, M.C. (Eds) (1990) *Encouraging Reflective Practice in Education: An Analysis of Issues and Programs*, New York: Teachers College Press.

FACULTY OF EDUCATION (1989) *Exploring and Mapping the Future: A Report on Alternatives for Issues Resolution by the Faculty of Education Strategic Planning Project*, Edmonton, Alberta: University of Alberta, Faculty of Education.

GREENE, M. (1988) 'Further notes on bloom and the new Bloomusalem', Phi Delta Kappan, **69**(2), 755–60.

GRIMMETT, P. and ERICKSON, G. (Eds) (1988) *Reflection in Teacher Education*, New York: Teachers College Press.

HEIDEGGER, M. (1968) *What is Called Thinking?*, New York: Harper Colophone Books.

HUEBNER, D. (1987) 'The vocation of teaching', in BOLIN, F.S. and FALK, J.M. (Eds) *Teacher Renewal: Professional Issues, Personal Choices*, New York: Teachers College Press.

MICHEFELDER, D. (1989) 'Derrida and the ethics of the car', in DALLERY, A. and SCOTT, C.

(Eds) *The Question of the Other: Essays in Continental Philosophy*, Albany, NY: SUNY Press.

PEPERZAK, A. (1989) 'From intentionality to responsibility: On Levinas' philosophy of language', in DALLERY, A. and SCOTT, C. (Eds) *The Question of the Other: Essays in Contemporary Continental Philosophy*, Albany, NY: SUNY Press.

SCHÖN, D. (1987) *Educating the Reflective Practitioner: Toward a New Design for Teaching and Learning in the Professions*, San Francisco, CA: Jossey-Bass.

SMITS, H. (1994) *Interpreting Reflective Practice: A Hermeneutically Inspired Action Research*, Unpublished doctoral dissertation.

ZEICHNER, K.M. and LISTON, D.P. (1987) 'Teaching student teachers to reflect', *Harvard Educational Review*, **57**(1), 23–48.

Chapter 12

Foxfire and Teacher Preparation: Practising What We Teach

Allan Dittmer and John Fischetti

The learning in school should be continuous with that out of school. There should be a free interplay between the two. This is possible only when there are numerous points of contact between the social interests of the one and the other . . . as a rule, the absence of a social environment in connection with which learning is a need and a reward is the chief reason for the isolation of the school; and this isolation renders school knowledge inapplicable to life and so sterile in character.

(John Dewey, *Democracy and Education*, 1914:358).

Regardless of how one describes the times in which we live, the post-modern era, the environmental renaissance, the communications bonanza, with its information highway and global village, or the age of consumerism, one thing is clear: not only are things greatly changed, but the speed at which things are changing seems to increase exponentially. Currently, experts agree that information is doubling every twelve to thirteen months. Clearly, in all facets of living, our ability to adapt, adjust, and remain flexible is necessary not only for keeping up with what's going on, but in many cases, just surviving.

The work of preparing teachers is no exception. From the beginning, when normal schools took over the responsibility of training teachers, to now, where colleges and universities have assumed that function, most teacher preparation programs have consisted of a specified number of courses taught on the university campus, culminating in a student teaching experience at a school site. Because of the major shifts in the social fabric of the United States, and our emerging understanding of teaching and learning this out of context approach no longer prepares teachers for the realities of current classrooms and the children who come to them – if indeed it ever did. At a time when both schools and universities are in the process of reinventing themselves, the presence of our students at the school site not only provides a valuable resource to assist with that change, but the students benefit as well by being in the middle of it. This type of involvement is similar to what Foxfire teachers do with their students in their classrooms. The difference is that we are doing it across institutions.

This chapter describes the change made in teacher education at Louisville, Kentucky, and the program now in place based on the Foxfire approach to teaching.

The Change at Louisville

In 1987, shortly after the authors of this paper arrived at the University of Louisville, the Department of Secondary Education began to revise the high school teacher preparation in light of a major convergence of factors which were either present or about to happen. The Holmes Group agenda was being vigorously debated, the ramifications of the major education reports dating to 1983's *Nation at Risk* were getting significant attention on the floors of state legislatures and in corporate board rooms, and in Kentucky, a new wide-ranging educational reform initiative was being shaped which would become the law in 1990. In addition to considering all these factors looming on the horizon, we brought several common beliefs and practices to the endeavor, many embodied in the Foxfire Approach to teaching. Guided by the eleven core practices (see Wigginton, 1986; 1989) and, in particular, core practice #1 which states,

> All the work teachers and students do together must flow from stu-
> dent desire, student concerns. It must be infused from the beginning
> with student choice, design, revision, execution, reflection and evalu-
> ation. Teachers, of course, are still responsible for assessing and min-
> istering to their students' developmental needs.

We set about the task of creating an experimental program to pilot some of our ideas about how best to prepare high school teachers in an urban setting.

Foxfire represents an approach to teaching grounded in the philosophy of John Dewey, particularly his notions about education, democracy and experi-ence. Although the approach has evolved over a twenty-five year period through increasing use and refinement by teachers with pupils, it has remained un-tested as an effective approach for preparing teachers.

Several assumptions about teaching and learning lie at the heart of the Foxfire approach to teaching. Students must be in charge of their learning, which means they must have choices about what and how they learn. Think-ing and learning must be connected to real-world problems and issues and grow out of a desire and need to learn. Learning must also be continuous, and new learnings must spiral out of previous learning. The process of learning by doing and reflecting on experience in order to grow in knowledge is funda-mental to the approach and stems from Dewey's notion that education and learning are growth. Knowing is a process, and the process of learning is far more important than the products.

These assumptions require a different role for the teacher. The teacher acts as a guide who assists students in their search for the right questions and the means to attempt to answer them. In this sense the teacher is not an answer or fact giver and knowledge is not a fixed quantity of information, dates, names, events or things. As such, the teacher must be well-grounded and knowledgeable in a wide range of content, and regard learning as a continuous, life-long process.

Generally, when the Foxfire approach to teaching is discussed in teacher preparation classes, it is frequently referred to as one way to teach among many, with little opportunity for students to see it modeled. We take the position that our students will probably adopt a mode of teaching with their students when they see it modeled while they are learning to teach.

When we began exploring how to change our approach to preparing teachers at the high school level through the Foxfire approach, we began a change process that regarded no currently-held assumptions as sacred, inviolable or true. To say the least, what we entered into was difficult, extremely stressful, and for some individual faculty members, cataclysmic.

For the most part, university professors come out of a tradition that respects individuality. Professors rarely work in groups. The system of ranks and promotion create a highly individualistic competitive system. The Doctorate is considered the highest level of educational attainment. When professors have completed it, they believe strongly that they know something valuable based on knowledge which has withstood the test of analysis and critical scrutiny. University cultures are highly political and 'getting along' in the system is something professors either learn, or they have unpleasant and sometimes brief careers. There is a strong mythology in universities about standards. The myth of objectivity rules and standards are considered absolute. The major vehicles for delivering content are courses, taught by experts who mostly lecture. In short, professors of education, known by their colleagues in the more prestigious colleges as *educationists*, and professors in general, are tainted by the cultural experience they have gone through to get to be a professor.

With the new experimental teacher preparation programs based around Foxfire, we changed the rules. We took colleagues out of their safety zones and asked individuals who felt very comfortable with what they knew to get uncomfortable and challenge some, if not all, of their intellectual, as well as cultural assumptions. Many of these same professors subject their students to a similarly unsettling experience in their classrooms by how and what they teach, and yet are dismayed and upset when it is practised with them. As we actively debated and discussed the issues of preparing teachers, it was clear there was no consensus about many issues.

A large part of the failure of cooperation inside schools of education relates to communication. Just as most teachers in schools know little about what takes place in their neighbors' classrooms, education faculty spend little time working together to synchronize their courses, integrate the important feedback of their cadre of graduate students,

Allan Dittmer and John Fischetti

or reporting on teaching practices that are successful or not. This behavior mimics our behavior as teachers in schools but contradicts both our intuitive desires and research findings (Fischetti and Aaronsohn, 1990:141).

The so-called *knowledge base* that guides teacher preparation was the first point of division. Some faculty argued that if there weren't empirical studies to back some aspect of practice, then that aspect of practice was worthless. Others held that the very term knowledge base implies a fixed body of immutable truths, rather than a constantly changing evolving body of questions and assumptions. These were tough discussions that left some individual faculty totally bewildered and shaken. And this was just the beginning.

Clearly, the university and school cultures are very different in many ways, as Seymour Sarason (1990) adeptly points out,

If you, as I have, ask teachers (for example, in an elementary school) how they justify the existence of their school, the answer you get is that schools exist to further the intellectual and social development of students. Now if you ask faculty members of a university how they justify the existence of the university, in one or another way the answer is that the university primarily exists to create and sustain those conditions that enable its faculty to learn, change, and grow. (You can have a university with few or no students.) The assumption is that if those conditions exist for faculty, it increases the chances that the faculty can create and sustain those conditions for students.

The two answers are polar opposites. The public school exists for students. Period. The university exists primarily for its faculty (Sarason, 1990:137).

When we made the suggestion that our teacher preparation programs be located at school sites and that we become an integral part of that school site's efforts to change, the reader can imagine the counter-reaction that began to take place. Colleagues began to stand on precedent, claiming ownership of *their* courses which they had always taught in a certain way and always on campus. Many colleagues didn't see the need to change, even though student evaluations of their courses frequently pointed out how disconnected they were from the realities of teaching in schools. They began to stand on formality and became obsessive about using Robert's Rules in all meetings and raising what we called the 'impossibility questions' which bogged down the discussions and significantly slowed the change process. They used rules and regulations to block proposed changes by either denying any knowledge of them or citing them to thwart doing something different from the way it had always been done. When it finally became clear that the process of changing the program wouldn't go away, and that the momentum was not on their side, a great insecurity and fear set in caused by the vast array of unknowns, and several individual faculty members began a slow but deliberate withdrawal from what appeared to them as the new centre of the work of the department.

The Program at Louisville

We have been operating for more than eight years and the goals and directions of the program continue to evolve. One thing is certain, the paradigm for preparing teachers at our institution has shifted from a campus-based, individual course/instructor delivery mode, to a school-based, collegial, collaborative and programmatic approach, one where students take a more active role in directing and evaluating their learning. The program consists of three completely school-based semesters, the first named *Exploring teaching* which is prerequisite to the Master of Arts in teaching semesters which follow this six-hour course.

The exploring teaching semester brings students preparing to teach at all grade levels into elementary, middle and secondary schools where they have the opportunity to confirm their hunches about teaching as a profession and the level they have selected to teach. During this exploring phase, the students work in classrooms with regular and mainstreamed special education students in the inclusion model currently in use in Kentucky schools; they are introduced to the theoretical concepts about learning and teaching, the philosophical questions that affect education, issues affecting urban schools, such as multiculturalism, diversity, demographics, and socio-economics, and the mandates of the state-wide reform initiative that will directly impact their teaching. They also begin assembling a teaching portfolio that will accompany them through and beyond the completion of the program. The students are also responsible for designing and participating in a major service learning project that puts them in touch with their students in their communities in a non-school setting. These strands continue throughout the program. The two-semesters of the Master of Arts in Teaching portion of the program are unimaginatively named *Pre-student teaching* and *Student teaching*. The students enter the Pre-student teaching course in the fall semester, and exit the program by presenting their entire portfolio in a Capstone seminar during the last week of the spring semester, at the conclusion of student teaching.

Of much more importance than the structure of the program, is the use of the Foxfire approach as the instructional mode to engage the students in their learning. The Foxfire approach begins with a set of *givens*, those concepts, ideas, issues, skills and attitudes that must be learned. Students spend time discussing the givens and have the opportunity to modify them if they agree changes are appropriate. Building teams and consensus are major features of the approach and the cohort structure of the program contributes greatly to that. As the students begin to shape the agenda with the assistance and guidance of the instructors, they constantly go back and check the givens to make sure they are pursuing their agreed-upon goals.

The givens for the secondary teacher preparation program are the course goals, the state of Kentucky's New Teacher Standards, and any other standards, such as NCATE or additional accreditation content area professional association standards. Because the courses are taught by teams of instructors, the instructional approaches vary, but co-planning and team teaching reduce the potential for fragmentation and discontinuity. The laboratory is the school; a real, typical urban high school that, itself, is in the throes of change. With fifty or more students in the building who are eager yet apprehensive about how to learn to teach adolescents, the need and desire to learn are there; they don't have to be artificially manufactured. The students reflect on issues and problems the moment they occur and can practise as well as test ideas or approaches they are learning in a supportive setting. The almost obsessive concern with content that dominates the thinking of secondary teachers is put into a more balanced perspective as the students work with actual high school kids inside and outside their classrooms. The concern for students and the complex lives they lead becomes a central part of the university student's thinking. Just a few specific examples of how this learning happens will help to clarify why this approach to preparing teachers is effective and desirable.

In our current regular secondary teacher preparation program, the Foxfire approach is imbedded in the course students take prior to student teaching. Offered on-site by a team of University faculty at two large urban high schools, the six-credit block is co-taught by teachers and administrators at the schools.

The starting point for the Foxfire approach is the establishment of clear goals for the class that become the basis for the students' portfolios as they proceed through the semester. These goals establish a wide range of choice inside of the academic expectations of the class, and as we stated earlier, student choice is a key element of the Foxfire approach. We continue to realize that if we give our students choices in how and what they learn, it will naturally follow that they will do the same with their students when they become teachers. As Constance Kamaii (1991) puts it,

> We cannot expect children to accept ready-made values and truths all the way through school, and then suddenly make choices in adulthood. Likewise, we cannot expect them to be manipulated with reward and punishment in school, and have the courage of a Martin Luther King in adulthood (1991:387).

During the Fall 1994 semester, for example, the section of Pre-Student Teaching had ten major goals or givens (Fischetti and Stroble, 1994); these goals and the projects are enlarged and expanded each semester by the evaluations of the graduates of the previous year's program. The people we work with at the school site, and the givens we mentioned earlier:

- understanding the complex lives of students and adults in schools;
- designing/planning; implementing/managing; creating/maintaining a positive learning climate;

- authentically assessing student learning and communicating results;
- effectively serving students with special needs;
- engaging in professional development related to Kentucky school reform and national educational initiatives;
- reflecting and evaluating specific teaching/learning situations;
- collaborating with colleagues/parents/community;
- applying appropriate content knowledge;
- developing leadership skills for success in a changing profession;
- preparing for student teaching.

Most college instructors use a text or series of readings around which they derive their syllabi and course content. This practice tends to limit student choice and access to performances for real audiences for the work in their classes. Students tend to *take* classes rather than *experience* them and have some say in shaping them. Consistent with the Foxfire approach, our Pre-student teaching class has moved to a project focus. Each semester there are between 8–10 projects developed out of the work of the previous cohorts. As a culminating activity of each project, there is an audience for the work; evidence of the reading, writing, collaborative and individual activities students have participated in; and a clear assessment process where self, peer, audience and instructor feedback is included. For the Fall 1994 cohort, the following are examples of the projects they worked on in groups:

Project 1: Organizing Pre-Student Teaching
Project 2: A Study of the PDS High School Site
Project 3: Teaching All Students
Project 4: Enabling School-Based Change
Project 5: Mid-term Assessment
Project 6: Professional Development
Project 7: To Be Determined as part of Project 5
Project 8: Preparing for Student Teaching
Project 9: Portfolio Exhibition and Performance Events

During Project 1, different groups in the class are responsible for determining what resources and facilities are available at the PDS site, organizing the class roster and administrative needs, recreating the school site classroom, assessing the level of knowledge about education reform, etc., among their peers, and finally teaching each other about what they have learned.

In Project 2, groups work with different facets of the community and develop a way to document the various components of a large urban school and its community setting. The students interview teachers, students, parents, bus drivers, custodians, secretaries, etc., and the demonstrations are produced so that the principal can use them as information pieces to educate audiences about the school and community. During this time, students read selections that address socio-cultural issues. The students then write letters to the authors seeking responses to issues they raise. Project 4 enables the class to be fully involved in some aspect of school restructuring and change by having them prepare written summaries, videos, case studies and presentations about one aspect of the school. For example, one group researched the impact of the Youth Services Center, a social services-community liaison office housed in the school. Another taught electronic mail skills to students and peers and developed curriculum to link high school students and college students to the emerging electronic highway. Other groups assisted teachers attempting to use alternative means of graduating students beyond the Carnegie Units, planned a conference with high school students to be held in the spring, and so on. The possibilities are only limited by the students' imaginations and creativity. These projects define clear student outcomes but give real choice and discretion to the groups as they develop the products they will put in their portfolios and final class Capstone demonstration. Every semester, at least one project is left open to be developed by the current class during the midterm. In fact, the midterm is designed to allow the groups to develop projects that will best serve the class interests in preparing for student teaching. The groups go through a consensus process to narrow a vast array of ideas down to one project.

One of the most discouraging, yet frequent, comments from veteran teachers is that they really learned to teach once they finished their teacher preparation program. As we have incorporated the Foxfire approach into our alternative and regular programs, we have found that a surprising number of our graduates report to us that they are using the approach in their classrooms with their students, and that they felt fully prepared to teach the very first day they stepped into their own classrooms. The following are just a few examples of how our graduates approached their subjects using the Foxfire approach. One third-year teacher organizes his English class around the production each week of a local access cable television show. A French teacher uses community members as the audience for her students' work. A chemistry teacher works with preservice teachers to develop and assess his students' projects that grow out of typical textbook topics such as 'The Solubility of Water' and 'Pressure/Volume/Temperature'. A Mathematics/Science team is teaching a 'Problem-based learning' curriculum linked to the school's public safety technical program.

At the end of the courses, we asked the students to reflect on their experiences focusing especially on how and what they felt they learned. These four quotes are illustrative of the comments we got back from them.

> We all had to work together. We had a lot of pressure. We got aggravated and frustrated with one another. And we can be delighted at the end product. Now we can look at our students and look at their frustration when we put them in groups and tell them to get it done and have real understanding of what they're facing.

When we went into the classes and worked with them on-site on our projects, it totally changed my viewpoint. If we had stayed on the campus and talked about lesson planning and how you plan an objective and initiate the lesson, move to assessment and closure, etc . . . I never would have understood that there are veteran teachers who have been there for years and who can't get lessons going in the first two minutes. Being on-site, being with the kids has made all the difference.

I think what you taught us and the way that you did it taught that there isn't a right answer when you are confronted with a teacher who is struggling to have success in her classroom. You don't just have 30 kids or 150 kids, you have society and the politics. You can't get that if you're not there and learn from the good and the bad. I was totally immersed with the journals and the sharing . . . You totally gave license to try things, gave us confidence and allowed us to learn from the good and the bad.

Being on site also showed me that I am always learning. There is no way that the instructors could tell us everything there is to know before we did it. We learned ways to learn. The example that best indicates that to me is that the last day of the fall semester, we rearranged our Pre-student teaching class into rows. That's the first time we were in rows. We all said, 'What?' That was an amazing experience. I realized that we couldn't have done the work of this class in rows. And yet, my classroom for visiting is mostly in rows. I'm still learning all the time. It is constant learning. When I am certified I am still going to be learning. I am afraid that a lot of people who are prepared the old way, think that they are done.

These quotations affirm our belief that working along with our colleagues at the school site allows us as teacher educators to practice what we teach.

Conclusion

We are continually reminded of the fragile nature of change. There are tremendous pressures from conservatives both inside our state and in the nation to undermine the reforms that are underway and return to the *tried and true* way things have always been done. There is constant infighting and posturing within the university, the schools and our units over trivial issues. These change efforts are extremely fragile and the smallest change in personnel can severely impede the progress already underway and erase the gains that have been made. Resources are always scarce and continually getting scarcer.

Most of our students fit the classic profile of the non-traditional student. They are older, bring with them significant life and work experiences, and are often in the process of making a major career shift. Recent studies confirm that over half of the individuals entering teaching will leave after six years. Non-traditional students require more collaboration with peers, a strong intellectual challenge coupled with real-world, hands-on experiences, and a clearly marked path to reaching their goals. In addition, the needs of children and families at this time in our nation's history are critical. The schools in our state have been slow to change, but with new legislated mandates and an agenda for change, we are now presented with an ever-increasing number of dynamic school settings in which our students can learn to teach. All of these factors and more have caused us to realize that we don't have the time or the resources to let new teachers test the water and learn to teach gradually, after their preparation program is completed and they have a few years of teaching experience under their belts.

Being a first-year teacher today involves many more responsibilities than simply being in 'your' room with 'your' students. Most of our graduates enter the profession immediately as members of an interdisciplinary team. Their schools have social service agency links in which they must participate. Most are asked to take a leadership role on a school council, or restructuring plan-ning committee. Most importantly, new teachers are being evaluated on how they serve all of their students, rather than on how quiet and orderly their classrooms are. The students in our program, and the people who hire them, report that they are better prepared to teach in the rapidly changing school settings.

Using the Foxfire approach takes a maturity and desire for change that challenges the most experienced teacher. Some would argue that encouraging new teachers to allow their students choice, to encourage real audiences for the work of the class, and to design interesting and compelling processes through which their students can make meaning is more than a new teacher can handle. What we don't know and hope to investigate is will our students remain in teaching any longer than the current national average, and will they continue to use the Foxfire approach to teaching that was such an integral part of their preparation program?

We use the Foxfire approach and continue to build upon it in the restruc-turing of our teacher preparation program because it honors what we know about learning and it establishes early on an experiential base upon which students can build their learning about teaching. Our view of restructuring is changing the rules, roles and relationships within a program. We have clearly changed the roles by immersing our students in area schools for the majority of their program and helping them become active participants in the school change process. We have come a long way, and have a long way to go, in changing the roles of faculty, both in the schools and university. We are team teaching at the school site and integrating the school restructuring agenda into the curriculum blurring the lines between the two. We have fostered a new set of positive relationships with school administrators, teachers, university col-leagues and state level officials. As one high school principal recently said when he learned that our students might not be at that school in the fall semesters, 'I can't start school without your students. They literally organized and conducted the entire first day of school registration, and our teachers are counting on them for assistance in their classes.' We see everyday, through the powerful examples of our graduates, that students can own their learning and that new teachers can learn to teach by working with students in schools as they grow in their knowledge, skill, and attitudes about teaching.

References

DEWEY, J. (1914) *Democracy and Education*, New York: The Free Press.

FISCHETTI, J. and AARONSOHN, E. (1990) 'Cooperation starts inside schools of education: Teacher educators as collaborators', *Collaboration: Building Common Agendas*: CTE, **10**, 140.

FISCHETTI, J. and STROBLE, E. (1994) *Pre-student Teaching Course Syllabus*, Louisville, KY: University of Louisville.

KAMAII, C. (1991) 'Toward autonomy: The importance of critical thinking and choice making', *School Psychology Review*, **20**, 387.

NATIONAL COMMISSION ON EXCELLENCE IN EDUCATION (1983) *A Nation at Risk*, Washington, DC: Government Printing Office.

SARASON, S. (1990) *The Predictable Failure of Education Reform*, San Francisco, CA: Jossey-Bass.

WIGGINTON, E. (1986) *Sometimes a Shining Moment: The Foxfire Experience*, Garden City: New York Anchor Books.

WIGGINTON, E. (1989) 'Foxfire grows up', *Harvard Educational Review*, **59**(1), 24–49.

Chapter 13

Reframing the Clinical Professor Role: The Faculty Associate at Simon Fraser University

A.J. (Sandy) Dawson

Introduction

The creation and development of collaborative and cooperative relationships between universities and school authorities concerns teacher education institutions throughout North America, Europe and Australia. These institutions struggle to build productive relationships with local school authorities and yet maintain their own central role in the preparation of future teachers. The role of clinical professor has been seen as one means of promoting closer ties between the university and the schools. Clinical professors, faculty associates, or teachers in residence as they are sometimes called, are teachers seconded to the university for periods of time to teach and supervise student teachers. This chapter examines that role drawing on the experience at Simon Fraser University where the faculty associate, as the role is called at that institution, has been central to the university's Professional Development Program (PDP) for thirty years.

Tensions and risks exist in these efforts to establish collaborative and cooperative relationships founded at least in part on issues of power and authority (Brookhart and Loadman, 1992; Cornbleth and Ellsworth, 1994). Tensions arise around questions of what the role of clinical professor should involve, and perhaps as importantly from a teacher education institution's point of view, what the role should not involve. The risks are both personal and professional. Clinical professors risk not being able to live up to the faculty's expectations. Professors risk having their positions usurped if clinical professors are able to fulfill the tasks normally carried out by professors. This can occur if the clinical professor becomes knowledgeable about the conceptual and theoretical issues confronting student teachers, the traditional area of professors' expertise. The professor's place in the institution may then be seriously threatened. From an institutional point of view, if the clinical professor role proves so powerful that it encompasses both the practical and theoretical aspects of teacher education, funding authorities may raise the question of why the university is needed at all to prepare teachers if the most significant work can be done by clinical professors. The experience at Simon Fraser University illustrates how these tensions, risks, and questions play out and how they can be approached and resolved in ways that can benefit all parties.

The Faculty Associate Role

The Professional Development Program began as a new program for preparing teachers in 1965, when Simon Fraser University opened. The founders of the program saw two needs in teacher education at the time. On the one hand, there was a strong need for the faculty of education to maintain credibility within the larger university community. The second need was to maintain a strong connection with the field. Both needs arose out of perceived weaknesses in teacher education at the time. The founders of the Simon Fraser program saw the existing campus-based programs at other universities as inadequate in terms of preparing teachers. They saw university courses as overly theoretical and largely irrelevant to the needs of beginning teachers. Furthermore, faculties of education which had just become part of the university did not enjoy a strong reputation in that setting. Thus, Simon Fraser would be different.

Gaining credibility within university would come through a careful selection of top scholars and a strong emphasis on research and publication. Sending such academics out to the schools to supervise student teachers for a few weeks each year did not seem to be the way to build that connection with the field or to use their talents wisely. It was also recognized that they may not be authoritative regarding classroom issues, principally because they lacked recent, on-going knowledge and contact with the day-to-day operation of classrooms. On the other hand, it was recognized that outstanding classroom teachers had well developed and oftimes clearly articulated personal/practical knowledge of classroom settings and children, though the terms used here (typically the ones used by Clandinin, 1986) are not the ones used in the 1960s when the university was founded. How could these two spheres of knowledge and experience be brought together in mutually productive ways.

One of the founders of the program reports having an Archimedean, eureka-type experience one evening, when he conceived the idea for faculty associates. They would be outstanding classroom teachers seconded to the university while maintaining the salary, benefits and seniority guaranteed by the local school authority from which they are seconded. They would assume the role of clinical professors within the faculty (Dawson, 1994).

When the faculty associate role was first conceptualized, it was thought that the research-based, theoretical focus brought by professors would be critically tested by the personal/practical knowledge brought by the faculty associates. At the same time the potential for faculty associates to expand, deepen, and verbalize their personal/practical knowledge would be greatly increased because of the challenge and prodding of professors. A dialectic was envisioned which would foster the growth of knowledge and understanding in both parties. Moreover, because direct supervision of student teachers would be left to faculty associates, professors would be free to pursue their research and writing programs. Student teachers would be supervised by faculty associates who had very recent classroom experience thereby removing the complaint that university supervisors were out-of-date and ivory-towerish! Faculty associates and school associates (the term the program used to describe cooperating teachers), both with deep roots in the classroom, could function collaboratively in their work with student teachers.

The program has now been in operation for nearly thirty years. Although it struggled to gain acceptance within the educational community of British Columbia in its early years, it has had a high degree of success, a conclusion attested to by a recently completed external review.

> They even appear to have slain the two albatrosses that hang around the necks of teacher education programs. The evidence is strong that the faculty is highly regarded across the university for the quality of its research, while the soundings that the College of Teachers took in other areas of its review of teacher education indicated that SFU confounded the literature, in that a large majority of its graduates see merit in its program. They have achieved academic excellence and professional respect and those are no mean accomplishments (BCCT, 1991:3).

The faculty works very hard at selecting and orienting new faculty associates and a primary objective of this process is to build a cadre of professionals who are held in high esteem by both their school and university colleagues. The fact that the faculty associate model has been successful derives from a number of factors described next, but the attribute of the high positive regard faculty associates enjoy stands out among many others. How is it, then, that the faculty is able to benefit year-after-year from the work of faculty associates?

Selection and Orientation of Faculty Associates

Faculty associates (FAs) spend two years associated with the faculty during which time they:

- plan and work with professors on both teaching and research functions;
- teach seminars and courses, singly and in teams with professors and other faculty associates;
- are directly involved with student teacher admission selection;
- assist with program evaluation and revision; and most centrally;
- supervise a small group of student teachers.

Though the initial identification of faculty associate candidates is by means of an advertisement in the newspaper, the intent is to select high quality teachers from around the province, and to then orient them to the role. From the 100 or more applications received each year, an initial selection of approximately 35 potential FAs is made. In recent years this group of candidates then took part in a one-day information session. In the late afternoon and evenings following this event, each candidate is given a forty-five minute interview by a team of faculty people composed of faculty members and current faculty associates. The interviews attempt to provide an opportunity for candidates to display their personal professional knowledge and how they might make use of that knowledge in their work with student teachers, faculty members, and other faculty associates. Typically, approximately fifteen faculty associates are appointed each year.

Very soon after being notified of their appointment, the faculty associate initiates are involved in, first, a one-day field experience with a current FA to get an overview of the supervision work which the role requires, and a second day to work with the professors to gain a sense of the theoretical aspects of the role. These two days provide the new FAs with their first taste of the academic requirements of the appointment. This process of initial selection and orientation takes place during the January to March period each spring.

These few days of early orientation are followed by an intensive three-week period commencing mid-August, when faculty associates partake in a variety of experiences designed to assist them with the supervisory nature of their job, as well as to begin the planning for their teaching role in a module with a professor. In a large measure, this orientation serves as an introduction to expectations of the university, and provides the time and (it is hoped) pleasant atmosphere in which they can become comfortable with their new work setting. Nonetheless, faculty associates testify that the orientation period is both energizing and tension producing. As the day approaches when the student teachers will come to campus, the level of nervous energy and stress rises noticeably, and the demand for more time to plan and prepare is heard to echo around the hallways of the faculty.

This orientation period is not conceived as an opportunity to remedy deficiencies in the background and education of the faculty associates. It is thought to be a time when the knowledge and experience of faculty associates and professors can be brought together in ways which will be mutually beneficial for them and for the student teachers with whom they will work. Though faculty associates are given opportunities to learn and practice supervisory skills, these are not approached in a mechanistic fashion. Rather, the conceptual issues and problems associated with supervision, assessment, and so on, are integral parts of the work at this time, and the dialogue which occurs is a sharing among faculty and faculty associates, each bringing his or her grounded knowledge to the discussion.

A.J. (Sandy) Dawson

Working With Professors

When student teachers commence the program, they are assigned to a module normally composed of a cohort of twenty-eight students teachers, two faculty associates, and one professor. The professor and the faculty associates begin planning the focus, activities, and content of their module approximately four months prior to the arrival of the student teachers, during that initial day of orientation back in the spring, spoken of earlier. Though they work within a broad set of goals established and approved by the faculty, each module has freedom to structure the experiences for their student teachers within the focus selected by the team. Time and support make it possible to do this advanced planning during the summer preceding the fall intake of students. The first task of this planning is the establishment of a dialogue between the faculty member and faculty associates. The nature of this dialogue and the focus the module selects can vary widely, but all modules attempt to blend the scholarly expertise of the professor with the practical expertise of the faculty associates (Dawson and Leyland, 1989; Dawson *et al.*, 1988; Norman *et al.*, 1989). The BCCT review commented on the module structure:

> The modules are loosely coupled to a very general philosophy. . . . There is a set of objectives to guide people who work in the program and to use in the evaluation of students but whether or not those objectives are strictly adhered to seems uncertain. In any case they are broad enough to cover almost any practice. That appears to us to be both the strength and weakness of the program and why it is so difficult to capture its essence.
> . . . the diversity in practice that is inevitable, is what gives the program its uniqueness and its strength. And if we had to make a stark choice between designing an ideal teacher education program and having great mentors without giving them much direction and less prescription, we know which we would choose (BCCT, 1991:13).

During the long practicum term, student teachers are expected to assume complete responsibility for the school associate's teaching assignment by the fifth or sixth week of the practicum, and to maintain this load for three to four weeks. During the final couple of weeks of the long practicum, the student teacher gradually withdraws from full-time teaching and the school associate reassumes responsibility for the class. During this term, the faculty associate will make weekly or bi-weekly visits to the student teacher and school associate. It is this triad of student teacher, school associate and faculty associate which jointly assesses the student teacher. This process has a self-evaluation focus. The grading system used during this term is simply pass or withdrawal (not failure!) from the program. Approximately 15 per cent of the student teachers withdraw from the program each year.

The foundation for the cohort support so critical for student teachers during their long practicum is developed from the day the student teachers begin the program. It is the first term of the program that departs most radically from more traditional teacher education programs, and it is in the preparation for and the operation of this term that the faculty associate role becomes defined. As noted earlier, the faculty associates and professor begin planning the module four months prior to its commencement. Establishing the dialectic among themselves is the first priority of their planning sessions, the outcome of which is the identification of the focus of the module. In some cases, the focus of a particular module (e.g., French Immersion or Fine and Performing Arts) is a built-in, on-going characteristic of the module. In other instances, particularly with primary generalist and secondary modules, this focus is invented by the module team. For example, one module may decide to focus on the building of a community of educators. This could involve the use of one particular school and all its teachers as school associates, the placement of the fourteen student teachers in that school (two student teachers per each school associate), and the everyday, on-site presence of the faculty associate. The faculty member associated with such a module might be giving a credit course for the school associates, other interested teachers, as well as district personnel.

The discussions which take place among the module team members are crucial not only for the development of the module's focus and ensuing program; this is the point at which the personal/practical knowledge brought by a faculty associate encounters the theoretical knowledge brought by a professor. It is in the working out of the module focus and program that the critical tension between theory and practice is confronted for the first time. For professors and faculty associates alike, this planning time is alive with potential for new learnings and vigorous debate as they struggle to place the personal/practical knowledge within a theoretical frame or to find a theoretical frame which can integrate the personal/practical knowledge. The movement is by no means in one direction only, and it is definitely a time when fruitful conceptual tensions and conflicts can be addressed. Over the years, professors and faculty associates have attested to the tremendous opportunities for renewal and growth that accompany the planning each year for the arrival of a new group of student teachers.

A number of years ago, in response to concerns expressed by professors that their involvement with a module was so time intensive (sixty or more contact hours during the first term, plus the planning time during the term previous to the commencement of the module), their research and publication projects were suffering. So while the program as conceived of over thirty years ago was successful in finding significant ways for developing university/school collaboration and cooperation by having professors establish a dialectic with faculty associates, the ability of professors to maintain their academic credibility within the university community was being undermined.

It was decided that one way to grapple with this problem was to add a research agenda to each module so that professors' research interests might be served through their work with a module. Results from this innovation are

A.J. (Sandy) Dawson

promising. A number of papers arising from this research have been presented at conferences and published in journals. One unexpected result of this change is that faculty associates, school associates, and student teachers are being involved in the action research projects proposed and guided by professors such as those Scott and Burke describe in Chapter 14. Nonetheless, the recommendation made by the British Columbia College of Teachers is well taken: that is, 'there is a need for more co-ordinated research on teacher education involving faculty and faculty co-ordinators/associates' (BCCT, 1991:16).

Teaching Courses Within the Faculty

In addition to the work just described, many faculty associates obtain employment with the university to teach methods courses during the semester when the student teachers are involved with course work exclusively. Most faculty associates have the background and expertise required by faculty to make them eligible to teach undergraduate courses. Hence, faculty associates are seen as full partners in the offering of the teacher education curriculum. They are not hired just to do the supervision of student teachers. In some instances, a professor and a group of faculty associates will work together in a team environment to offer a methods course. In other cases, faculty associates work alone, but with the ever-ready assistance of a faculty member should the faculty associate wish to have that help.

With that as background, I now wish to turn to some of the issues, concerns and questions regarding the role of faculty associate. These issues are set within the recent literature on the nature of collaboration between the university and local school authorities, a literature which points to difficulties with the role.

Questions and Issues About the Role

The work of Cornbleth and Ellsworth (1994), who examined the roles and relationships of clinical faculty in university teacher education programs, bears on the role played by the faculty associates at Simon Fraser. They examined seventeen teacher education programs to understand how these individuals contributed to teacher education within the university and what obstacles clinical faculty faced in becoming regular players in those programs. They identified three major forms of clinical faculty roles:

1 enhancement of the status of the traditional role of the cooperating teacher through title changes, increased preparation and perks, and role differentiation;
2 classroom teacher involvement in teaching university courses;

3   broad classroom teacher participation in teacher-education program planning, admissions, and other decision-making (1994:52).

Cornbleth and Ellsworth found that about one-third of the seventeen teacher education programs they reviewed offered clinical professors the first kind of role enhancement. Two-thirds of the programs reviewed allowed clinical faculty to have an involvement with university courses. However, very few programs provided opportunities for clinical faculty to engage more broadly in teacher preparation. It probably is clear by now that the role of faculty associate at Simon Fraser allowed for all three kinds of participation, though the degree to which this occurred was very much a function of the incumbent Director of the program, and the Dean of the faculty. As faculty associates became more involved in teacher education, conflicts began to emerge between them and professors. The role has been in continuous transition and has frequently been questioned and criticized by some faculty members. Faculty associates have also questioned the irrelevant theoretical stance taken by some faculty members. Perhaps part of the program's success has been due to the constant debate and argument that has occurred around the purposes behind teacher education and the role faculty associates might play in achieving those goals. The questions and issues about the role are discussed below under the categories of culture, knowledge and power.

Culture

It is when faculty associates begin their term with the professional development program that we see the beginnings of an interaction between two cultures, the school and the university. They were invited into a dialogue with professional colleagues regarding the nature of teacher education; some of those colleagues were professors and some were other classroom teachers who had come to the university to be faculty associates. In the words of Cornbleth and Ellsworth, the role ideally 'includes colleagueship with university faculty and is undertaken in a new setting' (1994:54). Many faculty associates testified that when their term was completed their experience in the role was the most profound professional development they had ever undertaken. A large part of that experience is the opportunity to have the time to discuss educational issues with faculty colleagues and teachers and to visit a tremendously varied and rich set of classrooms. But that opportunity has not been a constant over the thirty years experience of Simon Fraser with the faculty associate role. Periods of faculty control, which I discuss later, have changed this collegial atmosphere to one which can be characterized as a deficit model where the emphasis has been on training faculty associates for the role they are to assume.

A study by Brookhart and Loadman (1992) points out the difficulties that the lack of meaningful discussion between faculty and clinical professors can produce. They reviewed projects in the United States which had university/ school collaboration as a principal focus, and they used the concept of culture as the theoretical construct to analyze the literature they reviewed. This analysis seems relevant to the discussion here, because faculty associates and professors live in and come from two different cultures. Each of those cultures has its own set of meanings which the participants in that culture tend to treat as absolute. This makes breaking through the cultural barriers extremely difficult, doubly so if meaningful conversations are not promoted and do not take place between faculty and faculty associates.

> Without an awareness of these multiple systems of meaning, public school and university educators may each feel their perspectives are 'right', real, and true. Sensitivity to cultural differences is needed; both groups must recognize that their own work and experiences define 'reality' for them. To work together, they must negotiate what is real, what is true, and what things mean in this new relationship. Many efforts have faltered because participants were unaware of the need for this negotiation. Many more efforts faltered because participants were unprepared for the discomfort caused by changing the accustomed answers to questions of meaning (Brookhart and Loadman, 1992:55).

Sensitivity to the cultural perspective of the 'other' was certainly at the base of many of the difficulties which arose within the Simon Fraser program over the years, though the discussion which occurred at the time these problems surfaced tended to focus on: the status of personal, practical knowledge versus scholarly, academic knowledge; and power and authority. Brookhart and Loadman (1992:56) use slightly different terms – focus, tempo, rewards, and power – to describe the categories of assumptions which were brought into question when disagreements between faculty associates and faculty members happened.

Practical versus Academic Knowledge

Faculty associates face the significant challenge of placing their very considerable personal practical knowledge within a theoretical framework, within a rationale which they can elucidate. In short, they must concern themselves with broader issues than just the problems and questions of individual student teachers and their supervision. For some this transition to being a university teacher educator is a difficult one. Most faculty associates make the transition; some do not, however, and they may choose to return to their classrooms after one year as a faculty associate.

On the other hand, faculty members also have difficulties. Some faculty members view their academic knowledge base as being broader and more conceptual than the practical knowledge brought by the faculty associates. 'Universities traffic in theory; schools apply theories in practice. This oversimplification has enough basis in fact to cause long-standing school-university differences' (Lieberman, quoted in Brookhart and Loadman, 1992:56).

Complicating the issue is the fact that many faculty members working in the program have limited (and likely dated) school teaching experience, but nonetheless feel they too possess practical as well as academic knowledge. They therefore see themselves as having the benefit of a enhanced view of teacher education to that of the faculty associates. Even if they have not had classroom experience, some faculty members believe that because they have studied the broader issues in teacher education they are in a better position to judge what and how a teacher education program should be organized and operated. Faculty members with this view would agree with Brookhart and Loadman (1992:56) when they say,

> University thought about academic subject matter tends to be conceptual and come in big bites. School thought about academic subject matters tends to be chunked in the size of discrete instructional objectives . . .

Faculty associates tend to bristle at such a characterization of their knowledge because it implies that school thinking is not broad and conceptual.

The difficulties experienced by faculty associates and faculty members have had a variety of what we might term negative outcomes. Faculty associates have decided to not return for a second year with the faculty. Faculty members have recommended to the Director that particular faculty associates should be not rehired for a second year because the faculty associate in question is seen as being too skills-oriented, or not able to think broadly enough, or seems incapable of grasping theoretical issues.

In other cases, faculty members have assumed quasi-authoritarian roles within the module. Some modules are now defined and directed by the faculty member. The faculty associates in such a module follow the pre-set program established by the faculty member. In another instance 'when "what works" [became] synonymous with "good" and "theoretical" [became] synonymous with "bad" . . .' (Brookhart and Loadman (1992:57), the faculty member withdrew from working in the module for the balance of the semester. Over the years, a small number of faculty members have withdrawn from teaching in the program for a number of years, because they felt that their perspective was not being allowed to be the dominant one within a particular module.

Other faculty members, though working year-after-year in the program, pay a high price for that involvement, because the reward system of the university comes in the form of peer-reviewed publications, yet much of the work faculty do in the program is more suitable for presentation in practitioners' magazines, a far less prestigious outlet for ideas than research journals. Moreover, writing requires a quite different tempo of work than does direct work

A.J. (Sandy) Dawson

with student teachers and faculty associates, and faculty members who attempt to maintain a high level of involvement in both activities experience time conflicts in the extreme. Unfortunately, it is often high energy, relatively new, untenured scholars who wish to devote large amounts of time and energy to working with faculty associates and student teachers, yet they do so at the risk of their careers if they do not produce sufficient scholarly work to gain them tenure.

This involvement has ebbed and flowed, much like a sine curve, during the quarter of a century the program has functioned. In the early years, every faculty associate was a full voting member of faculty, for example, whereas currently, only two of forty-odd faculty associates are allowed to vote at faculty meetings. On the other hand, it was not always the case that faculty associates were involved with admissions decisions, but currently selected faculty associates are involved with the selection of prospective teacher candidates. Four faculty associates, five faculty members, and two students comprise an advisory/consultative body for the program, thereby providing faculty associates with input into the development and implementation of policy within the program. Once again, however, it is necessary to note that this body functions at the pleasure of the Director. Moreover, a recent report to the faculty recommended that the structure of this committee be modified so that it would not be possible for faculty associate and student representation to outweigh faculty votes on the Committee (Wassermann et al., 1993:23).

Power and Authority

In the previous sections where I dealt with culture and knowledge, the difficulties that arose may become ones of power and authority. In their review of teacher education programs which made use of the role of clinical professor, Cornbleth and Ellsworth (1994) note that there is

> ambivalence on the part of university faculty regarding the capacity of classroom teachers to play a greater role in teacher education programs. Ambivalence is evident in the shape of most clinical faculty roles and the language used to describe them. Subservience to 'the university', including its faculty and norms, is implicit if not explicit in most accounts of clinical faculty programs (p. 65).

The number of cases where faculty associates have not returned for a second year because of difficulty in making the transition to this new role, or of a faculty member withdrawing from participation in the program or of assuming an authoritarian leadership style within a module, have been very rare in the program. But when they have occurred, power and authority is a central attribute of the discussion which takes place around these actions.

The role of faculty associate within the Professional Development Program, at any particular time, is one marked by a constant state of transition and

184

redefinition. The fulcrum for the pendulum swing of this transition and change process rests on the issue of control. On the one hand, we have seen attempts to enhance the collegiality among faculty members, faculty associates and school associates, in ways that highlight the contributions of all individuals who work in the program. Control is worked out on a day-to-day basis. At the other end of the pendulum swing, we have seen attempts to reaffirm a hierarchical structure in which faculty associates are to be subservient participants in the program with faculty in control. This latter emphasis is contained in a recent document which examined the role of those faculty associates who become co-ordinators in the program. In that report, the words 'take back control of PDP' reflected the wish of some faculty to be more in control of the program which they saw as theirs (Wassermann *et al.*, 1993:9). Such shifts are often subtle and depend entirely on which faculty members are involved with the program at the time of the shift. The implications for faculty associates are quite direct.

Commenting on the recent administrative shift to a more hierarchical model for the relationship between faculty and faculty associates, a former faculty associate remarked:

> I think what [is being] demonstrated is that teachers from the field and those from the university are unable to establish a working relationship wherein 'real' decisions are reached collaboratively. I think that the model . . . so carefully nurtured was doomed to self-destruct as soon as real power was seen as being threatened. I am not even cynical about this; I see it as inevitable. Power pervades everything; it is not good or bad in itself; it is just the life force institutionalized through bureaucratic need (Personal communication to the author).

Prior to the shift in administrative style, however, the dialectic between faculty associates and faculty members had been rich and rewarding, even if stressful and tension ridden at times. Unlike the conclusion draw by Cornbleth and Ellsworth (1994) that 'clinical faculty have not had much to say in shaping their roles and relationships . . . [and that] . . . the roles and relationships have been created for them, usually by university personnel . . .' (p. 65), the experience of the majority of faculty associates and faculty members teaching in the program was that the roles and relationships are co-determined and mutually specified as the dialogue among module team members took place. What the future holds in this regard remains to be seen.

The faculty associate role as seen during the 1980s and early 1990s did not fit the pattern identified by Cornbleth and Ellsworth (1994) which argued that 'clinical faculty must become more "like us" . . .' (p. 66) [the us being university professors]. But stress had developed in the system over the past few years which was highlighted recently when a particular group of faculty associates (called coordinators) did become more 'like us' in that their scholarly/academic knowledge began to match that of the professors at the same time that their personal/practical knowledge remained current. This became a threat to a number of faculty members and the administration of the faculty. Statements by faculty members such as 'the . . . demand on coordinators to be "scholars" is, I believe, a misplaced function . . .' (Wassermann *et al.*, 1993:8). In point of fact, there was no demand on coordinators to become scholars. They did pursue graduate work out of self-interest, not because it was required of them. The Coordinator Report (Wassermann *et al.*, 1993), like all such documents, may or may not signal a shift in political power within the faculty. What becomes of interest with this document are the tensions which lie just below the surface. The report provided the opportunity for a number of faculty members to voice their agreement with the conclusion that Clandinin (1993) seems to be drawing when she contends 'how inappropriate it is to have university associates (clinical professors or faculty associates in other language) stand between university teachers and teachers, as go-betweens between theory and practice' (p. 186). The tension here is essentially one of power around who owns the knowledge that will be brought to bear on the process of learning to teach.

Change and Reform

The problem of school and university reform lies at the heart of our efforts now in education as others have argued in this work. Part of that problem, which teacher educators have sought to combat in many different ways over the years, recognizes that no matter how outstanding the university-based component of the program might be, it could be washed out by the student teacher's school experience (Zeichner and Tabachnick, 1981). The potential is great that a teacher education program such as the Simon Fraser's, which devotes fully one-half of the student teachers' time to school practice, becomes a prime agent for the maintenance of the *status quo* in schools.

However, the experience at Simon Fraser has shown that the role of the faculty associate can be a lever for change in the schools and within the university as well (Scott *et al.*, 1991). Two factors contribute to this. First, the individuals hired as faculty associates have typically been seen as change agents in their home districts. As such they are the 'fringe survivors' who argue for and enact change within the school system. Such people are attracted to the program at Simon Fraser. The experience there often provides them with the background and understanding to pursue reform once they return to their district. However, if this role is to flourish, it must have the support of the faculty and the administration. If power-brokers within the faculty are allowed to devalue the role of the faculty associate, then the potential of such reform will be lost. The tendency for faculty members to do that stems from the fact that frequently their own knowledge base is threatened by faculty associates.

Second, the modular structure of the Simon Fraser program provides a useful vehicle for ongoing experimentation with ways to link faculty, faculty associates and school associates in teacher preparation, teacher development and research, as Scott and Burke describe in Chapter 14. When a collaborative relationship can be maintained, and where the knowledge of academe can be combined with the personal/practical knowledge of the teacher in ways that benefit all involved with the program, then we approach having the best of all possible worlds at Simon Fraser. Moreover, when those elements are all brought to bear, the agenda is typically one which supports reform both in the schools and the university.

Conclusion

·The role of faculty associate within Simon Fraser University's Professional Development Program demonstrated in the 1980s and early 1990s that teachers from the field and university teachers can successfully establish collaborative and cooperative working relationships which benefit both the individuals involved and the student teachers whom they teach. The differentiated staffing model employed in the teacher education program at SFU has been judged by the teacher certification body of the province (BCCT, 1991) to be one which honours the knowledge and know-how of teachers, at the same time allowing the faculty of education professors to develop outstanding scholarly reputations. And the program is seen by its graduates and the employers of those graduates as being one which produces well-educated and highly-skilled novice practitioners. Based on the experience of the faculty associate role within the program, it would seem clear that this particular manifestation of the clinical professor role can function effectively. However, to work effectively, the role must be conceptualized within a framework that views the knowledge of the faculty associates as being on a par with that of university professors. Their knowledge may be different in kind but not in its value to the education of future teachers, and both must be honoured if the role of faculty associates is to achieve its potential. At times this has occurred at Simon Fraser University, but only when a collaborative, respectful climate is promoted in which the personal/professional knowledge of teachers is valued.

Nonetheless, tensions and difficulties have occurred over the years. The analysis provided here supports the view of Brookhart and Loadman who concluded that assumptions about focus, tempo, rewards and power are key attributes if successful university/school collaboration projects are to be created. Whether the program experience will continue to deal effectively with these attributes in the future is problematic at the time of writing. But it is clear that for a reconceptualization of teacher education to occur, a process which involves both universities and schools requires a dialogue between faculty, faculty associates and school associates. Only if such a dialogue happens might a bridge between the university and school cultures be constructed, a bridge of communication involving at the very least mutual respect and a sincere attempt to understand the point of views of the alternate culture.

A.J. (Sandy) Dawson

References

BRITISH COLUMBIA COLLEGE OF TEACHERS (1991) In BOWMAN, J. (Ed.) *A Report of the External Review Team of the College of Teachers*, Vancouver, BC: BCCT.

BROOKHART, S.M. and LOADMAN, W.E. (1992) 'School-university collaboration: Across cultures', *Teaching Education*, 4(2), 53–68.

CLANDININ, D.J. (1986) *Classroom Practices: Teacher Images in Action*, London: Falmer Press.

CLANDININ, D.J. (1993) 'Learning to collaborate at the university: Finding out places with each other', in CLANDININ, J., DAVIES, A., HOGAN, P. and KENNARD, B. (Eds) *Learning to Teach, Teaching to Learn: Stories of Collaboration in Teacher Education*, New York, NY: Teachers College Press, 177–86.

CORNBLETH, C. and ELLSWORTH, J. (1994) 'Teachers in teacher education: Clinical faculty roles and relationships', *American Educational Research Journal*, 31(1), 49–70.

DAWSON, A.J. (1994) 'A twenty-five-year-old professional development program for the twenty-first century', *South Pacific Journal of Teacher Education*, 22(1), 59–67.

DAWSON, A.J. and LEYLAND, J.L. (1989) *A comparative case study analysis of four approaches to improving the link between theory and practice*, Paper presented at the Annual Meeting of the American Educational Research Association, San Francisco, CA, March.

DAWSON, A.J., LEYLAND, J.L. and MONTABELLO, S. (1988) *Redefining the role of teacher as professional: The purpose of teacher education programs*, Paper presented at the Annual Meeting of the American Association of Colleges of Teacher Education, New Orleans, LA, February.

LIEBERMAN, A. (1980) 'Describers and improvers: People, process, and problems', in HALL, G., HORD, S. and BROWN, G. (Eds) *Exploring Issues in Teacher Education: Questions for Future Research*, Austin, TX: The University of Texas Research and Development Center for Teacher Education, 415–28.

NORMAN, P., MADOC-JONES, G. and DAWSON, A.J. (1989) *Revitalizing secondary schools: A study in university/district collaboration*, Paper presented at the Annual Meeting of the American Association of Colleges of Teacher Education, Anaheim, CA, March.

SCOTT, J.A., SKOBEL, B., BURKE, H., SPRUNGMAN, S., BUTLER, C. and ROBERTS, S. (1991) *Curricular integration: Teacher conceptions, concerns and creations*, Paper presented at the Annual Meeting of the Canadian Society for the Study of Education, Kingston, ON, June.

WASSERMANN, S., BEYNON, J., MAMCHUR, C., MARTAIN, J., SMITH, S. and ZOLA, M. (1993) *The Coordinator Report*, Faculty of Education, Simon Fraser University.

ZEICHNER, K. and TABACHNICK, B.R. (1981) 'Are the effects of university teacher education "washed out" by school experience?', *Journal of Teacher Education*, 32(3), 7–11.

Chapter 14

Collaborative Teacher Education: A Merging of Agendas

Judith A. Scott and Hugh Burke[1]

Raining. A west coast fog over our university. Get into the car, and head for the next observation of a student teacher. Traffic. Running late. Half-run into the school . . . up two flights of stairs into the classroom. Teacher turns; looks; 'Oh. You must be the supervisor from the ivory tower.' Slump. Have to figure out a better way of doing things.

(November, 1989).

The above words probably reflect the thoughts of many of us who supervise student teachers. This thought happens to be from Hugh Burke, a teacher seconded from a school district to work with student teachers, and one of the key players in establishing a collaborative project between a university and a school district in order to enhance the experiences student teachers have in a teacher education program. The focus of this chapter is on describing how the project came about and on the conditions and circumstances that led to its apparent success. It is not our intention to discuss what reforms must occur in school–university relationships, but rather how institutions can collaborate in order to discover and implement reform. We argue that successful institutional collaboration in teacher education can be fostered through the structure of teacher education programs.

Collaboration is necessary in teacher education because, typically, there exist two solitudes, one in the schools and one in the universities (Lieberman, 1988; Sarason, 1992). Rarely do schools and universities engage in meaningful conversation during research (Tikunoff and Ward, 1983) or during the conduct of teacher education (Clift and Say, 1988). Consequently, there has been a clarion call for school–university partnerships (Goodlad, 1988), 'organic collaboration' (Schlechty and Whitford, 1988), or networks, coalitions, and collaboratives (Lieberman, 1994; McLaughlin, 1994).

What, then, is collaboration? Collaboration can be defined as 'to work in combination with' (OED). Put differently:

Collaboration involves the mutual negotiation of purposes and interests by parties committed to the common goal of program improvement.

> Each of these parties has its own interests in and purposes for teacher education which, taken together, eventually emerge as the agenda for preservice teacher preparation . . . Collaboration, then, is the shared negotiation of purpose and task (Grimmett, 1993:200).

We take this to mean work accomplished through a mix of different people or institutions, as distinct from collegial work, or work that is done through members of a like institution, or body of colleagues. Implicit in this meaning of collaboration is that such a mix of people come to a task with a mix of reasons and a mix of motives or purposes for the collaboration. They typically agree to a unifying vision, but for different reasons. Moreover, they each bring their own abilities to the central task. A critical issue in developing collaborative projects, then, is how to bring people together who are not institutional colleagues, yet who have complementary strengths and interests, and can share common work and a common vision. A second issue involves setting the stage so that these people can work freely, yet each within the limits of their own particular personal and institutional set of circumstances. A third issue has to do with unravelling the motivation that might propel such a group in a common direction.

There have been many instances of successful collaboration in teacher education (Cochran-Smith and Lytle, 1993). However, much of this literature has been focused on the grand purposes of collaboration and on the programs developed, or on the outcomes of those programs. There has been less focus on the way that collaboration occurs, or on the circumstances that facilitate such collaboration.

In our case, the collaboration occurred largely due to the fundamental assumptions underlying the teacher education program at Simon Fraser University. These assumptions, for example about the validity of teachers' craft knowledge (Grimmett and MacKinnon, 1992), encouraged a collaborative project between the university and a neighbouring school district. Such a project brings together a mix of people, provides a motive for collaboration, and permits the freedom required when working through any innovation.

In this chapter, we first briefly describe the teacher education program at Simon Fraser University, then describe the development of our collaborative project. Finally, we analyze the interaction of the two so as to see how the structure of a teacher education program can facilitate both intra- and inter-institutional collaboration.

Simon Fraser University's Teacher Education Program

The teacher education program at Simon Fraser has been discussed (see Chapter 13). We would like only to call attention in this chapter to those parts of the program which enabled this collaborative project. These include differentiated staffing, cohort grouping, vertical staffing and a model of reflective practice

(Schön, 1983; 1987) and deliberate action (Kennedy, 1987) which underlies the other program assumptions.

There are three parts to the staffing at Simon Fraser University. The first part is composed of faculty who teach within the program as part of their regular teaching duties in the Faculty of Education. There are also seconded public school teachers, called faculty associates, who teach within the program for a while, typically two years. They are selected as outstanding teachers who are able to articulate their beliefs and demonstrate exemplary practices. Normally, two faculty associates are teamed with one faculty member to teach twenty-eight student teachers in what is loosely called a module.[2] The third part of the staffing consists of the teachers with whom the students are placed during their practicum, called school associates. Since the practica last for six out of the twelve months, the school associates play a very important role in the development of student teachers. At a structural level, then, the program already sets the preconditions for collaboration – it brings people with divergent backgrounds together who work to a common task. Importantly, the staff are not hierarchically differentiated. Each has a unique task, but there is no one who retains ultimate authority within the module structure. Even the task of writing an interim report on a student teacher calls for collaboration between the module team and the school associate. However, it is the case that the university-based personnel, that is, the faculty member and the faculty associates, have the prime responsibility for structuring the on-campus learning experiences for each module.

Another important part of the program lies in the grouping of students. They are placed in groups of twenty-eight students, called a module, and they travel through two of the three semesters together. Although the modules are loosely coupled, each module is able to function independently of the others for all practical purposes. Instruction is done by module, placements to schools are done by module, and both planning and evaluation are done by module. There is little overlap of module instructors, except when certain arrangements are developed through shared needs or interests. Modules operate as micro-programs within a larger programmatic context. The major implication of this structure for collaboration is to limit the number of people who have to be involved in any arrangements that the module may make. As we will outline, institutional collaboration can be arranged through the module structure, which affects only one cohort group of twenty-eight student teachers and does not require changes for the program at large.

Vertical staffing is the third structural component that allows for uncomplicated collaboration. As suggested by Tom (1995), vertical staffing means that a small group of instructors is responsible for all of the instruction provided to a specific group of students. This is the case at Simon Fraser University, as the module team is responsible for all instruction and supervision during the practicum semesters. In this arrangement decisions about curriculum and instruction in the module are limited in their effect to that group of instructors, which allows great internal flexibility within the module.

These structural decisions seem to be based on a central assumption about the nature of professional knowledge and learning. The Simon Fraser University program is built to allow students to learn through scaffolded practice, in the context of classrooms. It has long practica (amounting to six months of the professional year); the practica are concurrent with, or indeed precede, the theoretical frameworks offered by the university. The knowledge of the seconded public school teachers is seen as paramount in shaping the experience for student teachers, not as supplementary to university-generated knowledge (Cornbleth and Ellsworth, 1994). It is an assumption which is most closely described as one of deliberate action (Kennedy, 1987). Such an assumption does not merely lead to collaboration: It demands it. When a teacher education program involves as much practice as does Simon Fraser's, then collaboration with the field is a fact of life. The only questions to be addressed are about the scope and the explicitness of the collaboration, not about whether it will occur.

The module in which we taught serves as a good example. It consisted of a faculty member, two faculty associates, twenty-eight school associates and twenty-eight students. We had to work together, and we represented a microcosm of school–university relations. We were not bound by a prescribed curriculum or even a particular set of procedures; rather, we had to make sense of our situation together in light of the program's explicitly stated goals. Whether or not to collaborate was never at issue. The nature of the collaboration had to be worked out. There were, of course, routine ways of proceeding that were passed on from year-to-year by way of an 'oral culture.' From time-to-time, however, there would be triggers that caused us to rethink the routines and to take advantage of the degree of autonomy that existed. One such trigger was an initiative on the part of the Director of the Professional Programs to introduce action research into the program.

The Collaborative Project

We were assigned together as a module team. One of us, Judith, was a new faculty member, with a background in literacy research and education and a strong interest in teacher education. Bonnie and Hugh, the faculty associates, each came with over twenty years of teaching experience, as well as a strong background in staff development, having been on two different district staffs as program coordinators. We had each had a brief orientation to the program, and were confronting the challenge of preparing our students to teach, and the equal challenge of working out our various roles in doing so.

As we began to plan, we started talking about what each of us wanted from the experience, and how we could link our strengths and interests to the needs of the students so that everyone might benefit from what we could each provide. We were aware of the routinized pattern: teach three weeks on the campus; place students in classrooms; supervise them; teach some more;

supervise some more. It was fine, but we felt that such a pattern led to apprenticeship instead of reflection or deliberate action. We felt that the school associates were too far removed from what happened on campus, that teachers could have a stronger voice in both educational research and teacher education, and that teachers and schools alike would benefit from engaging with educational researchers and teacher educators in an ongoing dialogue about teaching.

All these thoughts are familiar enough to anyone who has been involved with teacher education. What caused us to attempt a more extensive collaborative effort to address these issues was the call from the Director of Simon Fraser University's Professional Development Program to engage in action research as part of our work in teacher education. As he made this call, it was not clear to us what precisely was meant by action research; we assumed it to amount to any codified attempt to inquire into our own practice as teacher educators, and to model such inquiry for our students. On reflection, it was a call to return to our beginnings as reflective practitioners in our own program, and to make that perspective clear.

During the initial planning stages, we shared what each of us might bring and what each of us might want from this involvement. It became clear that, although we had different agendas, we could help one another, and in the process create exciting conditions under which our students might learn. Judith was interested in studying cognitive change in student teachers. She wanted to study the factors which led to students' 'thinking like teachers'. Hugh was also interested in this idea, and wanted to pursue it as a possible thesis. Bonnie wanted to learn more about some of the foundations of the new curricula, as she planned to return to the classroom and wanted some insight into what might be most successful in working with her students.

These interests were balanced with strengths. Judith would be able to help with the research methodology. Hugh and Bonnie could bring their expertise in staff development and workshop presentation to the teaching of the students, and both were familiar with the new curricula. Together, we decided to articulate the assumptions of reflective, deliberate action in the program, and so ask the students to engage in action research on the new curriculum along with us. Finally, we would conduct our own research to see if this research carried out by the students helped them to think like teachers.

In order to do this, we faced several challenges. Where would we find school associates who would allow student teachers to try new practices in the classroom? In fact, we needed school associates who would not only sanction it, but also would become collaborative partners, prepared to spend much of their own time supporting the student teachers as they reflected on their efforts. We wanted to find school associates who would be interested in trying action research and who could model teaching as an active learning process in situations where the students could develop the personal practical knowledge so essential to becoming effective teachers.

Fortune was in the air. Hugh had recently spoken to a principal in his own school district, Delta, who had a vision of creating a teacher education site at his school. The school, a senior secondary school, shared grounds with a junior high school and an elementary school. That is, the site afforded the opportunity to work at varying grade levels with various teachers in differing buildings, yet all within a stroll of each other. We contacted the principal.

In addition, the provincial government in British Columbia was in the process of implementing a massive revision to the curricula for every grade and every subject in the public school system. They had called for research proposals from districts and schools, but not from universities. These proposals, if successful, would be funded to allow teachers to explore the new curricula in their classrooms. With the school district support and enthusiasm, we jointly applied for and received funding to engage in collaborative classroom research on implementing one of the components of the curricula – curricular integration.

At this point, we wish that we could regale you with tales of the difficulties that we encountered, and provide sage advice on how to overcome them. The bald truth is that the project fell into place quite easily when the various stakeholders met and realized the overlapping purposes and interests that could be met by involvement in one collaborative project. Of course, we had to make plans and conduct meetings and reach agreements. But all of this formality was conducted against a background where a few people from each institution had decided that they wanted to try collaboration. The formal arrangements between the institutions came after the real arrangements were in place. Formal arrangements were facilitated by the fact that no system-wide commitments were necessary; it only involved one school site and one Simon Fraser University module. The teachers had already indicated a willingness to be involved in the teacher education program, and they agreed to what was essentially an extension of that involvement as part of their professional growth toward understanding the new provincial curricula.

In the end, the Delta school district agreed to enter into a formal agreement of collaboration with Simon Fraser University, establishing our module and the principal's school as the collaborative units. The district, supporting their principal's original vision, saw it as an opportunity to assist their own teachers in trying out the new provincial curricula with support from the university. The collaboration was a way in which they could give teachers explicit permission to try out new approaches, and yet be assured that there would be considerable reflection on those approaches. The district provided funding so that teachers who were involved with the module could attend orientation and discussion sessions. In return, the university provided some release funding and a series of after-school workshops for teachers. Provincial Government wanted teachers to explore the new curricula and was willing to provide funding. This proposal was made through the school district, which was eligible for these grants, but was written by the university module team. This working together was, of course, facilitated by the connections with the field and with the Ministry that the faculty associates brought to the university.

That is, collaboration between the institutions was facilitated by the presence of people who personified an existing link between the institutions, and so brought the social and political connections that enabled joint effort. For example, the fact that one of us had worked in Delta meant that we had easy access to the principal of the school, the assistant superintendents, and the teachers with whom we wanted to work. Likewise, the faculty member brought the faculty into the collaboration, working with the Dean and the other faculty to explain the project, to secure additional university funding and to set up the workshop series. We always found ourselves working with friends. The formal agreement was, in the end, an extension of the working relationship built into the module as a result of the structure of the program. What was remarkable was the degree of trust the institutions placed in their representatives in this module. That, of course, was possible because of the limitations that the module structure placed on the size of the collaboration. It became, in effect, a safe place to try out a different relationship.

In this way, each of us benefitted through being able to pursue our own interests. Our students benefitted from being able to work in classrooms, freed from the common constraints of 'business as usual' instruction (Miller, 1990), and by learning to reflect on their teaching in both an informal and formal way. The schools benefitted by being able to examine the new curricula in a non-threatening way and by providing teachers with a way of responding to the new program through a provincial research grant. The teachers were also provided with in-service support from the faculty. The University gained clustered placements in a school district and financial support for their teacher education program in the form of release time for school associates. The Provincial Government gained valuable feedback on their new program.

This program led to a number of benefits for the participants. It became a case of what Cochran-Smith (1991) calls 'collaborative resonance', where novices and experienced professionals worked together in a situation; where power was shared among participants in the community; where knowledge about teaching was socially constructed; where, 'in the end, the power to liberalize and reinvent notions of teaching, learning and schooling [was] located in neither the university nor the school but in the collaborative work of the two' (p. 284).

This program enhanced the model of deliberate action through involving the students in action research (Liston and Zeichner, 1990). It provided clustered placements (Grimmett, 1988). It provided our student teachers with school associates who modelled teaching as an active learning process when they co-planned action research projects with the students who provided time for reflection and encouraged innovation. These benefits have been discussed elsewhere (Burke, Scott and Skobel, 1993; Burke and Scott, 1992), as have the results of the research (Burke, Scott and Skobel, 1991; Scott and Burke, 1991). Suffice it to say that the collaboration had significant positive results and few negative ones. As an assistant superintendent in the school district said, 'This project had no downsides.'

Judith A. Scott and Hugh Burke

The downsides that did exist were mitigated for this administrator, and for others, by the positive aspects of the program. However, there were some downsides. The amount of time devoted to this collaboration was extensive, as meetings were held regularly with the steering committee, the students, and district personnel. These meetings certainly smoothed the collaborative process, as concerns were dealt with before they became problems, but they did take an extraordinary amount of time. Many days the module team did not return home until late in the evening.

At the university, some of the other modules become jealous of the monetary support apparent in this project, and tension arose between our faculty associates and some of their colleagues. It was not a significant downside, but it did put a slight damper on their expression of enthusiasm for the project.

In retrospect, it seems apparent that the bicultural position of our faculty associates (Cornbleth and Ellsworth, 1994) put them in a unique position to understand and facilitate collaboration between the cultures of schools and universities. They had friends in both cultures, a vision of possibilities, and the expertise to pull these various groups together in a positive and productive framework.

On Facilitating Collaboration

Each collaborative effort takes place within a particular context and that context both limits and shapes the range of options available. This project can only be seen as one case in which collaboration was apparently successful, and is therefore limited in the lessons that can be learned from it. However, it can provide some useful insights into the conditions that did facilitate our collaboration. The conditions that seem important to us are those which enabled us to understand the various agendas held by the partners in the collaboration, subjugation of issues relating to power and authority, permission and a challenge to try new ideas, and the constant redefinition of our professional development program.

Such conditions are to be found within the structure of the teacher education program at Simon Fraser. They include differentiated vertical staffing, the lack of assigned roles, the dependence on a goal-driven program rather than on one with a prescriptive curriculum and the module structure. Each of these conditions seems worthy of individual comment.

Differentiated Staffing

Differentiated staffing is the condition that allowed us to collaborate in the first place. It provides for a continual flow of different ideas in the teacher education program through ensuring a regular influx of new people in the form of Faculty Associates. People of varying backgrounds are brought into the program

196

and share a similar set of circumstances and intents in the short term, yet vary widely in background and interests. In the case of our module, each member of the team faced a common problem – how best to structure the learning for student teachers in our module – yet each brought different personal and professional interests and networks to bear on that problem.

Differentiated staffing also puts institutions in touch with one another, by providing staff from those institutions with the opportunity to work closely together. Collaboration between the Delta school district and Simon Fraser University therefore came about at the policy-making level because their respective representatives lobbied for it. There had been no grand institutional talks beforehand, no formal overtures between institutions. Differentiated staffing thus made it possible for personal collaboration to lead to institutional collaboration, rather than the opposite, which seems to be more commonly the case and which, Hargreaves (1994) maintains, leads to 'contrived collegiality'.

Lack of Hierarchical Roles

The lack of assigned roles or hierarchical structure at several levels was another important element of our collaboration. For collaboration to be successful, it seems to us that each partner has to be considered with parity. When any imbalance occurs, considerations of power enter into the relationship, making it difficult for each partner to feel that his or her own agenda is equally important, thus reducing the motivation to collaborate.

Issues of power and authority present serious problems for relationships between faculty associates, or clinical faculty, and university faculty members in many settings (Cornbleth and Ellsworth, 1994). It is often the case that the craft knowledge of faculty associates is seen as supplementary to university-generated knowledge and of lower status. In the Simon Fraser University model, the three members of the instructional team are seen as partners, each contributing equal but different parts to the marriage of theory and practice. There is a joint responsibility to re-create instruction as new members join the team.

Entering a partnership with the district meant that the needs of both institutions needed to be considered. Neither took precedent, and both were necessary to complete the project. At the school level, the school associates were not held up as models to emulate, but as partners with the student teachers engaged in action research. This allowed the student teachers to explore issues of teaching with another, more experienced learner.

Permission and Challenge to try New Ideas

Permission and encouragement to try this innovation came from all levels of administration. At the university, the Director of the Professional Development Program called for module teams to engage in action research as part of our work in teacher education. We accepted this as a challenge and began to put together a plan. In addition, the Ministry of Education for the Province of British Columbia actively sought input for their new curricula and not only challenged teachers to try out the program, but provided funding to do so. The district, encouraged by the Ministry and the professional development potential for their teachers, fully supported the project with release days and personal commitment.

The fact that these projects were valued and supported seemed to help motivate the teachers and student teachers to explore teaching through action research in their classrooms. In the end, permission and challenge led to celebration and the presentation of the action research projects to all participants in the collaboration. Teachers valued this opportunity to see the work of the other teams, and to see what curricular integration might look like in Grade 4–12 classrooms.

Lack of Prescribed Curriculum

The lack of a prescribed curriculum within the program was another important condition which led to our collaboration. The goals of the program are explicitly laid out; the method of achieving them is not. This lack of a formal scope and sequence of curriculum creates a condition under which the teaching in the program is always problematic. Module members work as a team, and each year one faculty associate leaves while another arrives. As in any team-teaching situation, this means that the members of the team have to find what each module teaching member can bring, what understandings they have, and how they view teaching and learning, before successful planning can occur. Without constraints of authority of rank or of curriculum, the articulation of these abilities and beliefs leads to the annual reinventing of the program, and necessitates collaboration.

These three conditions – differentiated staffing, the lack of hierarchy, and the lack of a formal curriculum – are underscored by the fact that the staffing in the program is vertical, not horizontal. That is, every element of the teacher education program is the responsibility of the module staff. No formal compartmentalization of curriculum or role exists; each member of the module team is presumed to be capable of a number of different roles. What roles each will play is left up to the team. For example, in our module each of the team taught some classes, worked with school associates, and was involved in writing reports on the progress of students and the project. The Faculty Associates assumed the role of supervising student teachers, while the Faculty member assumed the role of writing about and organizing much of the work outside classrooms. At one time, one of us observed another, who was observing a student teacher, in order to give feedback on the quality of the observation process. To function well, we had to function as a team. Vertical staffing requires collaboration at a personal level, and such personal collaboration inevitably leads to collaboration between the various institutions represented.

The Module Structure

The module structure also seems to have been an important element in facilitating institutional collaboration. By freeing us from strong program constraints enforced through a timetable or other bureaucratic necessities, it enabled us to create a unique set of conditions without disrupting other students or faculty within the program. Certainly there are other advantages to cohort grouping (see Tom, Chapter 9; Anders, 1990), but the ability to try out alternative approaches quickly is an important one. It has the additional advantage of limiting any possible negative consequences of an innovation to a small group, rather than spreading them over a whole program. When an innovation works, it can be quickly adopted by other modules. For example, after our successful collaboration with the Delta school district, four other modules entered into similar collaborative arrangements with other school districts within the following twelve months.

Conclusion

We found that the teacher education program created in a module is a microcosm of what could happen in the larger world under ideal circumstances. Change is created by those people directly involved in it, rather than being an institution-wide affair in which large-scale consent is needed for any innovation. The relations between teachers and faculty are left open to negotiation. Rather than trying to impose a common agenda on all, the module structure allows for the merging of agendas. It leaves timetabling and teaching arrangements sufficiently open so that a module staff, as a microcosm of school and university relations, can create arrangements to suit the collaboration that must take place.

Because the participants can structure a module to engage their personal and professional agendas, motivation to collaborate as individuals is implicit. As the team members in a module have strong ties to their own institutions, individual agendas and small group collaboration lead to the merging of institutional agendas and, eventually, to institutional collaboration. In this way, personal and institutional renewal are naturally-evolving outcomes of the program.

The role of leadership cannot be discounted in this picture. The organizational arrangements at Simon Fraser have always been open to such collaboration, yet it did not occur. It took a Director who was open to change and trusted people to give a nudge in the right direction and open the program up to its own possibilities. Leadership, in this case, was less a matter of showing the way and more a matter of giving permission to others to find the way. He asked us to investigate and reflect on our own practice. We ended up in an institutional collaboration. The structure of the program made it possible; the request of the Director provided permission; the outcomes for all of us made it desirable.

Notes

1 The authors would like to acknowledge other key participants in initiating this project: Bonnie Skobel, Surrey School District (our second Faculty Associate); Sherry Sprungman, Campbell River School District (SFU campus coordinator); Neil Ingles (principal, South Delta secondary); and Bill Wakefield (Assistant Supperintendent, Delta School District).
2 Module here is meant to designate that each separate section is part of the larger Professional Development Program, but not a section of the program that different students may take at various times during the course of one academic year.

References

ANDERS, D. (1990) *Student teachers in a block program: Patterns and platitudes*, Paper presented to the Annual Meeting of the American Educational Research Association, Boston, MA.

BURKE, H. and SCOTT, J. (1992) *The Revision project: Restructuring teacher education*. Paper presented to the Annual Meeting of the American Educational Research Association, Atlanta, GA.

BURKE, H., SCOTT, J. and SKOBEL, B. (1991) *Emerging as teachers: What changes in perception occur along the way?*, Paper presented to the Canadian Society for Studies in Education, Kingston, Ontario.

BURKE, H., SCOTT, J. and SKOBEL, B. (1993) *Bringing teachers and teacher educators together*, Paper presented to the Annual Meeting of the American Educational Research Association, Atlanta, GA.

CLIFT, R.T. and SAY, M. (1988) 'Teacher education: Collaboration or conflict?', *Journal of Teacher Education*, **39**(3), 2–7.

COCHRAN-SMITH, M. (1991) 'Learning to teach against the grain', *Harvard Educational Review*, **61**(3), 279–310.

COCHRAN-SMITH, M. and LYTLE, S. (1993) *Inside/Outside: Teacher Research and Knowledge*, New York: Teachers College Press.

CORNBLETH, C. and ELLSWORTH, J. (1994) 'Teachers in teacher education: Clinical faculty roles and relationships', *American Educational Research Journal*, **31**(1), 49–70.

GOODLAD, J. (1988) 'School–university partnerships for educational renewal: Rationale and concepts', in SIROTNIK, K. and GOODLAD, J. (Eds) *School–university Partnerships in Action*, New York: Teachers College Press, 3–31.

GRIMMETT, P.P. (1988) 'Implications of research in teaching and teacher education for the content and delivery of teacher education programs', in GILLISS, G. (Ed.) *Extended Programs of Teacher Education*, Ottawa: Canadian Teachers' Federation, pp. 38–85.

GRIMMETT, P.P. (1993) 'Re-visiting collaboration', *Journal of Education for Teaching*, **19**(4–5), 195–203.

GRIMMETT, P.P. and MACKINNON, A.M. (1992) 'Craft knowledge and the education of teachers', *Review of Research in Education*, **18**, 385–456.

HARGREAVES, A. (1994) *Changing Teachers, Changing Times: Teachers' Work and Culture in the Postmodern Age*, London, UK: Cassell.

KENNEDY, M. (1987) 'Inexact sciences: Professional education and the development of expertise', in ROTHKOPF, E.Z. (Ed.) *Review of Research in Education*, Washington, DC: American Educational Research Association.

LIEBERMAN, A. (1988) 'The Metropolitan School Study Council: A living history', in SIROTNIK, K. and GOODLAD, J. (Eds) *School-university Partnerships in Action* (pp. 69–85). New York: Teachers College Press, 69–85.

LIEBERMAN, A. (1994) 'Teacher development: Commitment and challenge', In GRIMMETT, P.P. and NEUFELD, J. (Eds) *Teacher Development and the struggle for Authenticity: Professional Growth and Restructuring in the Context of Change*, New York: Teachers College Press, 15–30.

LISTON, D. and ZEICHNER, K. (1990) 'Reflective teaching and action research in preservice teacher education', *Journal of Education for Teaching*, **16**(3), 145–151.

MCLAUGHLIN, M.W. (1994) 'Strategic sites for teachers professional development', in GRIMMETT, P.P. and NEUFELD, J. (Eds) *Teacher Development and the Struggle for Authenticity: Professional Growth and Restructuring in the Context of Change*, New York: Teachers College Press, 31–51.

MILLER, L. (1990) *Teacher research: Practice and promise*, Paper presented to the Annual Meeting of the American Educational Research Association, Boston, MA.

SARASON, S. (1992) *The Predictable Failure of School Reform*, San Francisco, CA: Jossey-Bass.

SCHLECHTY, P. and WHITFORD, B. (1988) 'Shared problems and shared vision: Organic collaboration', in SIROTNIK, K. and GOODLAD, J. (Eds) *School-university Partnerships in Action*, New York: Teachers College Press, 191–204.

SCHÖN, D.A. (1983) *The Reflective Practitioner: How Professionals Think in Action*, New York: Basic Books.

SCHÖN, D.A. (1987) *Educating the Reflective Practitioner: Toward a New Design for Teaching and Learning in the Professions*, San Francisco, CA: Jossey-Bass.

SCOTT, J. and BURKE, H. (1991) *The SFU–Delta project: Synergy in Action*, Paper presented to the BC. College of Teachers Education Forum: Collaboration in teacher education. Richmond, BC.

TIKUNOFF, W. and WARD, B. (1983) 'Collaborative research on teaching', *The Elementary School Journal*, **83**(4), 453–68.

TOM, A.R. (1995) 'Stirring the embers: Reconsidering the structure of teacher education programs', in WIDEEN, M.F. and GRIMMETT, P.P. (Eds) *Changing Times and Teacher Education: Restructuring or Reconceptualization?* London: Falmer Press.

Chapter 15

Reconceptualizing Teacher Education: Preparing Teachers for Revitalized Schools[1]

Peter P. Grimmett

The challenge in compiling this edited volume was to explore why teacher education currently appears to be more in a state of turmoil – indeed, in some countries under attack – than in a state of continuous improvement. We set out to examine the issues confronting teacher education in selected Western countries in which restructuring efforts are taking place. What do we make of the efforts of policymakers to reshape the preparation of teachers in these different countries? Further, we saw the need to identify some policy directions for changing how we prepare teachers, and to provide examples of what that might mean at the level of action. We undertook this examination on the assumption that restructuring without reconceptualization does not lead to genuine change in teacher education. Put differently, we view the primary purpose of restructuring as opening up different opportunities for much-needed reconceptualization. Reconceptualization of teacher education is essential because we see the future of public education ultimately resting in the hands of efficacious teachers, and we believe that teacher efficacy is initially nurtured in challenging teacher preparation programs which are connected in some vital way to the university community.

In the introductory chapter, Marvin Wideen raised three important questions:

- What is the role of university faculties of education in teacher education?
- What kind of change in teacher education will represent a radical reconceptualization of current practice?
- Can teacher education meet the challenge? Can university faculties of education regain a central focus on teacher education?

A quick examination of the chapters in the book suggests the following response:

- that teacher education should be located in collaborative partnerships between faculties of education and the field on the one hand, and between faculties of education and university faculties of arts and science on the other;

- that such an arrangement calls for a radical reconceptualization of teacher preparation;
- that, provided faculties of education grasp the opportunity and reconceptualize both their mission and preparation programs, teacher education can meet the challenge that lies ahead.

In this conclusion chapter, I shall build on this response by attempting to show how a radical reconceptualization of teacher education will involve partnerships within and without the university and that these partnerships inexorably lead to interdisciplinary study and field-based teacher research in the preparation program. I begin by characterizing the intricate balance and tension between restructuring and reconceptualization as it emerges in the book. I then describe the current context of education and the kind of workplace setting – revitalized teaching in revitalized schools – for which teachers are being prepared. The aim here is to broaden the base of systemic reform of schools to include the systematic reconceptualization of teacher education, a necessary condition articulated by Howey and by Sheehan and Fullan. In so doing, I shall attempt to show how teacher education can contribute in constructive ways to actualizing the possibility of revitalized teaching in revitalized schools.

Tensions in Restructuring and Reconceptualization

David Imig[2] (1995) recently characterized five current trends in American education: 1) the nationalization of American education; 2) the transformation of schools; 3) increasing diversity in a multicultural context; 4) the professionalization of teaching; 5) the re-engineering of higher education. He concluded that the first four of these trends were now moribund and that the only one that mattered under the Republican 'Contract with America' was the last one. This did not fill him with a great deal of optimism about the future. He saw certain events as foreshadowing tremendous problems in teacher education. For example, the State of Colorado now has legislation in place mandating members of a faculty of education to undertake at least 15 hours per week in school classrooms. A further example lay in the move to place teacher licensure in the hands of local schools so that they can hire whomever they please, regardless of background and qualification. According to Imig, there are persistent threats to teacher education based in higher education. There is conservative sponsorship of anti-credential, alternative certification models for entry into teaching. Such sponsorship has spawned the belief that alternative certification programs are likely to be more responsive to minority recruitment. This is partially true but it also represents a right-wing co-optation of the language of diversity and multiculturalism. There is also strong support for school-based professional development programs and concerted efforts to uncouple teacher salary advancement from the accumulation of university credits.

This invidious picture from Washington reinforces the view emerging in this book that the future of university-based teacher education hangs in the balance. Restructuring efforts are already happening around the world at both the policy and the ground level of action. Policy and action must work in tandem for genuine change to occur. In many countries, however, these initiatives occur only at the policy level and represent *restructuring without purposeful reconceptualization*. When policy is used solely to coerce people at the ground level into working in ostensibly different ways, much resistance and little purposeful reconceptualization of teacher preparation takes place. In other countries, these initiatives also take place at the policy level but depict a more positive view of *restructuring in advance of reconceptualization* at the ground level. When policy is designed to pave the way for reconceptualization, there are grounds for optimism but still no actual evidence that teacher preparation will operate any differently. In very few places, then, are policy and action so closely aligned that policy initiatives represent a *restructuring arising out of reconceptualization* that has already been articulated at the ground level of action. When policy has ably reflected or successfully enabled reconceptualization at the action level, changes seem to have occurred that have effectively addressed the criticisms plaguing teacher education for the last thirty years or so.

Restructuring Without Purposeful Reconceptualization

Back in 1950, George Homans documented how changes in activity structures produce ripple effects throughout the human group. These changes affect the nature of the interactions that take place, which, in turn, influences the sentiments that people derive from their work. And these sentiments typically take on a normative force, governing what people may or may not do. Using today's language, Homans would have said that restructuring inevitably leads to some form of reconceptualization. In other words, even blunt forms of restructuring (the kind that is used euphemistically to describe corporate-style firings) provokes people to think about their work in different, though not always innovative, ways. Although it is possible to restructure in an adventitious and ultimately dysfunctional manner, the process nevertheless brings about some form of rethinking. The question thus becomes not one of whether restructuring occurs without reconceptualization but whether the kind of reconceptualization that restructuring precipitates is appropriately rigorous and purposeful.

Currently, many countries are re-introducing nineteenth century modes of teacher training with the United States, Australia and England in the vanguard. The rush to provide school-based training in these countries indicates scant critical examination of government motives for introducing such measures.

Nineteenth century industrialists made no bones about their motives. They wanted a work force skilled enough to operate their machines but not capable of questioning their place in the socio/political system. The idea of teaching children to think critically, to ask questions and solve problems would have seemed to them a recipe for their demise. They made sure that that did not happen by their control of the school system and its funding. Have things changed? Does it matter where teacher education takes place?

Howey's description of the situation in the United States suggests that teacher education is precariously balanced. He can find no national design for the reform of schools or teacher education. Indeed, the reform of schools occurs independent of teacher education. No incentive exists to bring the two together and the gap appears to be widening. This may be because preservice teacher education is regarded as a weak intervention and teacher educators are seen as being pedagogically limited. Howey criticizes American teacher education for not engaging in a fundamental re-examination of the nature of schooling in today's society, of the changing roles and responsibilities of teachers, and of the character of learning desired by today's youth. The cumbersome organization of American teacher education (over 1200 institutions, not all universities) and the idiosyncratic nature of the curriculum and lack of public accountability in the preparation process lamentably signal the need for externally imposed restructuring.

On this count, the situation in Norway is similar. The second of three big changes that Hauge reports taking place in Norwegian teacher education is an example of externally imposed restructuring without purposeful reconceptualization. All teacher education institutions outside of the university sector are being reorganized from 129 smaller institutions into 26 larger regional institutions. Such chronic inefficiencies in Norway and in the United States invite the external intervention of debt-conscious governments. Small wonder, then, that the conservative forces at work in both countries are considering and, in the case of the United States, encouraging a move towards alternative certification. Nevertheless, Howey firmly believes that reconceptualization of teacher education will only occur if it remains anchored in the university setting but closely tied to the realities and practical problems of schools. Regrettably, however, pedagogical cases that are grounded in domain-specific knowledge and state theoretical claims relative to the complexity of classroom life are all too rare in American teacher education.

The Australian context described by Tisher is equally in a state of disarray. Government restructuring has brought about numerous changes in teacher preparation: increases in the amount of school experience for preservice teachers; reduced supervision by university personnel; a phasing out of concurrent programs; a strengthening of subject discipline knowledge in elementary teachers; and the inclusion of business/industry experiences. Historically, the move of teacher education to university status from colleges of advanced education left a lingering question mark over the commitment of teacher educators to preparation within a university reward structure traditionally tilted toward research.

The preparation process therefore has many critics, but attempts to bring about change have largely ignored the calamitously docile and silent teacher educators. Education in Australia is a state concern that is funded federally. Consequently, federal restructuring initiatives are taken seriously. One of the aims of the national government is to renew the faculties of education – in Tisher's words, to eradicate 'obsolescent teaching'. Another is a national professional development program designed to renew teachers' knowledge of school curriculum subjects. A further one is to support the practicum supervision carried out by practising teachers through a teacher professional development fund. This has led to an emphasis on the training and accreditation of 'advanced skills teachers' as practicum supervisors and on an industrial model of partnership. Tisher views the result of this – a shift of decision making in teacher preparation from universities to local schools – as retrogressive. He posits that teacher education should remain university-based but become more connected with the pedagogy of the workplace.

The events in England provide a forbidding picture of what happens when radical restructuring is not accompanied by purposeful reconceptualization. Pimm and Selinger describe how government restructuring has essentially commodified schooling and teacher education in England. Disregarding important research findings, the national government has declared that the education system is in crisis and only market forces can save it. Any attempt by teachers and teacher educators to counter these assertions is treated with contempt. Schools, not universities, are seen as *the* place of learning to teach. Consequently, schools are given a dominant role to play in teacher preparation. The apprenticeship model is very much back in vogue. Universities become 'service providers' in the market place of education. Pimm and Selinger's critique is scathing. They liken the government to a neurotic constantly poking a fish called education to see how it is frying. They turn on its head the government's use of Orwell's phrase 'less is more', i.e., less government means more productivity. They show that less government in the form of privatization, heightened competition and reduced funding levels actually produces more government in the sense of increased regulation and intrusion into the practice and autonomy of professionals.

Alongside the myth of educational decline another myth has been cultivated in each of these three countries. This myth has it that so-called business people are capable of solving a variety of problems from the management of publicly funded hospitals to deciding the appropriate curriculum for the different levels of schooling. Such penetration of corporate interests into education is currently popular in the United States, Australia and England. At the same time, little opposition has been mounted by teacher educators against such interests. With few exceptions teacher education institutions in these countries appear to have accepted decisions about their place in the education system. In England the reaction by teacher education institutions to political depredation by the national government has been to fall into line and scramble for funds to do things with which they may not agree. While survival is clearly an important objective for any institution and any individual within an institution, this supine lack of critical resistance by teacher educators, particularly in England, is a predictable consequence of politically harsh restructuring that does not permit appropriately purposeful reconceptualization. Such restructuring represents change but not improvement. It is a first but huge step towards the eventual ravaging of university-connected teacher education.

Restructuring in Advance of Reconceptualization

When restructuring precedes reconceptualization, it often provokes a shallow, survival-oriented reaction. But restructuring of teacher education can also serve as an advance organizer for its subsequent reconceptualization. This is another theme emerging in the book. The chapters by Tuinman and Tom are central to it. Tuinman posits six propositions for restructuring that he believes will lead to a reconceptualization of teacher education. First, he suggests that formal agreements must be made between the university, its faculty of education and the field to operate jointly teacher education programs designed to meet local needs. Second, he insists that faculties of education make a public acknowledgment of their professional school status. Third, he is convinced that education faculty must be held accountable for an up-to-date knowledge of the profession. Fourth, he sees no reason why faculties of education have not and do not become models of good practice. Fifth, he stipulates that graduate education must include tougher requirements for methodology. And finally, he contends that universities must direct their scarce internal support for research specific to the mandate of each of their faculties. Such a policy, he claims, would foster the kind of research in teacher education he considers necessary (and currently lacking) in faculties of education. These are not idle ramblings; they are the carefully thought-out observations of an ex-dean of a faculty of education who is fundamentally committed to university-connected teacher education but who, from his particular vantage point, also sees the need for radical changes in its operation.

Tom contends that reconceptualization of teacher education will only occur when we attend to its deep structures and stop tinkering with its surface patterns. He challenges four sets of taken-for-granted structural assumptions around intensity, sequencing, staffing and grouping. He argues strongly for compressed teacher education experiences over the current gradualist approach. He suggests that practice must precede knowledge and that vertical staffing with faculty teams committed to the program (as distinct from a course) and to team teaching should replace the current emphasis on horizontal staffing, which he sees as exposing students in superficial and disorganized ways to more material than they can possibly absorb, thereby promoting breadth without depth. And he is convinced that students need to experience a shared ordeal with a cohort rather than the current emphasis on regrouping.

The case of Canada described by Sheehan and Fullan is one that contains many of the structural features suggested by Tuinman and Tom. Like the one in its neighbour to the south, the Canadian teacher education situation is also disconnected from school reform but it is contained in a relatively limited number of institutions. Thus the picture painted by Sheehan and Fullan is somewhat optimistic, relative to the harsh political restructuring taking place in England and Norway (and probably the United States). They see growing pressure points of restructuring that suggest great potential for future reconceptualization. In British Columbia, the creation of the College of Teachers and university colleges, together with province-wide curriculum reform, has acted as a catalyst for change and spawned numerous collaborative projects, like the one reported by Scott and Burke in Chapter 14. In Ontario, the lengthening of teacher preparation and the building of preservice-inservice links represent important steps forward. The Learning Consortium at the Faculty of Education at the University of Toronto (FEUT) has many of the structural features suggested by Tom in Chapter 9, such as, student cohorts, faculty team teaching, clustered partner schools, a focus on educational reform, embedded inquiry, 150 of 300 days in focused field placements and internships, but this represents action at the ground level rather than the policy level. Thus, despite considerable debate and some action, Sheehan and Fullan are unable to report significant breakthroughs. They trace this lack of breakthrough to the history of teacher education since its original move to the university setting. Although the governance of teacher education is essentially decentralized, faculties of education have tended to be reactive (as distinct from proactive) to the demands of both university and government bureaucracies. Up until recently, the location of teacher education in universities has therefore proved to be problematic because of the heavy emphasis in these settings on theory and research at the expense of practice. Other faculties typically downplay the importance of pedagogy in teaching in favour of an emphasis on subject discipline knowledge. Faculties of education have also placed little emphasis on induction or on schools as learning institutions, and teacher education programs have been slow to come to grips with the prevalent social issues (multiculturalism, mainstreaming, gender bias, ESL, etc.) of the day. Nevertheless, Sheehan and Fullan contend that locating teacher education in the university should be a strength and that breakthroughs are more likely to occur around the experience of university–field partnerships like the Learning Consortium and Professional Development Schools (PDSs).

The teacher education situation in Norway is mixed. Hauge reports on three big changes taking place in Norwegian teacher education, two of which represent attempts at restructuring in advance of reconceptualization. First, preservice elementary and secondary preparation programs are lengthened from six months to one year. This change paves the way for much program reorganization. Second, the curriculum of teacher education reform has two important thrusts: one towards increasing teachers' knowledge of the subject disciplines, and the other emphasizing reflective practice and collaboration. These restructuring measures provide opportunities for teacher educators in this country to do some serious revisiting of the preparation process.

Alarcão characterizes the Portuguese situation as being in need of and ready for reconceptualization of teacher preparation, but she fears that the government's debt-reducing political agenda might only allow for restructuring. The case of Portugal thus represents an example of restructuring in advance of a reconceptualization that did not occur in the previous two decades and that now needs to occur in the 1990s. Since the 1974 revolution, a discourse emerged among educational researchers influencing teacher education policy. This led to the expansion of teacher preparation in the 1970s and 1980s. This restructuring located it in higher education but with strong connections to schools and the community, emphasized the integration of academic and professional knowledge, and fostered a positive attitude towards research. The opportunity to reconceptualize teacher preparation was present but did not materialize. Instead, the discourse of the 1970s and 1980s became several discourses in the 1990s that confounded government policy. Consequently, this decade has witnessed a shift in emphasis from preservice to in-service education. In-service education is now regarded as a right for teachers and is seen as more relevant and more appreciated by politicians than preservice. Teacher preparation has suffered as a result of this shift. Large classes and a tendency to lecture about rather than demonstrate important pedagogical strategies have shown the need to reconceptualize the preparation process. However, the political reality may dictate what will happen via a restructuring process unaccompanied by appropriately purposeful reconceptualization. What was an optimistic picture appears, then, to be changing.

Both the Australian and American contexts have features of this use of restructuring. Tisher cites the two year post-baccalaureate Bachelor of Teaching degree at Melbourne University where students spend the second year in an internship. He also cites the not unproblematic double degree at Deakin University that is offered jointly by the faculty of education and other faculties. Howey finds limited cause for optimism in the United States' National Board's attempt to set standards of accomplished practice around self-reflection and classroom action. He also applauds the involvement of teacher leaders as clinical faculty in teacher preparation. He describes the Holmes group's attempts at restructuring as a wake-up call for American teacher education and documents the important but small efforts of the Renaissance, Goodlad, and UNITE groups to bring about change in teacher education. But none of these efforts equates to a fundamental reconceptualization of teacher education; rather, they represent valiant but small attempts to use new structures as a catalyst for rethinking the teacher preparation process.

Restructuring Arising out of Reconceptualization

The evidence of a progressive wedge of practice at the ground level in teacher education suggests a third way of viewing restructuring, namely, that which arises out of a reconceptualization process that is taking place or has already occurred in the action setting. In other words, the purpose of restructuring becomes one of changing the organization so that good ideas and strategies born in practice can flourish and not be stymied by existing bureaucratic forces.

Wassermann's use of case teaching is an example of this form of restructuring. Having become convinced of the need to engage students actively with content in a manner that stimulates them to think deeply about the issues, Wassermann sought out a strategy that has been successfully used to foster such learning in faculties of business, law, and medicine for over fifty years. This 'pedagogy for all seasons', as she refers to a case, is a complex educational instrument containing the *big ideas* of the curriculum in the form of a narrative accompanied by open-ended, higher-order study questions and a concluding *kicker*, a dilemma producing dissonance, that shifts the teacher educator's role from one of giving answers to one of elevating ambiguity and moving students from dependence to autonomy. In so doing, teacher educators facilitate student discussion and examination of the big ideas in all their complexity using small group work and total group debriefing. Thus, the decision to use case teaching in teacher education stemmed from Wassermann's fundamental reconceptualization of how students teachers best learn the craft of teaching. By restructuring the teacher education experience around cases, she succeeded in changing the learning outcomes. Students became actively involved and motivated to learn, they initiated their own questions of inquiry and developed better habits of thinking, and ultimately they became better prepared for handling the complexity and ambiguity of classroom teaching. Restructuring arising from a fundamental reconceptualization of how to prepare teachers not only brings about educationally defensible changes in teacher education practices but it also alters the outcomes, producing a teacher capable of entering the workforce with a much clearer initial grasp of the issues and complexity involved in teaching in today's rapidly changing social context.

Carson's use of reflective practice further illustrates this kind of restructuring. He attributes to traditional teacher educators a sense of misunderstanding their place in the world (by placing themselves at the centre) which has caused them to create an ever-expanding representational world, with research on teaching, that closes them and their students off from experiencing the world as it actually is. He is convinced, however, that he and his students need to re-think the preparation process from the vantage point of how they live together pedagogically. This fundamental reconceptualization leads him to embrace reflective practice as a way of restructuring the program to create spaces and open up places where such reframing can take place. He sees this restructuring as helping to forestall the usual shallow hyperactivity of teacher education, because the added structure of action research encourages students to understand the questions facing social education and to consider alternative ways of forging relationships with and between pupils, subject matter, and the milieu. But action research is a two-edged sword; teacher educators have to subject their own pedagogical practice to similar scrutiny. Accordingly, Carson relates how he learned that reflection repositions teacher educators as instructors who create uncertainties, that examining the taken-for-granted aspects of one's practice precipitates intense self-doubt in teacher educators as their role as so-called experts is destabilized and their self unsettled, and that the process of learning to teach for students is one of constitution and reconstitution of a professional identity. Preparing students to teach, then, is preparing them to live in the tension between vulnerability and competence, a tension that this form of restructuring (based on its reconceptualist assumptions) requires teacher educators to model and exhibit.

Dittmer and Frischetti's description of Wigginton's Foxfire approach represents a further example of restructuring that arises out of a reconceptualization of teaching and teacher education. The eleven Foxfire principles represent an attempt to restructure teacher education around Dewey's original reconceptualization of teaching as forging connections between curriculum and students' interests/needs. Dittmer and Frischetti relate how this restructuring proved cataclysmic for some of their colleagues causing much resistance and grief because it sanctioned an experimental approach to teacher education that changed the ground rules and challenged the intellectual and cultural assumptions undergirding their colleagues' image of themselves as a repository of expert knowledge. This leads Dittmer and Frischetti to question whether the university, if it exists for the faculty as they cite Sarason as suggesting, is the appropriate setting for teacher preparation. They go on to articulate how the Foxfire approach embodies the conditions under which preparation can be appropriately connected to the university. It involves a school-based, collaborative approach framed around the eleven Foxfire principles in a professional development school (PDS) where university and school personnel team teach courses with a project focus. The overall outcome reported by Dittmer and Frischetti is that students feel better prepared to enter the rigors of classroom teaching.

The faculty associate role at Simon Fraser University reported by Dawson represents an innovative restructuring of the clinical faculty role that derived from a reconceptualization of teacher education seeking to involve, honour and validate the work and knowledge of school practitioners. That this restructuring first occurred over 25 years ago is noteworthy. Indeed, it seems that the idea of involving school practitioners as central players in teacher preparation was so far ahead of its time that a small but dominant section of the faculty at this institution now appears prone to view it as a dated conceptualization. Given that many teacher education institutions around the world have recently begun to espouse the use of clinical faculty, the local trend described by Dawson is just a little ironic. Although the intended dialectic has, in some quarters, been interpreted as a threat – presumably by professors with similar worldviews to those at the University of Louisville for whom the Foxfire changes were cataclysmic – the chapter by Scott and Burke clearly shows that opportunities for collaboration with the field still abound in the Simon Fraser context. The project they report came about when additional restructuring by the program director and the provincial government introduced conditions that fostered the shared negotiation of purpose and task in the education of teachers. This additional restructuring arose out of the original reconceptualization that viewed teacher education as the joint property of the university and the profession. The project thus shows how an agreement reached between the university and school district with the blessing of the provincial government enabled them to set up a module framed around action research for students in clustered placements. In so doing, they illustrate some of the structural changes, such as vertical staffing, shared ordeal with a cohort, stress on practical knowledge, that Tom views as essential if teacher education is to meet the challenge it faces.

Differences in Restructuring and Reconceptualization: Another Look

It is intriguing to compare the effects of restructuring arising out of reconceptualization of teacher education with the effects of harsh, politically motivated restructuring that precludes purposeful reconceptualization. Whereas the latter was met with docility, silence, and little resistance, the former created inordinate stress and tension for those involved. What are we to make of this? I believe it suggests that teacher educators resist ardently when they recognize and disagree with a fundamental reconceptualization undergirding efforts at restructuring the preparation process. In other words, when their practice world is threatened and potentially destabilized by a competing set of assumptions about teacher education, they react in predictably conservative ways. At the same time, when restructuring is politically imposed in a manner that precludes reconceptualization around educational purposes, teacher educators appear not to resist because the rationale is typically stated as a response to fiscal exigency and seldom couched in the educational terms with which they are familiar. Consequently, the kind of stress and intellectual ferment that ought to accompany restructuring in whatever form it takes is lamentably absent when restructuring lacks and/or precludes an educational reconceptualization.

This state of affairs is as remarkable as it is deplorable. Granted there have been problems of disinformation in teacher education (Stones (1994) and public education (Berliner, 1992) where governments and other agencies appear to have set out to discredit education, but these actions surely call for considered, as distinct from supine, responses. What then can teacher educators do? Two broad courses of action come to mind. On the one hand, they could involve themselves in political action. This would involve them in seriously questioning how they can counter such disinformation and the naked use of political power. They must ask themselves honestly whether they are politically powerless but very good at beating the air? They must consider whether there are actions that need to be taken in opposition to current social, political and economic trends? These are important questions needing careful analysis if political action becomes the preferred option. On the other hand, teacher educators could work at reconceptualizing the preparation process at the ground level such that subsequent restructuring represents and reinforces the essential features of a reconceptualized process. It is to an examination of ways in which this third form of restructuring (arising out of reconceptualization at the ground level) could be nurtured and encouraged in teacher education that I now turn. I begin by characterizing the current context within which the education of teachers takes place. The purpose is to document succinctly the challenge facing teacher educators as they attempt to prepare revitalized teachers for revitalized schools.

Characterization of Current Context of Education

The Societal Context

The 1980s were not simply a decade of glitz and greed. More important, they ushered in a new era of American history – the triumphant conservatism of Reagan, Rambo and retrenchment. The Reagan revolution was a full-blown ideological response to the anemic liberalism of the Carter presidency that faltered in the face of runaway inflation, sluggish economic growth, and the relative erosion of North America's place in the global economy. The Rambo mentality harked back to a gunfighter readiness to do battle with an 'evil' empire at nearly any cost. And the unapologetic retrenchment has taken the form of making people more comfortable with their prejudices and reducing public focus on the disadvantaged. The '80s discouraged a serious national discourse on the deep problems confronting us . . . The unintended *cultural* consequence of this economic legacy was a spiritual impoverishment in which the dominant conception of the good life consists of gaining access to power, pleasure and property, sometimes by any means . . . and nonmarket values such as loyalty, commitment, service, care – even tenderness – can hardly gain a secure foothold in such a market culture . . . [and] that more and more of our children believe that life is a thoroughly hedonistic and narcissistic affair (West, 1994; 48; Emphasis in original).

West goes on to describe one of the telling moments of the 1980s came when a member of the Federal Communications Commission in the United States boasted that when television was deregulated, 'the marketplace will take care of children.' 'And, to a significant degree,' he writes, 'this unintentionally sad and sobering prophecy has come true. The entertainment industry, with its huge doses of sex and violence, has a disproportionately and often disgusting influence over us and our children' (pp. 48–9). Instead of reviving traditional values, then, the strong social conservatism of the 1980s has ironically yielded a populace in the 1990s that is suspicious of the common good and addicted to narrow pleasures.

The 1980s, then, revived a form of government mercantilism that brought a resurgence of neo-conservative thought and Reaganomics. This neo-conservative reaction, however, is only one aspect of the current circumstances of widespread disintegration of social and personal relationships, rampant un-certainty, and a discrediting of 'grand theories', such as rationalism, capitalism, and Marxism, etc. An equally important and contrasting aspect is the gaining of voice by previously marginalized groups and the unmitigated contestation – the uprising of ordinary people against experts – and lack of consensus that accompanies such circumstances (Grimmett and Neufeld, 1994).

The Educational Context

These two societal trends – the resurgence of the neo-conservative right and the gaining of voice by previously disenfranchized groups – have made deep inroads into the educational context, essentially foreshadowing the kinds of changes taking place in schools and classrooms (Grimmett and Neufeld, 1994; Hargreaves, 1994).

Considerable pressure currently exists for the reform of schools. This pressure is both political and economic and is usually applied from arenas of knowledge and social control, which are perceived as being outside particular school settings. It typically leads to a reactionary stance emphasizing central-ized policy making and control of resources, a concern with the delivery of subject-centered core knowledge and skills and an accompanying preoccupa-tion with external assessment of outcomes relative to national standards, and ultimately a reiteration of the teacher's role as 'curriculum-deliverer'. Marshall (1992) maintains that these reform efforts are steeped in behaviourist views of learning and consistent with the factory model of the 'classroom as a workplace'. 'Teachers/managers reward students/workers with praise or grades for pro-ducing worksheets/products as evidence that they have acquired the basic facts and skills that teachers have provided' (pp. 1–2).

At the same time, there is a call for the restructuring of schools from within as student-centered places of learning. This call is based on a view of knowledge as being humanly constructed and is framed around 'the need to redefine learning, to rethink the purposes of learning and the consequences for learners of different conceptualizations of learning, and to reconsider ele-ments essential to educational reform' (Marshall, 1992:3). The emphasis here is on 'classrooms-as-learning-places' (Marshall, 1992) where learning requires the active participation of the learner, taps into individual and social processes, assumes students to be constructors (as well as recipients) of knowledge, and ultimately views teachers as curriculum makers.

As society moves out of the economic, political, and organizational malaise of a modern, industrial age into a postmodern, information age dependent on flexible, globalized economies, sophisticated technology and service, and characterized by paradoxes, uncertainty, and unpredictability (Hargreaves, 1994), I believe that educated persons need to be perceptive, critical, creative, and empowered learners who are capable of handling uncertainty and turbulence. It is unrealistic to assume that the mind can store the vast quantities of information that are now readily available. Far more important in today's world is that people know where to search for pertinent information when it is needed to address novel problems and dilemmas (Wigginton, 1985; 1989). Knowing how to access information, and how to use it constructively become critically important. To do so, the human mind needs to develop a profound grasp of concepts and ideas. It is towards these ends that I envision revitalized schools working.

Characterization of Revitalized Schools

Revitalized schools will have an emphasis on processes of inquiry, a collaborative work context, and teachers' sentiments and voice, and a view of knowledge as humanly constructed.

Emphasis on Inquiry Processes

A primary purpose of revitalized schools is to encourage teachers to understand and engage the minds of learners. Teaching is not transmitting information or coercing students to learn; it is not a case of teachers *pontificating* and students *absorbing* all that they can. These teachers seek to know their students, to listen to them and reach out to them with care and understanding. Such understanding provides the basis for teacher–student engagement. This engagement, in turn, enables teachers to create opportunities and capacities for students to reach beyond what they currently know towards what is yet to be known (Greene, 1984). Teachers in revitalized schools set out to foster an insatiable desire for learning, a zestful curiosity about events, encounters and experiences (Kohl, 1986; 1988a; Wigginton, 1985; 1991). To do this, they attempt to connect with students' constructions of reality as a way of stimulating in them a desire to connect with other, more public constructions that are currently accepted as warranted knowledge. In this way they attempt to make learning memorable to students. Learning becomes memorable when it is driven by students' interests and choice, and when it connects to the real world outside the classroom as Dittmer and Frischetti describe in Chapter 12. Students become active decision makers and teachers frequently change their roles in the classroom. At times they are facilitators, then observers, sometimes confidantes and listeners, sometimes coaches, always learners, seldom content deliverers, and never autocrats (Wasley, 1990). And students' classroom roles change also. No longer desk-bound or unduly deferential, they become active explorers and co-teachers.

Engaging students' minds and fostering a zestful curiosity so as to make learning memorable leads imperceptibly to the emphasis in revitalized schools that depth and mastery within subject areas are more important than broad scope and coverage of curriculum content (Wasley, 1990). Thus, moments of pausing have to be taken to allow students to absorb insights and ideas; moments of silence have to be afforded to permit them the space to understand their being in the world. Understanding, not speed, is the essential aim (Kohl, 1986; 1988a). Doing less to achieve more involves risk-taking. The ultimate risk for teachers in revitalized schools is to become an advocate for students and their learning. This typically means refusing to believe that students cannot learn and striving with colleagues to ensure that no student is disadvantaged by unfair diagnosis, labeling, or institutional pressure.

These purposes are always pursued within the context of teachers' work. It is this context that also acts as a focus of inquiry for teachers in revitalized schools.

The Collaborative Work Context of Inquiry

An important aspect of teaching and learning in revitalized schools is that the work context of inquiry and student learning is collaborative in the sense that teachers and students negotiate meaning and work activities together. Further, the work context in the classroom is intimately related to the real world outside, as teachers see connecting points everywhere. To function in this way, teachers in revitalized schools have to prepare assiduously by anticipating some of the situations that could arise in classroom teaching. They gather materials, they note down ideas and activities, they hunt out different kinds of teaching resources, and generally prepare much more than they could ever use in any given lesson, unit, or year (Kohl, 1986). This preparation gives them a repertoire upon which they can draw as they engage the minds of students and negotiate with them potential work activities. It also permits teachers to act flexibly within the work context, as they engage in 'rolling' planning.

Anticipatory preparation happens before classroom teaching begins. 'Rolling' planning occurs when the teacher is actively involved in the engagement process with students in the classroom. Such preparation is not a prescription for action but a safety-net of ideas and activities that the teacher can fall back on as he or she rolls in negotiating work activities with the students. Rolling planning therefore involves teachers in observing, analyzing, hypothesizing, and responding as they attempt to create curriculum on-the-spot with their students. It consists of 'balancing teacher-initiated ideas with student-initiated ones' (Kohl, 1986:54) so that the work context of inquiry becomes one that truly facilitates student learning. Teachers in revitalized schools thus assume that all students have within them an inherent desire to learn. They work to ensure that all classroom work is infused by student choice, student volition, and student action (Dittmer and Fischetti, Chapter 12; Wigginton, 1989; 1991).

The purposes that teachers pursue in a work context of inquiry leads them to develop certain sentiments about their chosen vocation.

Teachers' Sentiments

Teaching is not just a job for teachers in revitalized schools; it is a vocation for which they have developed a passion. They are obsessed by the urge to 'help others learn and grow' (Kohl, 1988a:6). The drive to facilitate learning is very strong and is deeply embedded within their persons. They are not satisfied until they have succeeded in promoting learning in some way or another. Revitalized teachers therefore view themselves primarily as students of teaching and learning (Lieberman, 1994). The classroom is typically the setting in which they attempt to facilitate learning for students. It is also the setting in which they learn so much about the craft of teaching. But they also view themselves as co-learners with students in all of the learning adventures that they collaboratively undertake. These adventures in turn reinforce the passion with which they care for students as learners. Caring for students and nurturing them as persons involves loving students for their capacity and potentiality as a learner (Kohl, 1988a:65).

Revitalized schools address the purposes of teaching, the work context of inquiry in teaching, the sentiments that teachers hold about teaching, and ultimately sponsor the teachers' voice.

Sponsoring the Teachers' Voice

The purposes of teaching that teachers in revitalized schools pursue, the collaborative context within which they do their work, and the sentiments they hold inevitably leads to the emerging of a moral voice. They speak on behalf of students. They make promises to students they intend to keep; they reach out to difficult or withdrawn children to include them in the group (Kohl, 1986; 1988b); they involve students in curriculum-making; they insist that the work be that of the students and not an imposition of the teacher (Wigginton, 1989; 1991); they are prepared to take risks and face ridicule to contend for student-oriented opportunities to learn. Teachers also gain a critical voice when they express their views for the specific purpose of changing the ways in which teaching is conceived and enacted. They begin to challenge many of the instrumental assumptions embedded in schooling and in the curriculum guides. They are quick to point out fallacious assumptions about students as learners, for example, the view that students are empty vessels waiting to be filled. Moreover, in a time when there appears to be no shortage of advice on how teachers should do their jobs, they develop a political voice by standing up for the centrality of students' needs in the learning process. This standing up essentially contends with the external imposition of those initiatives, such as standardized testing, national core curriculum (see Chard, 1994), and basic skills in kindergarten, which are based on a narrow view of schooling and deliberately ignore the real lives of children.

Viewing Knowledge as Humanly Constructed

Teachers in revitalized schools view knowledge problematically, not as being given by external experts but as being constructed by human agents in the personal and social settings of learning (Paris, 1993). They therefore invite students to 'have encounters with learning that might transform their lives' (Kohl, 1994:64), as they attempt to understand the world's complexities. Duckworth (1987) suggests that teachers working in this way propose situations for learners to think about and then watch what they do. Students then tell the teachers what *they*, the learners, make of it rather than the teachers telling them *what* to make of it. This approach values the students' viewpoints and involves teachers in negotiating the curriculum so that students can take ownership of the learning experience (Boomer, 1992). This inevitably changes teaching from an act of posing questions for students to answer to one in which the teacher begins to answer the questions that learners pose. As Susan Hyde, a science teacher cited by Boomer, points out:

> *answering questions* beats teaching any day, *if you want the kids to learn and understand.* But stick to teaching and *asking questions if you, the teacher, want to learn* (Boomer, 1992: 12–13, emphasis added).

This view of knowledge has pedagogical implications for teaching. Teachers pose problems of emerging relevance; that is, they mediate the importance and relevance of the concepts to be learned. Interest can be created – there must be a *hook.* Teachers teaching in this way constantly search for meaningful hooks to create interest and connect curriculum content to the minds of the learners. They structure learning around primary concepts. This entails starting with the 'big ideas' that Wassermann talks about, instead of the broken down parts. Teachers seek and value students' viewpoints. Such action is important for finding out what students already know. Their viewpoints become windows into their minds and the way they think. Teachers who seek and value students' viewpoints are able to contextualize learning. Eliciting students' prior conceptions enables teachers to know how much the instruction must change students' minds. If students' viewpoints function as windows to the minds of students, teachers have to grapple with 'How do I open the window?' To do so, teachers often adapt or negotiate the curriculum to address students' prior conceptions. Even the most charismatic teaching is ineffective if it does not address students' prior conceptions. In all of this, there is a need to see prior conceptions not as errors but as part of a search that we call learning.

A further principle involves assessing learning in the context of teaching. Testing disconnected from the context of learning is like trying to make sense of a tapestry from the back. One sees all the threads but they do not together make up a meaningful picture. Assessing student learning in the context of teaching is an attempt to view the tapestry of student learning from the front. It is an attempt to connect assessment to student learning. It is seeing how the threads of learning connect in a learner's mind to the big ideas of the curriculum rather than looking at the disconnected threads in themselves. It is also seeing how students apply prior understandings to novel situations and construct new understandings.

Reconceptualizing Teacher Education

The current possibilities described by Howey for students in the United States to go directly into teaching after a baccalaureate degree raise the question of what influence teacher education can have on classroom practice. Grossman's (1990) study comparing three secondary teachers with no teacher education with three who undertook an additional year of professional preparation before entering teaching demonstrates trenchantly that the former, while they may know their subject matter well, are at a loss when it comes to transforming that subject-matter content into representational forms that connect with the minds of learners. Consequently, she argues, teacher education is vital if teaching is ever going to get beyond a dreary preoccupation with the transmission of sometimes dated facts.

How can teacher education bring about such constructive change in classroom practice? How can teacher education prepare empowered teachers of deep understanding capable of contributing fully to the culture of a revitalized school? With Jaap Tuinman and Alan Tom, I believe that current attempts at reforming teacher education (Carnegie Forum, 1986; Hoimes Report, 1986) miss the mark. These proposals include mandating a liberal arts degree, increasing professional studies in pedagogical thinking and educational foundations, making teachers pass a basic competency test in writing and mathematics, and creating career ladder ranks within teaching. As Ken Howey points out, these may have served as a major wake-up call to the leadership in most major colleges of education and positioned teacher education within a postbaccalaureate endeavour that has carried symbolic and political significance, but I am less sanguine about the effects of these attempts at improving the preparation of teachers and enhancing the professional image of teachers (as distinct from the interests of so-called major research universities). Other critics share these misgivings. Murray (1986) argues that these reform proposals will fail because they attempt to change teacher education 'by telling teachers (and everyone else) what to do, rather than by empowering them to do what must be done' (p. 29). Labaree (1992) argues that the teacher professionalization movement (which he attributes to the Holmes Group and Carnegie Forum) will inadvertently produce two effects that are not in the best interests of democratic education, namely, 'augmenting the influence of the university over elementary and secondary schools (by reinforcing the authority of those who teach teachers) and accelerating the rationalization of classroom instruction (by reinforcing a research-based model of teaching practice' (p. 125). Noddings (1990), Richardson-Koehler and Fenstermacher (1989), and Ceroni and Garman (1994) each set forth reasons why they are specifically against the formation of hierarchical arrangements within the teaching profession. Most teacher education practices (and the proposed reforms) do not facilitate the development of the empowered practitioners called for by Murray (1986). Consequently, I would contend that nothing short of a reconceptualization of teacher education will help bring about the fundamental changes in pedagogical practice I have characterized as representing revitalized schools.

The chapters in this volume representing the third theme of restructuring arising out of reconceptualization at the ground level propose fundamental changes in pedagogical practice that teacher education could address. The authors suggest a focus on the development in prospective teachers of reflective practice (Carson, Chapter 11) through university-field collaboration (Dawson, Chapter 13; Scott and Burke, Chapter 14) around teaching cases (Wassermann, Chapter 10) and the modeling of student choice (Dittmer and Fischetti, Chapter 12). Such conceptions of teacher education fit well with the strengths of higher education settings. As Fenstermacher (1992) points out:

> Colleges and university campuses are intended and designed for contemplation and reflection, for taking one's own experiences seriously and seeking to understand them in relation to the larger human conversation. In a professional school or college, this reflective and contemplative attitude is connected to practice in ways that permit a back-and-forth between thought and action, theory and practice, research and decision making. With this dynamic relationship between reflective consideration and considered action, the higher education setting is without peer (provided, of course, that it has not lost its own way) (p. 181).

I agree with Fenstermacher's position that teacher education is most appropriately located in higher education. I also agree with his implied criticism of traditional approaches to university-based teacher education that they have somehow lost their way. I believe that university faculties or colleges of education have a critical role to play in the education of teachers but, with Soder and Sirotnik (1990)[3], would counter that such a role will only materialize when they regain a focus on teacher preparation as their central mission.[4] How can this be done?

Tuinman argues in Chapter 8 that teacher education should not be 'owned' exclusively by the university, that the area of responsibility for teacher education that does properly belong to the university is *de facto* co-owned by the faculties of arts, science, and education which should be recognized *de jure*, and that teacher education is the joint property of the university and the profession. Tom contends in Chapter 9 that teacher education will only change when we attend to its deep structures and stop tinkering with its surface patterns. He argues strongly that practice must precede knowledge and that vertical staffing with faculty teams committed to the program and to team teaching should replace the current emphasis on horizontal staffing (faculty commitment to a course) because this exposes students in superficial and disorganized ways to more material than they can possibly absorb, thereby promoting breadth without depth. And he is convinced that students need to experience a shared ordeal with a cohort rather than the current emphasis on continual regrouping.

I would contend that two broad features are necessary for teacher education to prepare the kind of teachers characterized above in a manner consistent with the parameters set by Tuinman and Tom. First, there is a need for prospective teachers to engage in classroom-based action research into dilemmas of teaching, such as investigating problematic aspects of the curriculum, attempting to understand learners' conceptions of subject-matter content, examining difficult student behaviour, and exploring the beliefs students bring into teaching from their prior socialization in schools and how these beliefs affect their views of teaching and learning. Such collaborative inquiry is consistent with Tuinman's declamation that teacher education be co-owned by the university and the profession and with Tom's call for practice before knowledge in the shared ordeal of a cohort staffed vertically by team-teaching university and field-based personnel. It would enable prospective teachers and their school associates to reflect together on the pedagogy needed to bring about learner understanding of important curriculum concepts. Second, there would appear to be a need for rigorous integration – as distinct from the current reform emphasis on separation, i.e., disciplinary content is taught in the faculties of arts and science, and pedagogical processes are taught in the professional studies component in faculties of education – of liberal arts and sciences with professional pedagogy. Such a direction, underscoring both the co-ownership of teacher education between the faculties of arts, science, and education and the commitment to team teaching of instructors representing diverse perspectives, would call for an arrangement whereby professors from the different faculties plan and teach courses collaboratively in order to give prospective teachers opportunities to see and make connections between disciplinary subject matter and related pedagogy.

Reconceptualizing teacher education around teacher research holds much potential for developing empowered professional teachers (Cochran-Smith and Lytle, 1993). The chapters authored by Wassermann, Carson, Dittmer and

Frischetti, Dawson, and Scott and Burke illustrate the kind of research envisioned, namely, classroom-related collaborative inquiry around learning dilemmas in curriculum, pedagogy and assessment. These same chapters also provide a beginning basis for understanding how the integration of liberal arts and science academic content courses with pedagogical methods courses could provide preservice teachers with opportunities to engage in both the active exploration of content areas and purposeful reflection on appropriate forms of pedagogy and assessment such that they *learn how to represent knowledge in ways that make it comprehensible to learners.*

Conclusion

Three themes about restructuring and reconceptualization in teacher education have emerged in this book. In many countries, restructuring initiatives occur only at the policy level and represent *restructuring without purposeful reconceptualization.* In other countries, restructuring initiatives also take place at the policy level but depict a more positive view of *restructuring in advance of reconceptualization* at the ground level. In a few places, we see policy and action so closely aligned that policy initiatives represent a *restructuring arising out of reconceptualization* that has already been articulated at the ground level of action. Whereas the first and third themes seem diametrically opposed to each other, the second theme occupies a pivotal position and could therefore, along with the third theme, play a consequential role in determining the future of teacher education.

How could this come about? Can teacher education meet the challenge currently facing it around the world? I believe that it can, provided that restructuring initiatives in advance of reconceptualization lead to rather than prevent the subsequent rethinking from taking place, and provided that the examples of restructuring arising out of reconceptualization are maintained and increased. To facilitate these changes, I have argued that teacher educators need to reconceptualize their mission as preparing revitalized teachers for revitalized schools. Such a reconceptualization inevitably leads to restructuring – teacher educators align themselves with the systemic reform of schools and systematically seek out partnerships with other faculties and with the field. This restructuring arising out of a careful reconceptualization of teacher education would, I contend, lead to interdisciplinary study and field-based teacher research in the preparation program. Only then can teacher education contribute in constructive ways to enhancing the learning of society's young in a rapidly changing and disintegrating context. If, however, this challenge is not met quickly and decisively, teacher education will become increasingly subjected to the kind of harsh political restructuring that precludes any form of reconceptualization around educational purposes. Such restructuring would, I fear, represent the *coup de grâce* for university-connected teacher education.

Notes

1   This chapter is based, in part, on the research project, 'Teacher Development through Administrative or Collegial Processes of Instructional Consultation' (Peter P. Grimmett, Principal Investigator), funded by the Social Sciences and Humanities Research Council of Canada (Grants #410–85–0339, #410–86–2014 and #410–88–0747). It is gratefully acknowledged that this work could not have been carried out without this funding. The opinions expressed in this chapter do not necessarily reflect the policy, position, or endorsement of SSHRCC.

2   David Imig is the Washington-based Executive Secretary of the American Association of Colleges of Teacher Education (AACTE).

3   Soder and Sirotnik (1990) put it very pointedly: '[Faculties of Education] must rediscover their mission as professional schools, built around the moral and ethical responsibilities of teaching and preparing to teach and all the scholarly and service activities that would be expected to support, nurture and sustain this central purpose' (p. 400).

4   One of the most intriguing features of the Holmes Group is that it consists of a group of deans from research university based colleges of education who are arguing for the centrality of teacher education within their own institutions. Further, Goodlad (1990) notes that public policymakers and other faculties and administrators on university campuses show little interest in faculties of education, save for their function as preparers of teachers. Fenstermacher (1992) suggests that there would be little public lament if alternative routes to teacher certification became the predominant, if not exclusive, form of entry into teaching and faculties of education eventually ceased to exist. Labaree (1992) documents in a historical analysis how teacher education is no longer the center-piece in faculties of education but is forced to compete with a wide range of other programs whose prestige is frequently greater. Similar arguments are made by Clifford and Guthrie (1988), Judge (1982), and Fowler (1992).

References

BERLINER, D.C. (1992) *Educational reform in an era of disinformation*, Paper presented at the annual meeting of the American Association of Colleges of Teacher Education (AACTE), San Antonio, TX, February.

BOOMER, G. (1992) 'Negotiating the curriculum', in BOOMER, G., LESTER, N., ONORE, C. and COOK, J. *Negotiating the Curriculum: Educating for the Twenty-First century*, London, UK: The Falmer Press, 4–14.

CARNEGIE FORUM ON EDUCATION AND THE ECONOMY (1986) *A Nation Prepared: Teachers for the Twently-First Century: Report of the Carnegie Task Force on Teaching as a Profession*, Washington, DC: Carnegie Forum.

CERONI, K.M. and GARMAN, N.B. (1994) 'The empowerment movement: Genuine collegiality or yet another hierarchy?', in GRIMMETT, P.P. and NEUFELD, J. (Eds) *Teacher Development and the Struggle for Authenticity: Professional Growth and Restructuring in the Context of Change*, New York: Teachers College Press, 141–61.

CHARD, S. (1994) 'The national curriculum of England and Wales: Its implementation and evaluation in early childhood classrooms', in GRIMMETT, P.P. and NEUFELD, J.

Peter P. Grimmett

(Eds) *Teacher Development and the Struggle for Authenticity: Professional Growth and Restructuring in the Context of Change*, New York: Teachers College Press, 101–20.

CLIFFORD, G.J. and GUTHRIE, J.W. (1988) *Ed School: A Brief for Professional Education*, Chicago, IL: University of Chicago Press.

COCHRAN-SMITH, M. and LYTLE, S.L. (1993) *Inside Outside: Teacher Research and Knowledge*, New York: Teachers College Press.

DUCKWORTH, E. (1987) *The Having of Wonderful Ideas and other Essays on teaching and Learning*, New York: Teachers College Press.

FENSTERMACHER, G.D. (1992) 'The place of the alternative certification in the education of teachers', in HAWLEY, W.D. (Ed.) *The Alternative Certification of Teachers* (Teacher Education Monograph: No. 14), Washington, DC: ERIC Clearinghouse on Teacher Education, 155–85.

FOWLER, R.H. (1992) 'Reform and change in teacher education: A perspective from a Canadian dean's chair', Unpublished paper, Victoria, BC: University of Victoria.

GOODLAD, J.I. (1990) *Teachers for our Nation's Schools*, San Francisco, CA: Jossey-Bass.

GREENE, M. (1984) 'How do we think about our craft?', in LIEBERMAN, A. (Ed) *Rethinking School Improvement: Research, Craft, and Concept*, New York: Teachers College Press, 13–25.

GRIMMETT, P.P. and NEUFELD, J. (1994) 'Teacher development in a changing educational context', in GRIMMETT, P.P. and NEUFELD, J. (Eds) *Teacher Development and the Struggle for Authenticity: Professional Growth and Restructuring in the Context of Change*, New York: Teachers College Press, 1–12.

GROSSMAN, P.L. (1990) *The Making of a Teacher: Teacher Knowledge and Teacher Education*, New York: Teachers College Press.

HARGREAVES, A. (1994) *Changing Teachers, Changing Times: Teachers' Work and Culture in the Postmodern Age*, London, UK: Cassell.

HOLMES GROUP (1986) *Tomorrow' Teachers: A Report of the Holmes Group*, East Lansing, MI: Holmes Group.

HOMANS, G. (1950) *The Human Group*, New York: Harcourt, Brace.

IMIG, D. (1995) *A Washington bird's eye view: Trends in American education*, Presentation given to members of the Urban Network for the Improvement of Teacher Education (UNITE), Washington, DC, February 12.

JUDGE, H.S. (1982) *American Graduate Schools of Education: A View from Abroad*, New York: Ford Foundation.

KOHL, H.R. (1986) *On Teaching*, New York: Schocken Books.

KOHL, H.R. (1988a) *Growing Minds: On Becoming a Teacher*, New York: Harper & Row.

KOHL, H.R. (1988b) *36 Children*, New York: New American Library.

KOHL, H.R. (1994) *I Won't Learn from You: And Other Thoughts on Creative Maladjustment*, New York: New Press.

LARABEE, D. (1992). 'Power, knowledge and the rationalization of teaching: A genealogy of the move to professionalize teaching', *Harvard Educational Review*, **62**(6), 123–55.

LIEBERMAN, A. (1994) 'Teacher development: Commitment and challenge', in GRIMMETT, P.P. and NEUFELD, J. (Eds) *Teacher Development and the Struggle for Authenticity: Professional Growth and Restructuring in the Context of Change*, New York: Teachers College Press, 15–30.

MARSHALL, H.H. (1992) 'Seeing, redefining, and support student learning', in MARSHALL,

H.H. (Ed.) *Redefining Student Learning: Roots of Educational Change*, Norwood, NJ: Ablex, 1–32.

MURRAY, F. (1986) 'Goals for the reform of teacher education: An executive summary of the Holmes Group report', *Phi Delta Kappan*, **68**(1), 28–32.

NODDINGS, N. (1990) 'Feminist critiques in the professions', in CAZDEN, C. (Ed.) *Review of Research in Education*, **16**, Washington, DC: AERA, 393–424.

PARIS, C.L. (1993) *Teacher Agency and Curriculum Making in Classrooms*, New York: Teachers College Press.

RICHARDSON-KOEHLER, V. and FENSTERMACHER, G.D. (1989) 'Graduate programs of teacher education and the professionalization of teaching', in WOOLFOLK, A.E. (Ed.) *Research Perspectives on the Graduate Preparation of Teachers*, Englewood Cliffs, NJ: Prentice-Hall, 153–68.

SODER, R. and SIROTNIK, K. (1990) 'Beyond reinventing the past: The politics of teacher education', in GOODLAD, J.I., SIROTNIK, K. and SODER, R. (Eds) *Places Where Teachers are Taught*, San Franciso, CA: Jossey-Bass.

STONES, E. (1994) 'Editorial: Paranoids of the world unite!', *Journal of Education for Teaching*, **20**(3), 259–60.

WASLEY, P.A. (1990) *Stirring the Chalkdust: Three Teachers in the Midst of Change*, Providence, RI: Coalition for Essential Schools, Brown University.

WEST, C. (1994) 'The '80s: Market culture run amok', *Newsweek*, 48–9, January 3.

WIGGINTON, E. (1985) *Sometimes a Shining Moment: The Foxfire Experience*, Garden City, NY: Doubleday.

WIGGINTON, E. (1989) 'Foxfire grows up', *Harvard Educational Review*, **59**(1), 24–49.

WIGGINTON, E. (1991) *The Foxfire Approach: Perspectives and Core Practices*, Rabun Gap, GA: The Foxfire Fund, Inc.

Notes on Contributors

Isabel Alarcao is Professor of Education at the University of Aveiro, Portugal. A former foreign language teacher at the secondary level, she has continued to supervise secondary school teachers in teaching practise, supervision and foreign language teaching being for her two main areas of interest. She co-authored (with José Tavares) two books: *Psicologia do desenvolvimento e da aprendizagem e Supervisão da Práctica Pedagógica: uma perspectiva de desenvolvimento e aprendizagem*.

Hugh Burke is Vice-Principal at Vancouver Talmad Torak school. He also worked as a faculty associate at Simon Fraser University for three years. His area of interest is English education and teacher education.

Terrance R. Carson is Professor in the Department of Secondary Education at the University of Alberta. His teaching and research activities include curriculum theory, teacher education and action research. He maintains a strong interest in peace and global education and is the codirector of the Institute for Peace and Global Education at the University of Alberta.

A.J. (Sandy) Dawson, an Associate Professor at Simon Fraser was the Director of the Professional Development Program (PDP) at Simon Fraser University from 1985 to 1994. He was instrumental in the implementation of the model or structure described in two chapters of this book. In addition to his work in teacher education, his research interests lie within the field of mathematics education where he has written about the teaching and learning of mathematics and the philosophical underpinnings for mathematics education.

Allan Dittmer is the Chair and Professor of the Department of Secondary Education at the University of Louisville. In that position he pioneered the work that has resulted in the school-based teacher education program described in this book. His interests include psycholinguistics and all aspects of English education, applied linguistics, composition and writing. He has some 60 publications of various types and is currently writing a book about Grawemeyer award winners.

John Fischetti is Associate Professor at the University of Louisville. His interests lie in the area of social studies education and teacher education. He recently steered a state-wide initiative to restructure the high schools in the State of Kentucky.

Michael Fullan is Dean of the Faculty of Education, University of Toronto. He participates as a researcher, consultant, trainer, and policy advisor on a wide range of educational reform projects with school systems, teachers' unions, R & D labs and institutes, and government agencies in Canada and around the world. He was the first recipient of the Canadian Association of Teacher Educators Award of Excellence, and was a recipient of the Colonel Watson Award from the Ontario Association of Curriculum Development. He has published widely on the topic of educational change, including *Change Forces* (Falmer Press), and *The New Meaning of Educational Change* (Teachers College Press).

Peter P. Grimmett is Associate Professor of Education in the Faculty of Education at Simon Fraser University. His research interests focus on the relationship between teachers' development of their craft and the processes of reflection, collegial consultation, and classroom-based action research. His recent publications include *Craft Knowledge and the Education of Teachers* (American Educational Research Association, 1992, with Allan MacKinnon); and Teacher Development and the Struggle for Authenticity (*Teachers College Press*, 1994, with Jon Neufeld).

Trond Eiliv Hauge is a Deputy Head and Professor of Education at the Center for Teacher Education and In-Service Training, University of Oslo in Norway. Formerly he has been working as a teacher in secondary school and in college of teacher education, and as a consultant in the National Council for Teacher Education in Norway. In recent years his research interests focus on teachers' craft knowledge, mentoring, school effectiveness and improvement, and curriculum development.

Kenneth R. Howey, Professor in the College of Education at the Ohio State University. He is also Director of the Urban Network to Improve Teacher Education and Principle Investigator for the Research About Teacher Education Study (RATE) now in its eighth year. He is the author of numerous publications concerned with the education of teachers.

David Pimm is a senior lecturer at the Open University in Great Britain. He has authored two books and edited two books. He does research in the area of language and mathematics. He has been a visiting professor at both Simon Fraser University and The University of British Columbia.

Michelle Selinger is a lecturer in mathematics education at the Open University, currently working on the part-time, distance-taught, Post-Graduate Certificate of Education. Her research interests include teacher change, particularly as affected by Information Technology, and the teaching and learning of number.

Judith Scott is an Assistant Professor, with reading as a specialty area, in the Faculty of Education at Simon Fraser University. Her research in teacher education has focused on metaphors for teaching, and an integrated (K–12) community-based structure for facilitating the growth of preservice teachers. Her latest module is located in inner-city schools in East Vancouver.

Nancy Sheehan, an historian of education, is Professor and Dean of the Faculty of Education at UBC. She was educated at Mount St. Vincent University (BA, B.Ed), the University of Calgary (M.Ed), and the University of Alberta (Ph.D). She has published a number of articles and chapters and edited books on the role of organizations outside the schools and their influence on the curriculum and practice of the school. She is particularly interested in women's organizations in Canada in the first half of this century. Her more recent work has focused on the development of teacher education in British Columbia, particularly the changes caused by the move from normal school to university to the role of the College of Teachers.

Richard Tisher is a former Professor of Education and head of a group concerned with professional development, curriculum, teaching effectiveness, evaluation, and science, mathematics and computer education in the Faculty of Education, Monash University. He has also held posts with the Ministry of Education in the state of Victoria. His publications include articles on teacher induction, teacher education, classroom interaction, higher cognitive questioning, non-verbal behaviour and research on science teacher education. He is also co-author, with R.T. White, of 'Research in the Natural Sciences' in *The Third Handbook of Research on Teaching*.

Alan R. Tom is Professor of Education in the School of Education at the University of North Carolina at Chapel Hill. His teaching, program development, and research interests focus on the initial preparation of teachers and their career development. Tom is author of *Teaching as a Moral Craft*, and is completing a book, *Redesigning Teacher Education*, to be published by the State University of New York Press.

Jaap Tuinman is presently the Academic Vice President at Memorial University in Newfoundland. Prior to that he held various administrative posts at Simon Fraser University including the Dean of the Faculty of Education. He is a reading specialist and has developed a reading series for Canadian schools.

Selma Wassermann, Professor of Education and Director of Professional Programs at Simon Fraser University, is well known for her innovative teaching and pioneer work in case-method teaching in the secondary school. A recipient of the Simon Fraser University Excellence in Teaching award, her educational books include: *Serious Players in the Primary Classroom; Teaching Elementary Science: Who's Afraid of Spiders?; Teaching for Thinking: Theory,*

Strategies and Activities for the Classroom: Getting Down to Cases; and *Introduction to Case Method Teaching: A Guide to the Galaxy*.

Marvin F. Wideen is Professor in the Faculty of Education at Simon Fraser University where he works in the Institute for Studies in Teacher Education. Prior to his becoming involved in teacher education, he worked both as a teacher and as a principal in public schools. He writes and conducts research in the areas of teacher education, science education and school improvement. His recent works include *Staff Development for School Improvement; Becoming a Teacher*; and *The Struggle for Change*.

Index

94023095R00138

Made in the USA
Lexington, KY
22 July 2018